D0205804

Hostile Takeovers

Hostile Takeovers

ISSUES IN PUBLIC AND CORPORATE POLICY

Edited by DAVID L. McKEE

PRAEGER

New York
Westport, Connecticut
London

Library of Congress Cataloging-in-Publication Data

Hostile takeovers : issues in public and corporate policy / edited by
David L. McKee.
    p.   cm.
    Papers originally presented at a conference sponsored by the Kent
State University Graduate School of Management and the Dept. of
Economics, and held Sept. 28, 1988.
    Bibliography: p.
    Includes index.
    ISBN 0–275–93181–1 (alk. paper)
    1. Consolidation and merger of corporations—United States—
Congresses. 2. Consolidation and merger of corporations—Government policy—
United States—Congresses.   I. McKee, David L.
II. Kent State University. Graduate School of Management.
III. Kent State University. Dept. of Economics.
HD2746.5.H69 1989
338.8'3'0973—dc19   89–30900

Library of Congress Catalog Card Number: 89–30900
ISBN: 0–275–93181–1

First published in 1989

Praeger Publishers, One Madison Avenue, New York, NY 10010
A division of Greenwood Press, Inc.

Printed in the United States of America

The paper used in this book complies with the
Permanent Paper Standard issued by the National
Information Standards Organization (Z39.48–1984).

10 9 8 7 6 5 4 3 2 1

CONTENTS

TABLES AND FIGURES

TABLES

FIGURES

PREFACE

The chapters in this volume are the result of a conference, "Takeovers: Issues in Corporate and Public Policy," that was sponsored by the Graduate School of Management and the Department of Economics of Kent State University on September 28, 1988.

Most of the papers presented at the conference have been reworked for publication. The work of the conference and the chapters in this volume are largely the result of original research. The conference was supported in part by funding from Kent State University's portion of Ohio's Urban University Program. I am especially grateful to James Tinnin, director of Kent State's Urban University Program, for his assistance in obtaining that funding, as well as his continuing support, both moral and substantive, throughout the project.

The project could not have been successfully concluded without the support and encouragement of Acting Dean Michael Sesnowitz of the Graduate School of Management and Richard E. Bennett, chairman of the Department of Economics.

The editing of this book was simplified substantially through the efforts of Linda Poje. Brian Dawson and Karen Hahn made major contributions to the preparation of the bibliography.

INTRODUCTION

Foreign competition, rising labor costs, and changing product markets have been reworking the economic landscapes of advanced nations. Nowhere have such changes been more apparent than in the United States, where traditionally strong manufacturing industries have appeared to be in retreat, wreaking economic and social havoc on the regions and metropolitan complexes that have housed them. In the face of the relatively recent phenomenon of deindustrialization, planners both corporate and public have seemed to be impotent to stem the momentum of such presumably negative adjustments.

One can argue that many of the foreign-based manufacturing facilities are actually owned by U.S. companies and that the creation and operation of such facilities provides many well-paying employment opportunities in the United States. One can also point to the increasing number of foreign manufacturers who are locating plants (and thus creating jobs) in the United States, or to the service sector, which has become the leader in terms of domestic employment and which, despite its sometimes questionable image, appears to be providing increasing numbers of employment opportunities for skilled workers. Despite arguments and rebuttals, what has become increasingly apparent in recent years is that the economy of the United States has gone through what might be characterized as changes bordering on the revolutionary, while the thinking on the street seems not to have kept pace.

In the realm of public policy, the initiatives have often taken on crisis-response modes. States and metropolitan areas that have felt the negative impact of economic change have been increasing their efforts to attract new industrial facilities. Some successes have been noted, but not enough to suggest that such efforts can be expected to replace all the assembly-line opportunities that have been lost. In Congress, calls have gone out for protectionist legislation designed to shield domestic industry from foreign competition. Unionized labor has shown some willingness to forgo high wages in favor of job security. In some cases workers have expressed a desire to assume the actual ownership of production facilities as a way of preserving their jobs. Collectively, public and private initiatives that have been emerging demonstrate a general awareness of the structural changes that have been occurring. Unfortunately it is not yet obvious that such an awareness has generated the understanding that will be necessary if policy responses at all levels can be expected to facilitate continuing positive change while at the same time dealing with the social and economic dislocations that seem to accompany new developments.

In some industries, firms have sought diversification as a hedge against the uncertainties of the new competitive environment. That practice has led to the phenomenon of the corporate conglomerate, a type of enterprise that was scarcely contemplated by the private sector, much less public agencies charged with the oversight of the industrial environment. The rise of conglomerate mergers seems to have initiated a whole new way of thinking in the corporate United States with respect to the acquisition of ownership. Instead of a hedge against difficulties facing certain industries, interindustrial mergers and takeovers have spawned a whole new cadre of uncertainties.

In this new corporate climate, firms in various industries have had to alter their procedures to guard against unwanted suitors. Such alterations undoubtedly change corporate expansion patterns, financial procedures, and indeed the profit potential and perhaps even the very survival capabilities of specific enterprises. There has been considerable debate concerning the new form of corporate takeovers. Some maintain that they are well within the parameters of acceptability under a laissez-faire business climate and suggest that they may even contribute to greater efficiency in corporate operations. Others see them as little more than white-collar privateering and call for government regulations to curtail them.

Despite the continuing debate, what has sometimes been termed the "hostile takeover" has become a fact of life in the corporate United States, and enterprises large and small are adjusting their operating procedures to defend against it. The facilitation of the new form of takeover has encouraged new ranges of specialization in banking, finance, and related services. A new form of entrepreneur has emerged, feared and criticized in some circles, yet possessing a mystique that appears to have captured media attention and thus the public eye. An understanding of events chronicled in local media has necessitated the learning of a new vocabulary.

As the public learns about "golden parachutes," "greenmail," and "white knights," little is being added to anyone's understanding of the effect, real or potential, that specific takeovers may have on the economic base of metropolitan areas, states, or regions that house impacted corporate operations. What impact do takeovers have on the local economies of such areas? In regions where the industrial base is already at risk from the problems cited earlier in this discussion, how does the adding of takeovers to the economic equation affect the ultimate prognosis? Assuming that such questions can be answered, what will be the policy implications of those answers? What is it that state and local governments can and should (or should not) do? It is clear that such questions should be explored carefully, if for no other reason than to discourage ill-considered ad hoc actions in the face of real or perceived crises.

Nowhere do the questions raised above appear more relevant than in the traditionally strong industrial Midwest. Northern Ohio, for example, has already experienced an array of corporate takeover attempts, some successful, and others abortive. It would be hard to exist in that particular region without being aware of major examples. Unfortunately, an awareness of what has been occurring in steel, rubber, and various other industries in the industrial centers of Northern Ohio hardly seems to have developed the basis of understanding necessary for the formulation of sound policies to facilitate the economic viability of the region and, more specifically, its industrial centers.

The present volume makes no pretext of solving all the public and private policy issues that appear to be arising as a result of the new wave of corporate takeovers. Perhaps, however, it will highlight some of those issues and provide some background information that should be useful to those involved in actual policy formulation. To begin with, the arguments for and against takeovers will be presented. As is often the case with such debates, there are strong points to be made on both sides. With those points in place, the emphasis switches to the economic, legal, ethical, and spatial issues involved. With these discussions, interregional issues emerge, as do legal difficulties involving different levels of government, not to mention interstate differences. Issues relating to foreign direct investment and federal tax policy will also be considered. The volume concludes with an overview of the corporate impact of takeovers and some final policy reflections.

PART I

THE POSITIONS OF THE PROTAGONISTS

1

THREE CHEERS FOR THE CORPORATE RAIDER

Richard K. Vedder

Popular mythology leads us to believe that the free-wheeling laissez-faire environment of the Reagan years has led to the development of the modern-day equivalent of the pirates of the seventeenth and eighteenth centuries, the corporate raiders. Just as the pirates raided innocent ships for their gold, so, the mythology leads us to believe, the modern-day raiders engage in corporate piracy, skimming off the valuable assets of our leading industrial companies. Like the Robber Barons of the nineteenth century, the corporate raiders of the late twentieth century are portrayed as predatory creatures whose selfish pursuit of personal gain has ravaged great corporations, proud communities, and innocent and helpless stockholders. We are told that these modern-day corporate rapists have absorbed valuable capital that should have been used to rebuild our industries or our infrastructure. According to this view, the speculative misuse of money market funds by these financial parasites has further eroded our international competitiveness. Exploiting this mythology, politicians have passed legislation to protect us from these nefarious predators.

There is, however, another view. According to this alternative perspective, corporate takeover specialists are fulfilling a vital economic function, energizing corporate democracy in a way that gives society better use of its resources while protecting stockholders from the financial losses imposed by poor but entrenched management. The raider is the common investor's protection against corporate ineptitude, and fosters needed corporate restructuring that will make the United States

more competitive in the international marketplace. The takeover specialist is allowing the market to function more efficiently, and is serving
to reduce the specter of corporate dictatorships unresponsive either to
their stockholders or the needs of society. According to this view, the
role of public policy is to uphold the basic principles of corporate democracy but to otherwise stay out of private-sector battles for corporate
hegemony.

A SHORT HISTORY OF ANTITAKEOVER LEGISLATION

As an economic historian, I cannot resist pointing out that the current
debate is really nothing new. Major battles over the organization and
control of business enterprises have erupted throughout history. When
stock market speculation led to the rapid rise and then crash of the
shares of the South Sea Company in the early eighteenth century, the
answer of the British government was the Bubble Act of 1720, an act to
ban joint stock companies. The reasoning, apparently, was that there
cannot be a stock market crash if there is no stock. As the Industrial
Revolution proceeded, it became apparent that the benefits of stock
ownership exceeded the costs, and the Bubble Act was repealed.

Worried about the concentration of financial resources in a few hands,
the U.S. citizens of the early nineteenth century put an end to central
banking and, in a few state constitutions, even commercial banking. If
banks were institutions involved in an unequalitarian accumulation of
assets, and if bank failures hurt note-holders and depositors, then the
solution was to ban banks. As with the Bubble Act, that solution did
not last long: The cure was far worse than the disease (although I am
not entirely sure that this holds with respect to the banning of central
banks). Later, state and federal antitakeover laws in banking effectively
prohibited interstate banking by individual bank companies.

Almost precisely one century ago, an Ohio Senator led the movement
that led to the first national antitakeover legislation, the Sherman Act.
For the first time, the federal government made it illegal for a private
citizen or corporation to purchase another private corporation in some
circumstances. Even earlier, the Interstate Commerce Act of 1887 had
been passed, ostensibly with a similar antimonopoly motivation that
restrained private behavior.[1] While the Interstate Commerce Act, the
Sherman Act, and subsequent legislation remain on the books, there is
a growing body of economic and legal opinion that this form of anti–
corporate takeover legislation has not had any profoundly positive economic effects.[2] For example, transportation regulation, far from protecting consumers, has shielded inefficient producers from competition.
Similarly, a growing literature argues that antitrust law provisions sometimes actually impede competition.

Moreover, there is a growing realization that the old saying that "tariffs are the mother of trusts" is correct, and that the cure for monopoly is removing trade protection; the Japanese and Koreans will provide desired competition far more effectively than any antitrust laws that primarily benefit an already excessive number of lawyers.

Thus, public policy has long been concerned with financial transactions of private corporate parties. In one form or other, antitakeover legislation has been around for a long time. Furthermore, most of it has been so overtly absurd that it has been repealed, or has remained only in a weakened form to provide employment or income for certain special-interest groups long after its true effectiveness has ended or been disproven. If history is any guide, we should be skeptical of government attempts to restrain private transactions in the corporate sector.

THE CASE AGAINST ANTITAKEOVER LEGISLATION

While history suggests that it may be inappropriate to try to restrict corporate transactions, it also suggests that a basic function of government is to provide the legal and institutional framework that protects private property rights. We have laws against larceny, arson, and embezzlement, all acts that some individuals might use to steal or destroy another citizen's property.

All but the most extreme libertarian would agree that one of the functions of government is to provide an environment where incentives to accumulate income and wealth are not annihilated by private acts of plundering. For property rights to have operational meaning, they need to be enforced from intrusion by outsiders. Just as the U.S. Navy protects shipping in the Persian Gulf, so, generally, governments appropriately protect other property from acts of destruction and theft.

When the material rewards from one's work or property are taken away, incentives to work and accumulate wealth decline. Thus, excessive taxation tends to reduce economic growth. Similarly, private acts of piracy or theft have a similar impact; consequently, governments' police forces, and judicial powers of protecting ownership of human and physical capital are important to society's well being.

FOUR COMMON ANTITAKEOVER TACTICS

With this in mind, a strong case can be made for federal legislation that constrains states and corporations from engaging in legal strategems that are the equivalent of piracy or theft—acts that in effect destroy or prevent the growth of wealth of some corporate owners. What are those strategems? The litany is long, involved, and perhaps familiar, so I will mention just four.

First, a growing number of corporations have gone over, to classified forms of stock and directors. Typically, there are two classes of stock, each with different voting characteristics. This violates the concept of "one share, one vote," the corporate democratic analogy to the political concept of "one man, one vote" that prevails in virtually every governmental democracy. A person or family with 5- or 10-percent ownership of a business can effectively control the entire corporation by changing bylaws to permit two classes of stock. Under the new bylaws, the "old" stockholders (largely the founding family) get all or most of the Class A stock, and there may be perhaps 6 Class A stock directors on a board of directors of 11 persons. The majority of the company's stock owned by the "new" (largely non-family) Class B shareowners only elects, say, 5 directors. This is really not too different to a political scenario of giving white persons five votes for every one vote given to black persons—a repulsive, discriminatory and thoroughly undemocratic practice, yet it flourishes and is growing in the corporate United States.

Aside from classified stock and directors, there is the infamous practice of greenmail. An individual wanting control of a corporation buys a significant block of stock in the company. The management, not wanting to lose control of the company to this outsider, offers this individual a very high price for the shares, well above the current market price. Other shareholders are not given the same opportunity to sell. Thus the shareholders who own the bulk of the corporation's shares are in fact subsidizing the one stockholder who obtains a bribe for selling out. Stockholders are thus treated unequally.

Morally, one might argue that greenmail is not much different than blackmail, extortion, larceny, or a very severe case of shoplifting at the least. Payment is made to someone to prevent him or her from taking another action; one group of persons—the other stockholders—are providing an unwilling payment to another stockholder, which is what happens when one is robbed or involved in a kidnapping. The fact that the practice is legal in most jurisdictions in this country does not make it morally right, and speaks more to the imperfections of our legal system than to the appropriateness of this tactic.

Third, there are a variety of financial strategems that corporations follow and that come under the name of poison pill. To cite one common tactic, rights offered to existing shareholders are made in advance of any takeover attempt. These rights might offer existing stockholders the opportunity to buy company stock at a very low price if any one stockholder buys—or even offers to buy—more than, say, 20 percent of the corporation's stock. This discourages would-be buyers by diluting their financial stake and by lowering the value of shares after a takeover attempt is announced.

Last, there is the golden parachute. The company by-laws are changed so that the directors can make giant severance payments to key executives if an outsider is successful in purchasing the company. This protects a selected few stockholders, namely the chief officers of the company, and discourages suitors by forcing them to pay millions in cash in addition to the money expended to buying control of the company. Since in many cases takeovers are led by persons seeking to increase the value of corporate stock by ridding companies of incompetent or weak management, golden parachutes tend to provide massive rewards to incompetent persons, paid by the very shareholders who suffered the consequences of their poor management in the first place. Again, as with the other strategies, it favors one group of stockholders over the others, and is the moral equivalent of piracy in that it robs the large majority of stockholders for the benefit of a few.

The public-policy solution to the problem of corporate piracy is simple: Outlaw it, or at least make its use subject to approval of the shareholders who might suffer its consequences. Make poison pills illegal; enforce the principle of one share, one vote. Require special shareholder votes on any generous severance payments (equal to more than six-months salary, for example), and make it a felony to offer greenmail, just as we outlaw blackmail.

THE MODERN AUTHORITARIAN CORPORATE LEADERSHIP

The ideal behind the corporation is that it is an efficient means of amalgamating the interests of diverse individuals who are unknown to each other. Modern capital-intensive economies are most efficiently developed by business organizations that are large in scope, usually requiring resources beyond the capabilities of individuals or small partnerships. Corporations have an unlimited life, and provide limited financial liability for their owners. The managers of corporations are chosen, indirectly perhaps, by shareholders to manage their interests. According to the ideal, the managers invest most of their own assets in the company, and thus have an incentive to improve the corporation's fortunes, serving the interest of all shareowners.

Over half a century ago, Adolph Berle and Gardiner Means wrote a book in which they claimed that the corporate democratic ideal was a myth.[3] According to Berle and Means, there has been a divorce between the ownership and the control of the modern corporation. A few top executives, working with a board of directors with whom they have close ties and may even control, run the company. The tens or hundreds of thousands of shareowners are individually each so insignificant in terms of their ownership that they are effectively ignored. The managers run the company in an authoritarian, non-democratic fashion, concerned more about their own interests than the interest of shareowners. Only when things go so badly that the stockholders might revolt or sell to a hostile management do the managers pay much attention to shareholders.

The reason for this state of affairs is simple: stockholders are "rationally ignorant." Consider a typical stockholder. She or he might be worth $500,000 and have $300,000 in stocks divided between a dozen or more companies. Perhaps a typical stock investment would be $25,000—only 5 percent of total net worth. How much time is the stockholder willing to spend monitoring that investment? Not too much. She or he probably will follow the stock price fairly regularly, read annual and quarterly reports, and so on; but beyond that, the stockholder is not going to take the time to be a watchdog of management; even if management proposes a poison pill provision in the corporate bylaws, the stockholder is not likely to invest more than a few minutes studying the issue, probably voting with management since she or he does not fully know the negative consequences. The shareowner thus is rationally ignorant of much that goes on in the corporation.

Therefore, there is in corporations a situation analogous to what goes on in government. In both cases, on most issues and decisions the voters are rationally ignorant of what is going on. In both cases, special interest groups, for whom the decision means a great deal, are fully informed and will lobby. In the case of government, a business may lobby for tariff protection with the Congress; with corporations, the executives may lobby the board of directors for golden parachutes. In national politics, the Congressmen depend on the lobbyists for contributions and honoraria; in corporate politics, the directors are initially chosen by the very executives they are supposed to monitor. In both cases, the special interests use their clout to triumph over the general interest, and both groups of voters, on balance, are losers.

In this environment, it is desirable to have institutional arrangements, or rules of the game, that restrict the ability of special interests to thwart democratic principles. At the federal level, a line item veto is one example of a device that could be used to prevent payments being made to certain special interests. At the corporate level, provisions against golden parachutes, poison pills, and greenmail would restrict some of the most harmful forms of special-interest piracy.

The analogy between public and private behavior is most appropriate. Antitakeover laws are a perfect example of special-interest pleading. A company's management wants job security and goes to the legislature, spending thousands if not millions of shareowner money to lobby for legislation that makes it difficult for shareowners to sell their stock to outsiders who would oust existing management. Corporate leaders misuse their corporation's funds to get legislation enacted that serves their special interest against the general interest of the thousands of corporate shareowners and the public in general.

The major objection to antitakeover legislation from the stockholder perspective is that it blocks opportunities to sell shares at an advantageous price. For anyone to buy control of a corporation, they must induce sufficient numbers of shareholders to sell their shares, meaning, of course, that they must offer a price above the market price that exists before the takeover is announced. If laws prevent some or all such takeovers from taking place, then shareholders miss out on the opportunity to cash in on high-price tender offers that provide capital gains. One estimate is that in the 1977–1986 period, selling shareholders gained $346 billion from merger-and-acquisition activity (not all of which were hostile takeovers), and that the gains to buying stockholders, while smaller, were nonetheless positive.[4] Empirical studies have amply demonstrated that takeover offers, in general, lead to higher stock prices. Shareholders of target companies receive premiums associated with the takeover of somewhere between 15 and 35 percent on the average.[5]

From a broader social perspective, antitakeover laws impede the mobility of financial capital, and prevent corporate restructuring which is desirable from the standpoint of economic efficiency. Suppose the XYZ Corporation's stock is selling at $30 a share, well below its book value. The reason for the low price is that existing management has refused to make the hard decisions that would enhance corporate profits. A takeover bid at $40 a share, if successful, would financially benefit shareowners. Why would anyone offer $40 for stock whose current value is $30? They would do so because the bidder plans managerial changes and asset redeployments that should enhance the value of the stock by more than $10 a share.[6] Besides aiding stockholders, more generally, takeovers typically help society by leading to improved entrepreneurial activity and a redeployment of assets from low-yielding to high-yielding activities. Resources will move where their return is greatest; that is to say, to activities that society values more highly.

Antitakeover legislation, then, fundamentally involves the restriction of the mobility of resources. It tends to constrain the migration of capital, and, to some extent that of labor. The law is used to prevent market forces from being allowed to operate. Antitakeover laws are somewhat analogous to laws the British tried to impose on the North American colonies in 1763. They tried to restrict the movement of human and physical capital resources in colonial North America with the Proclamation of 1763; this attempt to stop the westward movement failed, and so should modern-day attempts to restrict entrepreneurs from seeking rewards and opportunities by moving their resources from one activity to another.

EVALUATING OTHER ARGUMENTS FOR
ANTITAKEOVER LAWS

One argument for antitakeover laws that has strong intuitive appeal is that in some instances they can save jobs for certain workers. It may well be true that had Sir James Goldsmith purchased control of Goodyear, many employees in the Akron area, from Chairman of the Board Robert Mercer on down to rank-and-file blue-collar workers, would have lost their jobs. Accordingly, it is probably correct that it served the good of the Akron area to prevent the takeover, although even that statement is not entirely obvious since it is possible that many shareholders in the area may have been net losers because the transaction was not consummated.

However, that view is both myopic and wrong. The appropriate question to ask is, on balance, do restrictions on corporate takeovers create jobs? The answer is "no." If a relatively inefficient company is able to avoid takeover, productivity-enhancing restructuring probably will not occur. In the short run, some employees will keep their jobs, since restructuring typically means eliminating some jobs. At the same time, the company that thwarts takeover and does not restructure will suffer a loss of profits from continued inefficiency; consequently, the firm will not make as large a capital investment as it could if it were more profitable, and will not pay as large dividends to shareholders. The capital formation done by a restructured company would create jobs and enhance corporate competitiveness through greater labor productivity. The higher dividends would lead to more consumer spending that would additionally create jobs in a whole variety of different types of enterprises. The job creation would be far less obvious than the job destruction that sometimes comes with the corporate takeovers, but it is nonetheless real and measurable, and almost certainly greater in magnitude than the jobs destroyed by the corporate restructuring that accompanies new management.[7]

Restricting corporate restructuring in the name of saving jobs is a form of Luddism—the equivalent of destroying machines. We all know that the development of industrial robots, for example, has led to some workers being displaced by machines, namely robots. Why, then, do we not outlaw robots? We all know that Henry Ford's assembly line saved immense amounts of labor compared with earlier production techniques. Why then, did we not outlaw the assembly line and mass-production techniques? Outlawing or destroying machines would have prevented our national industrial development. Prohibiting efficiency-enhancing moves that make underperforming U.S. corporations more profitable and competitive would have a similar devastating impact.

Another argument for restricting takeovers is that they absorb much of the nation's financial capital, which should be used to finance machines and tools needed to revitalize and strengthen U.S. industry. While that argument has a certain intuitive appeal, it too is based on false assumptions. If Drexel Burnham Lambert issues $5 billion in so-called "junk bonds" to enable a corporate raider to finance a takeover of a U.S. corporation, the shareholders of the taken-over company will receive the $5 billion in payments, which they typically will promptly reinvest in the economy. All that happens initially is that paper changes hands—the corporate raider gives Drexel Burnham paper called bonds; Drexel Burnham gives the raider paper called money; the raider gives the shareowners that paper in exchange for other pieces of paper called stock certificates. Paper assets move around, but real assets are not used up or destroyed. There is little evidence that the rise in issuance of junk bonds and corporate takeovers has been accompanied by a decline in real capital formation: If anything, the opposite is the case. Investment as a percent of GNP is every bit as high in the takeover era of the 1980s as it was in the previous decade.[8]

Indeed, on balance, restriction of corporate takeovers would probably reduce capital formation. First, to the extent that it would restrict corporate restructuring (which would otherwise raise corporate profits), it would lower the aggregate rate of return on capital in the economy and reduce incentives for capital formation. Second, antitakeover laws restrict the ability of foreigners to invest in our economy. Foreign investment involves net new creation of financial and ultimately physical capital in the United States, and by keeping the Bridgestones and the BP Americas from making takeover bids, the country deprives itself of funds that increase national savings and capital stock, and ultimately the standard of living.

WHY NOT LEAVE THE MATTER TO THE STATES?

As a person with a strong libertarian bent, I have a hard time ever favoring the government passing new legislation. Even worse, when government intervention is needed, philosophically I believe that the best government is the one closest to the people, namely at the state or even local level. Even if legislation outlawing antitakeover activity were enacted, why should it be enacted in Washington, D.C., instead of in the individual states?

The answer to that question resides in the fact that corporations are fictitious entities. This chap "General Motors"—in what war did he fight? In fact, there never was a military figure called "General Motors," or any other individual by that name. General Motors is hundreds of thousands of shareholders who live throughout the country and even beyond, and who own shares of assets likewise widely dispersed beyond the state of the corporate headquarters or the state in which they are chartered. General Motors is chartered in Delaware, but almost no one would argue that in any meaningful sense is General Motors truly a Delaware corporation. A much better case can be made that it is a Michigan corporation, since that is where its top executives work most of the time. However, most likely only a minority of the company's assets are in that state, and certainly a majority of the company's stock is owned by non-Michiganders.

If the concept of interstate commerce has ever meant anything, it certainly applies to the operations and ownership of modern corporations. When the Ohio legislature passes legislation that makes it more difficult for Sir James Goldsmith to buy Goodyear, that body is adversely affecting thousands of stockholders who live outside Ohio, and who probably control a majority of that company's stock. It is also impacting on thousands of non-Ohioan consumers of Goodyear products who might also ultimately benefit from restructuring that raises labor productivity.

In my way of thinking, Goodyear is not an Ohio corporation, regardless of where its top executives may work. The chief executive may think "Goodyear, c'est moi" in the manner of Louis XIV, and the directors may think, "Goodyear, c'est nous." In an environment of democracy and protected private property rights, however, Goodyear is not its chief executive officer (CEO) or even its directors, and the CEO and the directors are not Goodyear. The principle must always be: "Goodyear of the stockholders, for the stockholders, and by the stockholders."

If one state, say Ohio, restricts the ability of persons to buy large quantities of a firm's stock for purposes of taking control, it does so typically in response to special-interest pleading from citizens of that state. A small number of persons, measured in the dozens, hundreds, or a few thousands, have a lot to lose if the company is taken over by outsiders. Those individuals will spend huge sums of money to convince the legislature of the need for legislation. They will give generously to the campaigns of lawmakers, and will then harass them for support. A community where most of the losers from a takeover live will lobby as well, with the local mayor testifying before the legislature. Aside from the affected community, however, most individuals are indifferent—rationally ignorant—about the issue, so the state legislature will typically give in and vote for antitakeover legislation.

It is possible, and even probable, however, that the costs of the corporate takeover are concentrated in a single state, say Ohio, while the benefits are disbursed geographically across the country—to millions of stockholders and consumers living elsewhere. Within Ohio, the costs of the takeover (lost jobs for some executives and other employees) possibly exceed the benefits, so the state quite rationally prevents it from happening, even though on a national level the benefits of the takeover exceed the costs. The Ohio General Assembly lowers the welfare of individuals in other states, and indeed the value of their property (company stock). That violates both sound economic principles and the principles of jurisprudence on which our system of federalism is grounded. Tyranny by state legislators who deprive us of our property must be stopped by federal legislation that invalidates state laws violating the principles of free interstate commerce and economic efficiency.

Without national legislation, we will see states bidding to win corporate charters by changing state incorporation laws to permit all sorts of antitakeover strategies. Delaware, the premier state in the lucrative business of corporate chartering, has bowed to the pressure of vested special interests within corporations and allowed more antitakeover strategies to be included in corporate bylaws. Other states no doubt will follow rather than see companies flee to Delaware. The only way we can prevent this tawdry practice from continuing is to impose federal rules on what are fundamentally interstate and even international forms of economic activity.

While society as a whole ultimately benefits from preventing greedy, entrenched managers from engaging in strategies for enhancing their job security, the major immediate beneficiaries are stockholders. Most people think of stockholders as elderly plutocrats, people who do not engender much sympathy. That picture is completely fallacious. To begin with, as of 1985, over 47,000,000 U.S. citizens directly owned stock. This is almost 20 percent of the total population and about 27 percent of the adult population.[9] There are not that many extremely rich U.S. citizens. Indeed, almost three-quarters of the adult shareowners in 1985 earned less than $50,000 a year.[10] A majority of those stockholders were not even college graduates. In general, the typical stockholder was a fairly ordinary citizen, only moderately more affluent than the mean for the entire population.

Additionally, however, millions of other U.S. citizens indirectly own stock through their pension plans, life insurance, mutual funds, or annuities. In 1986, pension-fund reserves "owned" by households approximated $2 trillion, almost as much as the value of corporate equities owned by households, which was $2.35 trillion. Of these pension assets, over one-half-trillion dollars was invested in corporate stocks.[11] Almost 50,000,000 workers, many of whom owned no stock directly, were covered by pension plans. All told, clearly a majority of the 65,000,000 U.S. families own a piece of U.S. business in some form or other, as do many individuals living outside of family units. Many of these are the proverbial widows and orphans, and many are relatively low-income persons working at unskilled jobs that provide a pension. In 1985, two out of every nine shareowners made less than $25,000 a year. When legislatures enact antitakeover laws, they may be lowering the wealth and potential prosperity of these millions of modest-income individuals.

Antitakeover legislation is often incorrectly viewed as protecting the ordinary citizen from the deleterious effects of corporate plundering by plutocratic corporate raiders. More accurately, however, such legislation protects a small number of autocratic and entrenched corporate executives from facing the consequences of their own incompetence or contempt for the persons they supposedly are working for, the stockholders. Antitakeover legislation is antidemocratic, antipatriotic, and promotes inefficiency and incompetence. The so-called corporate raider makes the most wonderful mechanism ever devised for allocating resources, the market, work even more efficiently. Whether you like it or not, what is good for T. Boone Pickens and Carl Icahn is good for the country. Long live the corporate raider!

NOTES

1. For a generation, economists and historians of quite different perspectives have questioned the actual antimonopoly intent or effect of the Interstate Commerce Act. See, for example, Gabriel Kolko, *Railroads and Regulations, 1877–1916* (Princeton: Princeton University Press, 1965), and Paul MacAvoy, *The Economic Effects of Regulation* (Cambridge, Mass.: MIT Press, 1965).

2. A representative study showing skepticism about the economic efficacy of antitrust laws is Richard A. Posner, *Antitrust Law: An Economic Perspective* (Chicago: University of Chicago Press, 1976).

3. Adolph A. Berle and Gardiner C. Means, *The Modern Corporation and Private Property* (New York: Macmillan, 1933).

4. Michael C. Jensen, "Takeovers: Their Causes and Consequences," *Journal of Economic Perspectives* 2 (Winter 1988): 21–48.

5. See Gregg A. Jarrell, James A. Brickley, and Jeffrey M. Netter, "The Market for Corporate Control: The Empirical Evidence since 1980," *Journal of Economic Perspectives* 2 (Winter 1988): 49–68, for a review of empirical studies. Positive and generally similar returns are observed for hostile takeovers and leveraged buyouts.

6. Of course, this assumes that markets are efficient; that is, that they incorporate in an appropriate fashion all available public information. The literature tends to support this view: see, for example, E. Elton and M. Gruber, *Modern Portfolio Theory and Investment Analysis* (New York: Wiley, 1984), for an exhaustive review of studies on this topic.

7. I know of no authoritative study of the employment effects of corporate mergers or takeovers. I would observe, however, that the great rise in merger activity in the mid- to late 1980s was accompanied by an extremely large increase in employment. Employment in mid–1988 was more than 14 million persons higher than in 1983, and the employment-population ratio rose from 58.3 to 62.6 percent. During the previous five years (1978–1983), which were a period of modest merger activity, employment rose by less than 5 million, and the em-

ployment-population ratio fell. While these trends are strongly influenced by business-cycle developments, one would be hard put to argue that the mergers reduced employment in light of the extraordinarily high rate of jobs created. See also Jarrell, Brickley, and Netter, "Market for Corporate Control," p. 57; and Charles Brown and James L. Medoff, *The Impact of Firm Acquisitions on Labor*, National Bureau of Economic Research Working Paper (1987).

8. In four years of high takeover activity, 1984 through 1987, gross private domestic investment averaged 16.27 percent of gross national product; in the previous decade, 1974 through 1983, investment's share of GNP was slightly less, 15.94 percent. Numerous other changes occurred between those periods, so the data need to be interpreted cautiously. It seems very unlikely, however, that the takeover boom impacted in a significantly negative fashion on national capital formation.

9. This is based on New York Stock Exchange information. A 1984 U.S. Census Bureau survey reported 20 percent of households directly held stock, with the median holdings worth $3,892. This is exclusive of indirect holdings through pension funds, life insurance, and so on.

10. See the *Statistical Abstract of the United States: 1988* (Washington, D.C.: U.S. Government Printing Office, 1988), p. 487 for interesting statistics on stock ownership.

11. This is based on Federal Reserve System flow-of-funds data. See, *Statistical Abstract*, p. 345.

2

HOSTILE TAKEOVERS: A U.S. FALKLAND ISLANDS WHERE THE ARGENTINES ALWAYS WIN

Leigh B. Trevor

Hostile takeovers are primarily the result of a drive for power.[1] They have no more to do with sound economics—nor with civilized values or a healthy future—than did the German invasion of Poland nearly 50 years ago. This is why I often say in my talks on the subject—in criticizing the 20-business-day minimum period that Federal law establishes for a tender offer—that Hitler took Poland in 20 business days and that it is embarrassing for a sophisticated nation to tolerate a legal system under which it takes a century to build a Goodyear but only 20 business days to tear it apart.[2]

It is for these reasons that I have called this discussion "Hostile Takeovers: A U.S. Falkland Islands Where the Argentines Always Win." I seek to establish the validity of that title by drawing together and enlarging upon certain thoughts of mine that have been expressed in articles and speeches over the last three years. After reviewing the evidence, I also set forth a simple, although highly controversial, proposal for reform that, if enacted, would put U.S. takeover-Argentines out of business.

The scope of merger-and-acquisition activity in this country is enormous. Over the last three years, there have been 15,497 deals, aggregating $757 billion dollars—21 deals every business day and 3 deals every business hour. In 1987 alone, total merger-and-acquisition activity amounted to $225.2 billion dollars. The most surprising and, I think, the most distressing fact is this: That number ($225.2 billion) is nearly ten times the nation's total 1987 investment in all the initial public offerings of common shares ($23.8 billion) by all of the 533 U.S. companies that sold shares to the public for the first time in 1987.

In 1987 we spent an amount of money greatly exceeding the entire federal budget deficit on merely rearranging the ownership of existing firms, but barely 10 percent of that same amount to raise fresh capital in the equity markets through initial public offerings. That same year, by the way, was the best year in history for initial public offerings. It was also the year in which the British and the Japanese spent about as much money buying companies in the United States as we accumulated through capital formation in the public-equity markets throughout the nation.

It is true that the number of hostile deals remains a relatively small part of the total number of transactions. However, in aggregate dollar terms—and in terms of their social and economic impact—the hostile deals are vastly more important. There were 21 billion-dollar or greater transactions in 1987, 13 of which resulted in one way or another from hostile initiatives. Those 13 transactions involved $24 billion: more than 10 percent of all merger activity in 1987 and, once again, more than all the capital formation reflected in initial public offerings. The market crash of October 1987 has had no retardant effect on hostile transactions. Indeed, quite the opposite appears to be the case. By one highly respected count, there were 99 substantial hostile contests for control during the first half of 1988, up sharply from 67 in the second half of 1987 and 77 in the first half of that year.[3]

By my own count, from March 1, 1985, through September 15, 1988, a period of 184 weeks, there have been 198 major hostile contests for control of U.S. companies. They are only the big ones—involving at least $100 million in each case and in most cases (such as Federated Department Stores, Macmillan, and Polaroid) involving vastly more.

Under our legal system, we are putting more than one major U.S. company "in play"—which is the language of the trade—each and every week. Furthermore, I think it's important to note that, during this same 184-week period, there have been no hostile contests for control in Japan or the Federal Republic of Germany. Of the 198 large contests that have occurred here, the outcome is known in 181 of them. Of those 181 target companies, 87 percent are either dead and gone or have become so burdened with debt incurred in leveraged buyouts or some other defensive maneuver that their ability to withstand the next economic downturn is open to grave doubt, and surely, after a six-year expansion, that economic downturn cannot now be far away.

During this same period, U.S. non-financial corporations increased their aggregate indebtedness by well over $650 billion—much of it directly related to hostile bids and to the defense against them.[4] Borrowing by non-financial businesses continued to grow (at a 6.4 percent annual rate) in the first quarter of 1988. It is therefore scarcely surprising that 64 percent of all corporate credit changes in 1987 were downgrades, and that bond-rating downgrades may well exceed upgrades in 1988 for the third consecutive year.

"Do not worry about junk bonds," we have been told repeatedly during the 1980s, and yet, what is now happening? The first big company has at last entered Chapter 11 (Revco). More generally, before the end of August 1988 we have already seen as many junk-bond defaults and credit downgrades as there were in all of 1987. The ultimate consequence of too much leverage in too many speculative hostile deals is finally beginning to emerge.

The principal argument in favor of hostile takeovers is the contention that they make target stockholders rich, even though they have undisputed adverse effects in other directions—on jobs and communities, for example. That is the position, in any event, of SEC (Securities and Exchange Commission) Commissioner Joseph Grundfest, who issued a study of his own in 1987 in which he claims that hostile takeovers during the period 1981 to 1986 created $167 billion in stockholder wealth.[5] He says the figure might actually be as high as $209 billion given certain assumptions—and he refers to unpublished work of Professor Michael Jensen of Harvard, who estimates that total target-stockholder gains might actually be as high as $400 billion for this same six-year period.

However, whatever the number may be, on October 19, 1987, the equity markets in this country wiped it out—altogether eliminating an amount of value exceeding six years of takeover profits. We are, nevertheless, left with all the undoubtedly adverse effects of hostile takeovers on companies, on communities, and on employees—and of course we have seen a good deal of that in Ohio in the recent past at Federated, Goodyear, and Owens Corning.

It is also sometimes claimed that hostile takeovers promote productivity. This is a complex subject. There can be no final conclusion until there is a proper study of a representative sample of target companies to see what has in fact happened to them. Macroeconomic data for the economy as a whole will not necessarily tell us the result for the specific population of target companies.

However, the Labor Department's figures for 1987 are interesting. That year's non-farm productivity increase was a sorry pittance; 0.9 percent for all of 1987 and 0.3 percent for the fourth quarter. The year-to-year improvement was barely half what it had been in 1986, and represented the most lethargic annual gain in five years. At the same time, real non-farm hourly compensation in 1987 actually declined by 0.8 percent, prompting one to wonder who in fact are the beneficiaries of the modest productivity advance that did occur. In the manufacturing sector, the real decline in wages was a good deal more—1.5 percent.

In addition, the revised productivity data for the second quarter of 1988, announced on September 1, 1988, reflect a 2.5 percent decline in the business sector and a 1.4 percent decline in the non-farm business sector, notwithstanding a 3.6 percent productivity improvement for manufacturing. Although the pace of hostile takeovers has been at or near its historic peak throughout the period, these productivity declines in the business and non-farm-business components of the economy are the first since 1986—a circumstance that scarcely supports the notion that, in any meaningful macroeconomic sense, more hostile bids and enhanced productivity are the inevitable consequence of one another.

Consequently, if there is a productivity benefit to hostile takeovers, it is quite apparent that such a benefit has yet to be demonstrated. There has been a vast amount of emotional rhetoric about the impact of hostile takeovers on jobs. Here, as in the case of productivity, the literature suffers from the absence of a proper study specifically directed to the population of target companies.

T. Boone Pickens and his allies like to talk about a paper written last year by Professors Charles Brown at the University of Michigan and James Medoff at Harvard.[6] In my opinion, it proves nothing. It resembles an Argentine General Staff Plan drafted for the war that could not be won. The data are derived from only a single state, the State of Michigan. The data do not separate privately held and publicly held companies, nor do they separate hostile deals from negotiated deals. The data include few of the big transactions, those that are most likely to have broad economic and social consequences. The data do not even include acquisitions of Michigan firms by companies based elsewhere. So much for Professors Medoff and Brown and for the claim that hostile takeovers create jobs; so much for the Argentine General Staff.

Here again, Commissioner Grundfest has studied the issue.[7] He argues that there is not necessarily a causal connection between job losses and a hostile bid that precedes them. While I agree that further scholarly attention to the jobs problem is desirable, Commissioner Grundfest's position strikes me as the equivalent of claiming that there was not necessarily any causal link between H.M.S. Sheffield (a Royal Navy destroyer sunk during the Falklands Campaign) and the Exocet missile that destroyed her.

I have recently done a study of my own to test the arguments on the employment impact of hostile takeovers that were advanced by Professors Medoff and Brown, Commissioner Grundfest, and Mr. Pickens himself. I find that in just 18 of the 198 hostile contests for control to which I have referred—a mere 9 percent of the cases—the identifiable job losses, the ones that are easy to find and can be readily located in publicly available information, come to 139,800. Quite a few of them have arisen in Ohio—in Akron, Cincinnati, Granville, Newark, and Toledo, for example.

The impact of hostile bids on communities is often very severe. It is not limited to job losses on the factory floor. To remove any doubt on this point, one need only refer to the words of Justice Lewis Powell (retired in 1987 from the United States Supreme Court), who wrote this in a celebrated takeover case in 1982:

When corporate headquarters are transferred out of a city and State . . . the State and locality from which the transfer is made inevitably suffer significantly. Management personnel—many of whom have provided community leadership—may move to the new corporate headquarters. Contributions to cultural, charitable and educational life—both in terms of leadership and financial support—also tend to diminish when there is a move of corporate headquarters.[8]

One can readily appreciate the accuracy of Justice Powell's conclusion for Northeastern Ohio by recalling such long-forgotten names as Clevite, Glidden, and Warner & Swasey—fine companies with fine products and people that are no longer much in evidence here or anywhere else.

If the theories of stockholder wealth, productivity, and jobs fail to support the argument that hostile takeovers produce economically and socially useful consequences, and if their impact on target-company communities is materially adverse, what do the hostile bidders have to say for themselves?

It is appropriate to revert to T. Boone Pickens in searching out the answer to this question. He is clearly the most articulate of the takeover bidders and by far the most persuasive advocate of hostile takeovers and forced restructurings. He is a clever and capable man, and he should, therefore, be the most qualified man in the United States to answer the most relevant questions about the hostile-takeover phenomenon.

These are the questions that I have put to him, in person and on paper:[9] Where is the evidence that takeover bidders have created any jobs in the United States? Where is the evidence that takeover bidders have built, expanded, or modernized any productive facilities in the United States? Where is the evidence that takeover bidders have added anything to U.S. technology?

I have represented managements for 26 years, and so I have been perfectly prepared to agree with Mr. Pickens that there are some bad managements in existence. However, when I have asked him these questions, he has replied—not with substantive answers—but with this statement, which he has repeated all over the country: "Not all Chief Executives in America are incompetent; only 80 percent of them are." Nevertheless, what Mr. Pickens will not tell you is this:

- The third-quarter 1987 net income of his own company, Mesa Limited Partnership, was down 90 percent from the prior year.
- Mesa's net income for the first nine months of 1987 was down 64 percent from the prior year.
- Mesa's funds from operations during those nine months were less than half its annual dividend requirement.
- Mesa did a little better in the fourth quarter because, when you average all the 1987 quarters together, Mesa's net income for the full year of 1987 was down by only 55 percent from the full year 1986.

Moreover, what Mr. Pickens also will not tell you is whether, based on Mesa's 1987 operating performance, he puts himself in the 80-percent group of incompetent U.S. chief executive officers or in the 20-percent group. Until Mr. Pickens—and hostile bidders generally—can answer these questions, there can be no credible claim that hostile takeovers provide any economic benefit to the nation. On the contrary, the evidence proves that these bidders have brought this country very much the same sort of senseless warfare that the Argentine Forces inflicted on the Falkland Islands in the spring of 1982. All that we are lacking is the resolve of the Thatcher government and the Royal Navy to deal with the problem.

What is the evidence, and what does it tell us about the impact of hostile takeovers? In the first place, tender-offer targets in the 1980s were not, on the whole, poor performers. If you look at Gillette, for example, or Firestone, Goodyear, Marathon Oil, or Unocal, these companies were, when attacked, solid companies. They were not sick. The definitive study of these matters has now appeared. It is a book, published at the beginning of summer 1988, by Professor Louis Lowenstein of the Columbia Law School, and entitled *What's Wrong with Wall Street*.[10]

Lowenstein, who in former incarnations has been both a Wall Street lawyer and the chief executive officer of a publicly traded company, analyzed 56 major hostile transactions during the early years of this decade and reached these conclusions:[11]

- Target companies in the 1980s have had "excellent profit histories . . . with little unused debt capacity." They are hardly, therefore, citadels of "entrenchment."
- In the case of consummated hostile transactions, "returns on equity for the bidders dropped from 14.1 percent in the year before the bid to less than 9 percent in the first three years after the takeover."
- *"In short, after the takeover, the bidders performed well below the level of either the bidders or their targets during the years before the bid."* (Emphasis in original)

Somewhat similar results have been arrived at by Professor F. M. Scherer at Swarthmore College. Scherer has studied 95 transactions resulting from hostile bids initiated over a substantial period of time ending in 1976. He summarizes his work in this way:

Since the acquired companies had slightly inferior profit performance before takeover and . . . the acquired lines continued to have slightly inferior cash flow/ sales performance after takeover, one must conclude that operating performance neither improved nor deteriorated significantly following takeover. *The hypothesis that takeovers improve performance is not supported.*[12] (Emphasis added)

Moreover, Lowenstein summarizes the work of other scholars who have looked deeply into the question of what really happens to the stockholders of the bidder in cases where a hostile takeover succeeds. The conclusion here is that, if the data are extended out for a meaningful period of time (say, three years), the bidder's stockholders are markedly worse off than they would have been had the bidding company pursued its historic course without making the hostile acquisition at all.[13] Indeed, there is evidence to support the proposition that

If the time horizon [of stock market event studies] is not artificially restricted to two years, the stock price performance of targets defeating tender offers exceeds that of the Standard & Poor's 500 index.[14]

There is only one adjective adequate to describe generalized short-term stock market event studies. That word is "silly." These studies are one of many unhappy by-products of the computer age. They call up Winston Churchill's definition of golf: a dismal way to ruin a pleasant walk in the country. They are among the clearest possible manifestations of why business schools often go wrong. They stand for the proposition that, once you have included the computer in your capital budget, management insists that you compute something with it. They represent the triumph of yuppies over truth.

These studies (even the occasional one that is congenial to my convictions) have nothing to do with the key issues surrounding hostile takeovers: meaningful, sustained, and sustainable stockholder wealth on both sides of the deal; productivity; jobs; and community and other corporate-constituency impacts. One example is enough: The 1987 study conducted by the SEC's Office of the Chief Economist concerning 1986 Ohio legislation that was claimed to have an antitakeover effect. If you actually read this entire piece of bureaucratic, computer-driven trivia (which few have had the courage to do), you will find the argument that the pendency and passage of this Ohio Bill caused a $1.45-billion "wealth loss" to stockholders over an 11-day period ($754 million over a 3-day period). It is important to note how fiercely these numbers are qualified:

- "A complete analysis of the impact of the Ohio law must wait until the courts have interpreted the law."
- "Also, the law does not protect target management from control contests using the proxy mechanism."
- "We note that the results are *not necessarily conclusive*."
- "Stock market returns of this nature are the market's first best *guess* as to the impact of this legislation."
- "Finally, news of the Boesky scandal was also breaking at this time period. . . . *[W]e do not know if* Ohio firms were more or less affected by this news."
- "The impact of the Ohio takeover legislation *may not be detrimental to Ohio*."
- "The law may have the effect of *preserving jobs in Ohio and keeping firms located in Ohio cities*."
- "No one has yet studied the *employment effect* of the Ohio takeover law."[15]

It is doubtful that any business executive, university administrator, or other serious decision maker would commission, act on, or even willingly pay for a study leading to such flimsily supported and totally hedged conclusions. If you ask the wrong questions, you will always get the wrong answers. It was for these reasons—notwithstanding the best computer studies of the Argentine Admiralty—that the British forces sunk *General Belgrano*, the only Argentine capital ship capable of getting up steam in time to participate in the Falklands War.

There is, by the way, a simple explanation for the mountain of qualifications in the SEC's Ohio study. You can find it in the work of Professor Donald Margotta of Northeastern University.[16] By appropriate adjustments to the portfolio and by extending the study period to include the first day after Governor Richard Celeste signed the Ohio Bill—the SEC study terminated before the bill was signed—he concludes that the Ohio legislation had no significant effects on either average stock prices or stockholder wealth. Finally, in assessing the evidence, one cannot overlook the fact that hostile bids and the response to them have resulted in recent years in the very substantial depletion of pension surpluses— $12 billion.

If all this is the result of hostile bids over a period of modern economic history sufficient to measure their impact, surely one must ask: Why are we doing this to ourselves when the Japanese and West Germans are not? Why do we behave as though we are as vulnerable as the Falkland Islanders before the Royal Navy Task Force sailed from Portsmouth? One must also ask: How do the directors of target companies respond in the face of these kinds of circumstances? Is the U.S. traditional form of corporate governance up to the task?[17]

In seeking to assess the role of corporate directors confronted with an unsolicited bid, one is reminded of the significance of two trenchant sayings that illustrate the practical issues. The first is a remark that Winston Churchill made to his doctor toward the end of his political career: "I'm glad that I've not my life to live over again; there's been such a dreadful degradation of standards."[18] The second is a quip of Carl Icahn's, uttered much more recently in his failed attempt to take over Phillips Petroleum: "The only way to get them [incumbent directors] off the golf course is to file a Schedule 13D."

Together they frame the impossible dilemma that confronts directors of U.S. public companies when they are called upon to react to their corporation being suddenly put in play. The dilemma is even sharper when one recalls that, for the directors, it is not their corporation at all because they only sit by the delegated authority that is granted and periodically renewed by the stockholders. They are very much like Rex Hunt, the colonial governor of the Falklands, confronted by the invading Argentine Forces with only a company of Royal Marines at his disposal.

The dilemma is this: How can men and women whose training and experience equip them to exercise the uniquely civilian task of industrial and financial leadership conceivably manage effectively under the "degraded standards" that govern economic warfare as practiced in hostile contests for control? How can they do so when the rules of engagement in that warfare require their decisions to be made in a legal setting where the right questions are never permitted to be asked—where the driving force is not what will ultimately aid the enterprise and the lives it impacts, but rather what responses are available to deal with a hostile initiative that can begin and end within the space of 20 business days?

Mr. Icahn's quip is a brilliant (though whimsical) statement of the issue, because it presupposes that ethically and economically useful results depend on a single Securities and Exchange Commission filing and its immediate aftermath. It is the modern equivalent of "Let them eat cake." Just as the French Queen Marie Antoinette never bothered to ask why the France of her day dissolved in bloodshed, so the takeover bidders of our time neither raise nor answer the relevant questions. "Let us enhance stockholder value" has been substituted for "Let them eat cake."

I have already set forth the relevant questions and supplied a representative sample of what passes for an answer from the bidders. I have also provided a brief summary of the scholarly evidence on the managerial record of successful bidders and the path of their own shares in the marketplace. In the face of this evidence, it is both farcical and dangerous to require that hostile contests for control be disposed of within the 20-business-day standard—a standard that can be avoided only by surrender within the period or extended only by a mountain of wasteful litigation. Such litigation contributes nothing toward making the enterprise under siege more productive in terms of its own performance or when measured by its impact on employees, communities, and other corporate constituencies. Deposition transcripts and interrogatory answers do not build superior machine tools.

The ordinary civilian director of a public company cannot make and execute sound business decisions within the blitzkrieg time constraints that govern hostile takeovers. The ordinary director is not a talented litigator, and it is the litigator who is, of course, the military leader in the economic warfare of control contests. One cannot expect Bernard Baruch to be General George Patton, nor could one expect General Patton to preside over a great U.S. company's future as we approach the third century of the Industrial Age. Similarly, the courtroom tacticians—and, indeed, lawyers generally—are the wrong people to hold in their hands the fate of a complex modern corporation when it has been put in play.

Moreover, the ordinary civilian director is virtually defenseless in the face of insider trading and the clandestine "parking" of stock. Civilians can confront and deal with known enemies when the contest is carried out under civilized rules, but they are helpless when matched against secret guerrillas who operate either without rules or beyond them. While we do not yet know the full extent of unlawful trading and parking in takeover contests of the recent past, it is apparent from the guilty pleas that have been entered up to now that it is widespread.

Furthermore, control contests should not be decided either by the payment or receipt of greenmail or by the use of pension surpluses. While it is not my purpose to criticize any particular transaction or its participants, I have no doubt that we will operate under degraded standards of the worst sort as long as our legal system countenances such devices by either side in a takeover situation.

Last, the conception of a modern corporation as being made up of nothing more than a paper charter and a transient group of stockholders must be replaced by a more sophisticated model. That is the problem with the Grundfest approach. No social or economic utility attaches to his $167 billion of "stockholder value" (which can, in any event, be obliterated in a single hour of trading) unless it can also be shown that there has been some resulting benefit to the nation as a whole that offsets the job losses, community disruptions, and other adverse effects that have resulted from the hostile-takeover movement.

The modern U.S. public corporation is a complex creature. Its acts and omissions have a broad impact on our society as a whole. It can no longer be viewed as existing solely for the benefit of trading profits on the part of the short-time holders of its securities.

Having now observed hostile takeovers and their consequences at first hand for half my life, it is quite apparent that there exists a compelling (indeed, I would say, an overpowering) need to deal legislatively with this unhappy infection in the life of the republic.

U.S. stockholders and the public generally are entitled to demand and enjoy a legal system that repudiates the blitzkrieg approach to corporate control contests, demilitarizes the process, eliminates the dominant role of lawyers in it, and acknowledges the complexity of the modern publicly traded corporation in the last days of the twentieth century.

For a long time I believed, along with many others, that the best hope for reforming the takeover laws required acceptance of three conventional notions:

First, that the Congress would control the process and that the Congress would never do more than revise, in a number of particulars (such as, for example, by enlarging the minimum offering period), the regulatory scheme it established in the Williams Act 20 years ago.

Second, that the Congress would, nevertheless, legislate for at least a reasonable number of those particulars if given a suitable interval to do so.[19]

Third, that, in the meanwhile, one must make do with carefully drafted state statutes seeking to discipline the hostile takeover phenomenon within the limits imposed on the states by the Commerce and Supremacy Clauses of the United States Constitution.[20]

Each of these three notions has proven to be wrong. Far from controlling the process, the Congress has ignored it. The House and Senate have refused—in the 98th Congress (1983–1984), in the 99th Congress (1985–1986), and now in the 100th Congress (1987–1988)—to deal with the issue. Indeed, in reflecting on the failure of these three Congresses to act, one is reminded of Harry Truman's criticism during the 1948 campaign of that "Do-Nothing 80th Congress." In addition, although a number of states (led by Ohio) have enacted statutes—and although some of those statutes (such as Ohio's) have enjoyed some substantial local success—the trend toward ever more and ever larger hostile takeovers has, on a national basis, sharply accelerated throughout the 1980s.[21]

Between the opening of the 98th Congress in 1983 and the imminent expiration of the 100th Congress later this year, we have come to learn a great deal more about hostile takeovers. If hostile takeovers do not improve the efficiency of the combined enterprise, do not benefit stockholders over the long haul, do not enhance productivity in any discernible macroeconomic way, do not create jobs, often inflict materially adverse effects on target-company communities, do not enhance the economic performance of target firms, dissipate pension funds, and reduce corporate governance to trench combat of a kind not seen since the Great War, why do we permit them at all?

Members of Congress could once plausibly argue that they could not legislate because the various data were in conflict. That argument no longer stands in the face of the scholarly evidence, which is now sufficient to establish, as a matter of fact, that hostile takeovers are destructive—both to those directly impacted by them and to society at large—and that they produce no countervailing economic or social benefits.

That being so, hostile takeovers should be abolished. This abolition must be effected by federal statute because modern Constitutional theory and the decided cases will not allow the states to do it. Although some technical legal phrases would ultimately be needed to harmonize it with other parts of existing law, the statute would be a simple one—two short sections, each made up of a single sentence:

ABOLITION OF
TENDER OFFERS ACT (1989)

Sec. 1. It shall be unlawful for any person to make a tender offer or a request or invitation for tenders.

Sec. 2. The Williams Act of 1968, as heretofore amended, is repealed except for Section 13(d) thereof [imposing certain disclosure requirements when any person or group acquires 5 percent or more of the shares of a publicly traded company].

Would such a statute inhibit legitimate corporate combinations? It would not. Tender offers are scarcely ever launched except as the vehicle for a hostile bid or in response to a hostile bid or the threat of one. Truly consensual transactions, preceded by careful planning and effected only pursuant to deliberative stockholder approval, would once again become the standard. Corporate control—the most valuable collective asset of the stockholders—would be disposed of only after allowing for the collective voice of the target-company stockholders to be expressed in a vote.

Would such a statute "entrench" poor management? It would not. It might have done so years ago when the individual investor was the dominant force in the market, but this is no longer the case. Most substantial public companies now have a majority (and often a very large majority) of their stock held by large institutions: mutual funds, pension trustees, bank trust departments, money managers, and the like. These institutions have the resources and, because of the size of their holdings, also possess the incentive to change bad management in the proper way—by means of a shareholder vote conducted through a proxy contest. Proxy contests are vastly cheaper to mount than tender offers. Moreover, a proxy contest, no matter how ferocious or prolonged, does not destroy the company. When it is over, there will still be something left for the management (whether incumbent or insurgent) to manage.

That these conclusions are accurate can best be demonstrated by the fact that there were, in the first half of 1988, 17 proxy contests for control (nearly three times the number that occurred in all of 1987).[22] In 9 of these cases (53 percent), the insurgents achieved, in one form or another, a material part of what they sought—including 5 radical financial restructurings. In 5 other cases, (29 percent), management got considerably less than 60 percent of the vote. In addition, there were another 43 sharply fought battles over specific corporate governance issues (poison pill rescission, confidential voting, equal access to proxy materials, and greenmail).[23] It is true that the insurgents did not succeed in any of these latter cases. Nevertheless, in many of them the antiincumbent vote was quite appreciable. For example, 49.1 percent of Santa Fe Southern Pacific's outstanding shares were voted in favor of rescinding Santa Fe's poison pill. The important point, however, once again comes from the analogy of warfare: No aggressor will ever take a fair vote seriously if he has a better chance to win by invasion. The Argentines had no interest in a Falkland Islands plebiscite. The 20-business-day blitzkrieg will inevitably take priority in corporate control contests for as long as the law allows it.

It is commonly and truly said that the outrageous nature of hostile tender offers has produced equally outrageous target-company reactions: poison pills, highly leveraged recapitalizations, management-led defensive buyouts, and serious issues of conflict of interest and self-dealing, for example.[24]

An inevitable and altogether healthy consequence of the adoption of the proposed Abolition of Tender Offers Act (1989) would be the elimination of most if not all of these defensive strategies in most if not all cases. These defenses are permitted solely by reason of a special body of jurisprudence that the courts have quite recently created.

The courts, correctly recognizing the hostile bid as a harsh departure from traditional methods of acquiring firms or changing their control, have authorized an equally harsh departure from traditional concepts of a director's duty. Although shrouded in classic language from historic opinions issued in a quieter time, the judgments rendered in takeover cases since 1985 have permitted a target board to treat a hostile bid as a unique threat to the corporation and its constituencies and therefore to open up with extremely aggressive (and often quite destructive) counter-battery fire so long as the court can be persuaded that the target's artillery barrage is "reasonable" in relation to the threat posed.[25] Unhappily but necessarily, reasonableness comes down essentially to whether the directors have asked the right questions, consulted the right advisors, and created the right record of their proceedings. Process takes precedence over products and people. The ultimate consequences of what target directors do or fail to do is successfully questioned only in the most unsavory situations.

The situation is like that of Flanders Field in 1915. Once the Germans let loose with the poison gas, anything went. One abomination inspired another. I agree with the outcome in these cases, just as I agree with President Truman's decision to drop the atomic bomb. Nevertheless, what works in war is often forbidden in peace. Every student of takeover law must agree that if the hostile tender offer goes, the resulting defenses go with it. The proposed Abolition of Tender Offers Act (1989) will procure exactly this result. When the Argentines go home, the Royal Navy will too.

Only two questions remain. The first is the question every responsible legislator must always ask: If the bill passes, who will be hurt? The answer is: no one; because the bill will not restrict changes in control that target stockholders approve, it will not disadvantage them. Because the bill will not allow entrenchment, it will not protect target management.

The only adverse impact will fall on arbitrageurs, speculators, other market players, and their advisors. As a group, they cannot command majorities in the Congress except by political contributions. If they can rule the Congress in this way, then we have an urgent national problem that is vastly more dangerous than hostile takeovers. It would be an ironic disaster if the campaign financing reforms of the 1970s, once regarded as bringing virtue to our political system, were to result in yet another failure of the Congress to address hostile takeovers and their consequences.

Finally, would serious congressional consideration of the bill (to say nothing of its enactment) provoke another "Black Monday"? Of course, it has been claimed by some that the mere fact that certain restrictive tax provisions were approved by the Committee on Ways and Means early in autumn 1987 either caused, or contributed mightily to, the market "meltdown." If that is true, then the case for the Abolition of Tender Offers Acts (1989) becomes all the more compelling. If the level of takeover speculation has become so intense that the modest possibility of a denial of the interest deduction on debt incurred to finance hostile deals and related tax-law changes can bring the equity markets to the threshold of collapse, then it is just as well that the threshold be crossed so that investment in those markets can once again be based on the real progress and realistic prospects of particular firms and specific industry groups. Enactment of the bill would ensure that such a farfetched result, if it actually did occur, would happen only once. If the act did indeed burst a speculative bubble created by the existence of the tender-offer process, that particular bubble would never again recur.

In grappling with the takeover question, the United States ought today to be thinking a good deal about Stanley Baldwin. Baldwin was three times prime minister of the United Kingdom in the 1920's and 1930s. There is no doubt in the minds of students of the period that Baldwin's patience, poise, tact, wit, common sense, and general toughmindedness saved Great Britain from the threat of revolution at the time of the General Strike in 1926—and also saved Great Britain from a grave constitutional crisis ten years later when King Edward VIII surrendered the throne and abdicated.

Baldwin's words now sound antique. His causes are largely forgotten, yet many of his speeches are as relevant today as they were when he made them. He remains, by the way, the only senior corporate executive officer throughout the entire history of Great Britain to serve as prime minister. He ran a steel company before he went to Parliament. Here is what Baldwin told the House of Commons in 1925, a time of great industrial difficulty throughout the United Kingdom:

I always want to see, at the head of these organisations on both sides [labor as well as management], men who have been right through the mill [and here he means the factory—the shop floor, the workplace—not the slogan], and who themselves know exactly where the shoe pinches, and who know exactly what can be conceded and what cannot, and who can make their reasons plain; and I hope that we shall always find such men [in management and labor alike] trying to steer their respective ships side by side, instead of making for head-on collisions.[26]

I would suggest that this is the kind of economic and industrial climate that we very badly need in the United States as we prepare ourselves for the twenty-first century, and I believe it can be done. I believe that we can have such a climate if we recognize that Mr. Pickens's ideas, and the ideas of takeover bidders generally, are the wrong ideas to guide our country as we enter into the third century of the Industrial Age.

At the start of the 98th Congress, the first of the three recent "Do-Nothing Congresses" insofar as hostile takeovers are concerned, a comprehensive history of the British Campaign in the Falklands appeared in London.[27] The authors, two distinguished British journalists, assessed the outcome of the British victory in this way:

This was a war which the British people should not have had to fight. Yet after so many years of what seemed like national failure and decline, they were confronted with a disaster which they still had the strength to rectify. They were reassured by the way the services had performed. They were pleased that a job which had to be done was done so well. They felt justified in renewed national pride and self-confidence.[28]

When, but not before, the Abolition of Tender Offers Act (1989) becomes law, similar words will accurately capture the state and spirit of this country.

NOTES

1. Portions of this chapter have previously been printed in *Directors & Boards* (Winter 1988): 6, and in *Corporate Growth* (July/August 1988): 14. They are reproduced here with permission.

2. Organized Polish military resistance to the German invasion ceased on September 28, 1939—on the 28th day of the campaign. Twenty-eight calendar days are, of course, exactly equivalent to 20 business days. The "bust up" of Poland, a common consequence of a hostile takeover, occurred on the following day upon the execution of a Russo-German Treaty that partitioned the country. See, W. S. Churchill, *The Gathering Storm* (Boston: Houghton Mifflin, 1948), pp. 447–448.

3. *Corporate Control Alert* (July 1988): 5.

4. U. S. Congress, Senate, *Report of the Senate Committee on Banking, Housing and Urban Affairs on the Tender Offer Disclosure and Fairness Act of 1987* (S. 1323), 100th Cong., 1st Sess. (December 17, 1987), p. 73 (additional Views of Senators Sasser, Sanford, and Chafee).

5. Hon. Joseph A. Grundfest and Bernard S. Black, *Stock Market Profits from Takeover Activity between 1981 and 1986: $167 Billion Is a Lot of Money* (September 28, 1987).

6. Charles Brown and James Medoff, *The Impact of Firm Acquisitions on Labor* (February 1987). Compare Richard S. Belous, *The Impact of Mergers and Acquisitions on Labor Markets* (March 31, 1987).

7. Hon. Joseph A. Grundfest, *Job Losses and Takeovers*, address to the University of Toledo College of Law, Third Annual Colloquium on Corporate Law and Social Policy, March 11, 1988.

8. *Edgar v. MITE Corp.*, 457 U.S. 624 at 646 (1982), J. Powell, concurring.

9. See, for example, "The Great Takeover Debate" (Pickens versus Trevor), *Financial Executive* (March/April 1988): 50 and 55.

10. Louis Lowenstein, *What's Wrong with Wall Street: Short-Term Gain and the Absentee Shareholder* (Reading, MA: Addison-Wesley Publishing Company, 1988).

11. Ibid., pp. 136–137.

12. F. M. Scherer, "Corporate Takeovers: The Efficiency Argument," *Journal of Economic Perspectives* 2, no. 1 (Winter 1988): 69–81.

13. Lowenstein, *What's Wrong with Wall Street*, p. 130.

14. Martin Lipton, "Corporate Governance in the Age of Finance Corporatism," *Univ. Penn. L. Rev.* 136 (1987): 27 n.117, citing a paper by D. Margotta and F. Marston.

15. Office of the Chief Economist of the Securities and Exchange Commission, *Shareholder Wealth Effects of Ohio Legislation Affecting Takeovers* (May 18, 1987), pp. 6, 17, 22–23 (emphasis supplied).

16. Donald G. Margotta, et al., "An Analysis of the Stock Price Effect of the 1986 Ohio Takeover Legislation" (in press). The authors state:

An issue relevant to a study's validity which we feel does not receive enough attention in the literature is the degree of *sensitivity* of the study's conclusions to alternative choices. If the conclusions change dramatically when net-of-market analysis is used in place of market model analysis, when an event window is extended or contracted by a single day, when the estimation period is changed slightly, or when a single firm is deleted from or added to a portfolio under consideration, then those conclusions are weak at best. (pp. 13–14; emphasis in original)

17. Adapted from Leigh B. Trevor, "The 'Blitzkrieged' Director," *Directors & Boards* (Winter 1988): 6.

18. In Britain, the standards have not yet become thus degraded. "Bids remain open longer, usually more than fifty and often as many as seventy-five days after the first announcement, long enough to produce reasonable, workable alternatives on which shareholders can then vote" Lowenstein, *What's Wrong with Wall Street*, p. 177.

19. Thus, I played a major role in drafting H.R. 1480 (the Shareholder Democracy Act of 1985), 99th Cong., 1st Sess., introduced by Hon. Edward J. Markey of Massachusetts on March 7, 1985. See also Leigh B. Trevor, "The Dingell-Markey Bill," *Buyouts & Acquisitions* (September/October 1987): 53. See also Leigh B. Trevor, "Hostile Takeovers in Perspective: Boethius, Boone and Baldwin," 525; *Corporate Growth* (July/August 1988): 14–18 and 53–55.

20. I have been involved for many years in the drafting of (and the defense against Constitutional attack on) state takeover laws. See Leigh B. Trevor and John W. Edwards II, "State Regulation of Corporate Takeovers: Developments since *Edgar v. MITE Corp.*," *Buyouts & Acquisitions* (April/May 1985); Leigh B. Trevor, John W. Edwards II, and Robert S. Walker, "The Takeover Laws: The Debate Continues," *Petroleum Management* 10, no. 1 (January 1988): 49; and Leigh B. Trevor and John W. Edwards II, "CTS Reaffirms State Role in Corporate Affairs," *The National Law Journal* (February 8, 1988).

21. *Veere, Inc. v. The Firestone Tire and Rubber Co.*, (No. C–88–0571A, N.D. Ohio, E. Div., March 16, 1988).

22. *Corporate Control Alert* (July 1988): 5.

23. *The Georgeson Report* no. 351 (2d Quarter 1988): 3.

24. *Norlin Corp. v. Rooney Pace, Inc.*, 744 F.2d 255 (2d Cir. 1984); *Bass Group, Inc. v. Evans (In Re Macmillan, Inc. Shareholders Litigation)* (Del. Ch., July 14, 1988).

25. *Unocal Corp. v. Mesa Petroleum Co.*, 493 A.2d 946 (Del., 1985).

26. Rt. Hon. Stanley Baldwin, *On England and Other Addresses* (Freeport, New York: Books for Libraries Press, 1971), p. 49; *Hansard's* (House of Commons) (March 1925).

27. Max Hastings and Simon Jenkins, *The Battle for the Falklands* (London: Michael Joseph, 1983) [Reprinted by permission of W. W. Norton & Co., New York, holder of the U.S. rights].

28. Ibid., p. 340.

3

MERGER-MANIA: AN EMPIRICAL CRITIQUE

Walter Adams
and James W. Brock

Get money, money still
And then let virtu follow, if she will.

—Jonathan Swift

Since 1980, the U.S. economy has been ensnarled in a maelstrom of merger-mania. The annual value of corporate acquisitions and takeovers has skyrocketed, from $33 billion in 1980 to $204 billion in 1986. New all-time records have been set—and broken—in recent years. The number of megamergers, valued at $1 billion or more, has exploded by tenfold. All told, the cumulative value of corporate mergers and acquisitions has topped two-thirds of a trillion dollars since 1980.[1]

Apologists have embraced this corporate feeding frenzy, and even celebrated it, on three main grounds. First, they assert that it benefits small investors by disciplining substandard managements and by transferring corporate control to more competent hands. Second, they hypothesize that it benefits the nation, too, by "restructuring" the corporate United States, and by unleashing efficiency, innovation, and productivity gains. Third, they confidently insist that, at worst, merger-mania is harmless because corporate deals can always later be undone if they fail to work out.

However, what does the evidence tell us? Do small investors really benefit from corporate deal-mania? Do mergers and acquisitions really promote superior economic performance? Is merger-mania really benign? The weight of the empirical evidence strongly suggests that it is not.

ADVERSE IMPACT ON SMALL INVESTORS

Far from being the prime beneficiaries of merger-mania, small investors lose, on balance, and in a variety of important ways. First, numerous studies reveal that the stock value of acquiring firms typically falls—an average of 1 percent to 7 percent in the first year, and a cumulative 16 percent over the three years following corporate takeovers.[2] This fact is not disputed, even by the most doctrinaire defenders of takeovers.

Second, these declines typically cancel out any gains in the stock value of acquired firms at the time of takeover. Murray Weidenbaum, President Reagan's first chairman of the Council of Economic Advisers, reports that:

The data do *not* support the notion that owners of acquiring firms generally benefit from takeovers. The available evidence of aggregate returns further suggests that acquiring firm losses on average are large enough to completely offset the gains made by owners of target firms.[3] (emphasis added)

In other words, considered as a group, stockholders typically lose.

Third, an in-depth study by Edward S. Herman and Louis Lowenstein reveals that typically the targets in corporate takeovers have significantly better performance records than the acquirers—that is, the targets are, on balance, better managed than the acquirers seeking to buy them.[4] This finding suggests that corporate deal-mania is transferring control of the nation's resources from more to less competent hands.

Fourth, leveraged buyouts (LBOs) are not a boon for small investors. When publicly held companies are bought out and "taken private" by a tiny coterie of insiders, only to be later sold back to the public, the small investor seldom shares in the bonanza. For example, the Gibson Greeting Card Co. was taken private in 1982 by a group that paid stockholders $80 million; a year and a half later, the firm was sold back to the public for $290 million—more than three times the amount paid to the original stockholders. More generally, a recent study of LBOs found the difference between the value paid to original stockholders and the value obtained when the assets were later retaken public to average 281 percent—spectacular gains that did not accrue to small investors.[5]

Fifth, bondholders also lose, as high takeover premiums, high debt-equity ratios, and astronomical fixed-interest charges combine to degrade the quality and value of their bond holdings. In the aftermath of the recent buyout of Colt Industries, for example, the firm's outstanding long-term bonds plunged as much as $200 for every $1,000 in face value.

The RJR Nabisco mega-buyout of 1988 has triggered lawsuits by bond-holders who have suffered multi-million-dollar losses on the firm's bonds. With bond-rating agencies like Moody's and Standard & Poor's downgrading record numbers of corporate bonds, one analyst points out that merger-mania is "slaughtering" bond holders.[6]

Sixth, the lion's share of the booty is captured by a small number of Wall Street marriage brokers—investment banks, corporate executives, professional arbitrageurs, and (at times) criminally knowledgeable inside traders.[7] Consider the Beatrice buyout in 1986. Who were the big winners? They were Drexel Burnham, providing junk-bond financing for the deal for $86 million in fees plus projected profits of $810 million; Kohlberg, Kravis, Roberts, arranging the buyout for $45 million in fees plus projected profits of $2.4 billion; Kidder, Peabody & Co., advising Kohlberg Kravis for $15 million in fees; Lazard Freres & Co., advising Beatrice for $8 million in fees; and Saloman Brothers, advising Beatrice for $8 million in fees.[8] For these five participants, the fee packages alone amounted to more than a quarter-billion dollars.[9] For two of them, projected profits totalled $2.3 billion.

Top management also seems to have comfortably accommodated itself to merger-mania. In the Beatrice deal, the firm's former chairman will receive an estimated $20 million in fees plus a $1.3-million annual salary and projected profits from the deal of $277 million. The chairman of dressmaker Leslie Fay netted $60 million on his initial buyout investment of less than $1 million. The chairman of Uniroyal expects to receive $20 million on his buyout investment of less than $750,000. Finally, the chief executive of Metromedia has garnered profits estimated at $3 billion from the buyout of his firm—without investing any cash at all.[10] Thus, merger-mania is a financial shell game played for the sake of greed merchants on Wall Street, not for small investors on Main Street.[11]

ADVERSE CONSEQUENCES FOR ECONOMIC PERFORMANCE

The wrecks and failures littering the corporate merger trail contradict the claim that deal-mania enhances economic performance. First, hyperactive acquirers, who gorged themselves on mergers and acquisitions in the 1960s and 1970s are today divesting scores of previously acquired operations. They are concentrating on what they know best, jettisoning the rest, and boosting their economic and financial performance in the process.[12]

Thus, ITT—the preeminent conglomerateur of the 1960s, which grew through acquisitions from an obscure Caribbean telephone company to one of the nation's very largest industrial concerns—has recently sold off 95 businesses, including an oil and gas company, Canadian timberlands, Continental Baking, and soda-bottling operations.[13] Gulf & West-ern—another leading conglomerateur of the 1960s—has recently shed more than 60 businesses. The divested operations range from sugar and zinc production to cigar manufacturing and racetracks.[14] General Mills has sold off some 26 businesses in the wake of its loss-ridden merger spree—a takeover binge that featured acquisitions of restaurants, Play Doh, and costume jewelry, among others.[15] Transamerica, through its diversification program, has, according to one financial analyst, dem-onstrated "that if you diversify enough you can keep your earnings low."[16]

United Airlines has reversed course, abjuring its grandiose plans to merge itself into a one-stop, full-service travel conglomerate. In a major reorientation of direction, in 1987 United announced its decision to divest its acquired hotel operations (Westin and Hilton International), to spin off its acquired rental car division (Hertz), and to scrap its short-lived "Allegis" logo.[17] Westinghouse Corp., after undertaking numerous ac-quisitions (including a mail-order house, a watchmaker, and a housing developer), has recently spun off dozens of operations in an effort to improve its performance.[18] Raytheon Co.'s merger-and-acquisition binge, according to the *Wall Street Journal*, has diluted the firm's overall profitability and generated mediocrity and recurrent losses for its ac-quired units.[19]

Big oil has struggled to extricate itself from a series of disastrous forays into merger-induced expansionism: ARCO has disposed if its ill-fated investment in Anaconda Minerals and absorbed a $785 million write-down in the process.[20] Mobil has finally found a buyer for its money-losing Montgomery-Ward subsidiary. Mobil also has divested its Con-tainer Corp. paperboard and packaging subsidiary.[21] Exxon has written off hundreds of millions of dollars of failed investments in Reliance Electric and office-equipment systems.[22] Amoco has spun off Cyprus Mines (a copper producer).[23] Sohio has divested non-oil acquisitions.[24] Finally, Schlumberger has sold Fairchild Semiconductor, absorbing a $200-million write-off in this failed merger.[25] Big Steel's recent merger record is no more reassuring.[26] Armco's acquisition of insurance oper-ations has produced more than a half-billion dollars of financial losses.[27] National Steel's diversification into oil, pharmaceutical distribution, and five-and-dime retailing (Ben Franklin stores) is foundering.[28] U.S. Steel has divested chemical operations that languished under the firm's tu-telage.[29]

Second, generalized statistical analyses corroborate these results. In their massive, recently published study of 6,000 corporate mergers and acquisitions, for example, Ravenscraft and Scherer find that the average merger is followed by deteriorating profit performance, that these pro-ductivity and efficiency losses cast doubt on the efficiency-enhancing faith in mergers, that there is no credible evidence that mergers enhance R&D (research and development) and technological innovation, and that the adverse performance-consequences of mergers have been responsible for a not insignificant portion of declining productivity in the United States.[30] Other researchers report similar findings.[31]

Third, the startlingly high merger failure rate further contradicts claims that merger-mania promotes good economic performance. According to *Business Week*, "A half to two-thirds of all mergers don't work; one in three is later undone. In 1985, for every seven acquisitions, there were three divestitures."[32] Similarly, a recent McKinsey & Co. study of the merger record of 56 large U.S. firms over the period 1972 through 1983 concluded that most (39 of 56) of the firms that embarked on diversification programs failed.[33] As summarized by Peter Drucker, 2 mergers out of 5 are "outright disasters," 2 "neither live nor die," and 1 "works"—a less than stirring testimonial.[34] Particularly revealing is a recent study by Michael Porter, who examined the merger record of 33 large, prestigious U.S. firms over the 1950–1986 period. Porter found that the

corporate strategies of most companies have dissipated instead of created shareholder value. . . . [O]n average corporations divested more than half their acquisitions in new industries and more than 60% of their acquisitions in entirely new fields. . . . The track record in unrelated acquisitions is even worse—the average divestment rate is a startling 74%.[35]

Specific firms and their failure rates include: ITT (52 percent), General Foods (63 percent), General Electric (65 percent), Xerox (71 percent), General Mills (75 percent), RCA (80 percent), and CBS (87 percent). In all, it is a performance that Porter terms "dismal."[36]

THE "OPPORTUNITY COST" OF MERGER-MANIA

Finally, merger-mania is not merely benign, as its defenders assume; nor is it costless. This is because for mergers, as elsewhere in economic life, there is no such thing as a free lunch. Instead, the iron law of "opportunity cost" applies. As economists know, opportunity cost refers to the inescapable fact that every choice unavoidably entails sacrifice— that choosing one course of action necessarily means forgoing other alternatives or opportunities. A pitcher who chooses to throw a fastball sacrifices the option of throwing a curve. A quarterback who calls for a forward pass forgoes the alternative of engineering a fullback plunge into the line. In the same way, a nation that devotes itself to merger-mania forgoes the opportunity to engage in economically productive pursuits.

Thus, two decades of managerial attention devoted to playing the merger game (organizing raids, devising poison pills and shark repellants, and constructing golden parachutes) are, at the same time, two decades during which management attention has been diverted from the critically important task of building new plants, bringing out new products, developing new state-of-the-art manufacturing techniques, and creating new jobs. Hundreds of billions of dollars spent shuffling paper ownership shares are, at the same time, hundreds of billions of dollars not spent on productivity-enhancing investments to reindustrialize the United States and to restore its international competitiveness. So, too, the billions of dollars absorbed in the legal fees and investment banking commissions integral to the merger game—expenses incurred at the initial corporate nuptials as well as at the subsequent divorce proceedings—are, at the same time, billions of dollars not plowed directly into the nation's industrial base.

Placed in an opportunity-cost context, corporate deal-mania represents a monumental diversion, dissipation, and misallocation of scarce resources, talents, and entrepreneurial energies. In 1986, for example, the corporate United States spent more on mergers and acquisitions ($204 billion) than it did on industry-financed research and development ($56 billion) and net new plant investment ($81 billion) combined. For a nation struggling with record foreign-trade deficits, losses of markets at home and abroad, and a global competitiveness problem of sizeable magnitude, the opportunity-cost consequence of mergers requires no adumbration. It is tantamount to rearranging deck chairs on the Titanic.[37]

CONCLUSION

In sum, the evidence has not been kind to merger-mania and its fuglemen. Contrary to their claims, small investors are, more often than not, the victims—not the beneficiaries—of corporate deal-mania. Economic performance suffers, and far from being benign, merger-mania imposes a heavy (and possibly intolerable) opportunity cost on the economy.

Perhaps the elder Henry Ford best grasped the nub of the problem. During the Roaring '20s, in the midst of that earlier era of speculation, manipulation and corporate consolidation, Ford pointed out that "some of the most successful money-makers of our times have never added one penny-worth to the wealth of men," asking: "Does a card player add to the wealth of the world?" He concluded that: "Speculation in things already produced—that is not business. It is just more or less respectable graft."[38]

NOTES

1. "1987" Profile, *Mergers & Acquisitions* (May/June 1988): 45. For an expanded analysis, see the authors' forthcoming book on mergers, takeovers, and buyouts (Pantheon).

2. See Judith H. Dobrzynski, "For Better or for Worse?" *Business Week*, Jan. 12, 1987, p. 39. For a painstakingly thorough confirmation of these findings, see Ellen B. Magenheim and Dennis C. Mueller, "Are Acquiring-Firm Shareholders Better Off after Acquisition?" in John C. Coffee, Louis Lowenstein, and Susan Rose-Ackerman, eds., *Knights, Raiders, and Targets* (New York: Oxford University Press, 1988), pp. 171–93. Magenheim and Mueller estimate changes in the value of stock held in acquiring firms over various time periods following merger. Evaluated relative to pre-merger trends, they estimate share prices to decline by 42 percent over the three-year period following acquisition (Ibid., p. 181).

3. Murray Weidenbaum and Stephen Vogt, *Takeovers and Stockholders: Winners and Losers*, St. Louis, MO: Center for the Study of American Business no. 83 (Dec. 1987), p. 6.

4. Edward S. Herman and Louis Lowenstein, "The Efficiency Effects of Hostile Takeovers," in Coffee, Lowenstein, and Rose-Ackerman, *Knights, Raiders and Targets*, pp. 218–33.

5. U.S. Congress, House, Subcommittee on Oversight and Investigations of the Committee on the Judiciary, *Committee Print: Leveraged Buyouts and the Pot of Gold: Trends, Public Policy, and Case Studies*, 100th Cong., 1st sess., 1987, pp. 9, 28–29.

6. U.S. Congress, *Leveraged Buyouts and the Pot of Gold*, pp. 58–60. For additional examples, see John Brooks, *The Takeover Game* (New York: E. P. Putnam, 1987), pp. 232–233. At the same time, the sharp escalation of corporate debt, concomitant with mergers, takeovers, and leveraged buyouts, renders the corporate sector more fragile and the general economy more vulnerable to business downturns. These high debt levels also constrict the Federal Reserve's capacity to conduct monetary policy operations. See Lindley H. Clark and Alfred L. Malabre, "Takeover Trend Helps Push Corporate Debt and Defaults Upward," *Wall Street Journal*, March 15, 1988, p. 1.

7. "For big banks, lending for mergers and leveraged buyouts is rapidly becoming one of their biggest businesses. Indeed, for some, more than 40% of their commercial and industrial lending is now merger-related" Sarah Bartlett, "Need a Quick Billion or Two?" (*Business Week*, October 26, 1987, p. 98). On the machinations of the insider traders, see Mark Stevens, *The Insiders* (New York: Putnam, 1987).

8. See U.S. Congress, *Leveraged Buyouts and the Pot of Gold*, pp. 68–71, and James Steingold, "Shaking Billions from Beatrice," *New York Times*, Sept. 6, 1987, sec. 3, p. 1. See also Richard B. Schmitt, "If an Investment Bank Says the Deal Is Fair, It May or May Not Be," *Wall Street Journal*, March 10, 1988, p. 1.

9. In the Texaco-Getty takeover, one investment banker was paid the equivalent of $126,582 per hour (Brooks, *The Takeover Game*, p. 20). These fees "may do more to explain current merger mania than all the blather about synergy and diversification" Richard Phalon, "Fuel for the Flames," (*Forbes*, Nov. 18, 1985, p. 122).

10. U.S. Congress, *Leveraged Buyouts and the Pot of Gold*, pp. 29, 89.

11. "Advocates of mergers and acquisitions argue that they are advantageous to stockholders because of the premium, often very large, that is paid by the acquirer. But in practice, most of that profit almost always goes to arbitrageurs" (Brooks, *The Takeover Game*, p. 143). For an incisive analysis of the victimization of small investors in one recent buyout, see Benjamin Stein, "Leveraged Buyouts: On the Level?" *New York Times Sunday Magazine*, Jan. 17, 1988, p. 40.

Such speculations worked upon small investors are not new. Examining the four major merger movements in the United States between 1897 and 1987, Professors Richard Du Boff and Edward Herman find each marked by

varying but significant degrees of misinformation, manipulation, the outcropping of fads, euphoria, and speculation. . . . Most important, there is a consistent historical record that the merger gains of promoters, investment bankers, and corporate insiders have been "more unequivocal" than those of shareholders. (Richard B. Du Boff and Edward S. Herman, "The Promotional-Financial Dynamic of Merger Movements: A Historical Perspective," *Journal of Economic Issues*, 33 (March 1989): 108–109.

Of the turn-of-the-century merger movement, Du Boff and Herman report that "the function of the publicity supplied to investors was not to elucidate but to sell, and it was so misleading as to constitute, in effect, a disinformation campaign." The "interests of the shareholders at large were, at best, an afterthought" (ibid., pp. 110–111).

Of the 1920s merger movement, Du Boff and Herman report:

Many of the holding company structures and investment companies of the 1920s were organized to take advantage of bull market psychology and to feed the demands of the extensive security selling apparatus built up in the late 1920s. Hard sell tactics and misrepresentation on a very large scale characterized this market. The financial establishment encouraged the new army of investors to believe that everyone could get rich in the ever-upward market of the New Era. (Ibid., pp. 116–117.)

In regard to the "Go-Go" conglomerate merger wave of the 1960s, they find that the

movement was initiated and promoted mainly by conglomerate entrepreneurs, with investment bankers, commercial bankers, and the brokerage community serving more as advisers, finders, and cooperative lenders and security salespeople. The bankers and brokers were important gainers. . . . The insider-managers-promoters were major winners. . . . [However, the] shareholders of the acquiring firms, as we have seen, were on the average nongainers. (Ibid., pp. 120–121.)

12. Generally, see Walter Adams and James W. Brock, *The Bigness Complex* (New York: Pantheon, 1987). In addition, see Leslie Wayne, "Fleeing the Corporate Stable," *New York Times*, Nov. 15, 1981, sec. 3, p. 1; "Big Goes Bust," *Economist*, April 17, 1982, p. 67; "Small is Beautiful Now in Manufacturing," *Business Week*, Oct. 22, 1984, p. 152; Steven E. Prokesch and William J. Powell, "Do Mergers Really Work?" *Business Week*, June 3, 1985, p. 88; Stewart Toy, "Splitting Up: The Other Side of Merger Mania," *Business Week*, July 1, 1985, p. 50; and Claire Poole and Jeffrey A. Trachtenberg, "Bear Hug," *Forbes*, Nov. 16, 1987, p. 186. These articles detail the failures of mergers and, especially, the debilitating effects of merger-induced corporate bigness.

13. See Geoffrey Colvin, "The De-Geneening of ITT," *Fortune*, Jan. 11, 1982, p. 34; "Behind the ITT Deal: Will Araskog's Radical Surgery Work?" *Business Week*, July 14, 1986, p. 62; Christopher Power, "How Cleaning House May Help ITT Clean Up," *Business Week*, March 23, 1987, p. 64; and Randall Smith, "ITTs Stock has Outpaced the Market Lately, and Some See More Gains as Firm Pares Lines," *Wall Street Journal*, June 5, 1986, p. 51.

14. See Laura Landro, "Davis Reshapes G&W into an Entertainment and Financial Concern," *Wall Street Journal*, June 10, 1985, p. 1.

15. See Steven Prokesch, "New General Mills is Lean and Mean," *New York Times*, Jan. 5, 1987, p. 19; and Steve Weiner and Janis Bultman, "Calling Betty Crocker," *Business Week*, Aug. 8, 1988, p. 88. For a detailed examination of General Mill's failed acquisition of Parker Brothers toys and games, see Ellen Wojahn, *Playing by Different Rules* (New York: Amacom, 1988).

16. See "Transamerica: Making a Monkey of Itself?" *Economist*, Sept. 27, 1986, p. 72; and Andrew Pollack, "Streamlining Transamerica," *New York Times*, Aug. 14, 1986, p. 32.

17. See Robert Johnson, "Full Service Just Didn't Fly," *Wall Street Journal*, June 11, 1987, p. 10; and James E. Ellis and Chuck Hawkins, "The Unraveling of an Idea," *Business Week*, June 22, 1987, p. 42.

18. See Gregory L. Miles and Dave Griffiths, "How Westinghouse is Revving Up after the Rebound," *Business Week*, March 28, 1988, p. 46.

19. See Laurie P. Cohen, "Raytheon is among Companies Regretting High-Tech Mergers," *Wall Street Journal*, Sept. 10, 1984, p. 1; and Gary Putka, "Forecasters Expect Raytheon to Shed Some of Its Units," *Wall Street Journal*, Sept. 13, 1988, p. 6.

20. Thomas C. Hayes, "Arco Has $785 Million Charge," *New York Times*, August 28, 1984, p. 31.

21. Julia F. Siler, "$3.8 Billion Buyout Set for Ward," *New York Times*, March 8, 1988, p. 27; and Allanna Sullivan, "Mobil Will Sell Packaging Unit for $700 Million," *Wall Street Journal*, July 28, 1986, p. 2.

22. See Lewis Beman, "Exxon's $600-Million Mistake," *Fortune*, Oct. 19, 1981, p. 68; Steve Swartz, "Exxon to Shed Reliance Electric Unit," *Wall Street Journal*, Dec. 12, 1986, p. 2; and Richard P. Schmitt and Laurie P. Cohen, "Humbled Giant: Exxon's Flop in Field of Office Gear Shows Diversification Perils," *Wall Street Journal*, Sept. 3, 1985, p. 1.

23. Daniel F. Cuff, "Indiana Standard's Strategy," *New York Times*, Jan. 28, 1985, p. 21.

24. Ralph E. Winter, "Standard Oil Agrees to Sell 2 Copper Mines," *Wall Street Journal*, Sept. 12, 1986, p. 10.

25. Richard B. Schmitt, "Schlumberger Reaches Accord to Sell Fairchild," *Wall Street Journal*, Sept. 1, 1987, p. 2.

26. It is instructive to remember that the largest U.S. steel companies have been built up through 80 years of sustained merger, acquisition, and consolidation. U.S. Steel Corp.—the combination of combinations— was created in 1901 as the product of a succession of mergers and combinations, collectively representing approximately 170 formerly independent plants and operations. Bethlehem Steel was incorporated in 1904 as a combination of 10 steel producers; over the years 1914 through 1945, Bethlehem acquired 33 more steel concerns.

Republic Steel was incorporated in 1930 as a consolidation of 4 formerly independent producers; Republic subsequently acquired 6 additional firms. Jones & Laughlin Steel was incorporated in 1902, and acquired 9 additional steel operations thereafter. Armco Steel grew in similar fashion. See Federal Trade Commission, *The Merger Movement: A Summary Report* (Washington, D.C.: Federal Trade Commission 1948), pp. 70–134; and U.S. Congress, House, Select Committee on Small Business, *Hearings: Steel—Acquisitions, Mergers and Expansion of 12 Major Companies, 1900 to 1950*, 81st Cong., 2d sess., 1950.

Consolidation in steel has continued apace. In 1968, Wheeling Steel (then the nation's 10th largest steel firm) merged with Pittsburgh Steel (16th largest). In 1971, National Steel (4th largest in the nation) acquired Granite City Steel (13th largest). In 1978, Jones & Laughlin Steel (7th largest) was combined with Youngstown Sheet & Tube (8th largest), and in 1984, LTV (the operator of the combined Youngstown/Jones & Laughlin facilities, and the nation's 3d largest steel producer) merged with Republic Steel (4th largest), to create the 2d largest steel firm in the country. See Walter Adams and Hans Mueller, "The Steel Industry," in Walter Adams, ed., *The Structure of American Industry*, 7th ed. (New York: Macmillan, 1986), pp. 80–81.

Clearly, merger-induced corporate giantism has not ameliorated Big Steel's perennial performance problems—a point that the bankruptcy of the LTV-Republic combination in 1986, only two years after its formation, seems to underscore.

27. Gregory L. Miles and John A. Byrne, "Smeltdown at Armco: Behind the Steelmaker's Long Slide," *Business Week*, Feb. 1, 1988, p. 48.

28. J. Ernest Beazley, "Steelmaker Has the Diversification Blues," *Wall Street Journal*, June 30, 1988, p. 24.

29. Gregory L. Miles, "The Alchemy That Turned Aristech into Gold," *Business Week*, Sept. 19, 1988, p. 154.

30. David J. Ravenscraft and F. M. Scherer, *Mergers, Sell-Offs and Economic Efficiency* (Washington, D.C.: Brookings Institute, 1987).

31. See, for example, Dennis C. Mueller, "Mergers and Market Share," *Review of Economics and Statistics* 67 (May 1985): 259; Dennis C. Mueller, "The Effects of Conglomerate Mergers," *Journal of Banking and Finance* 1 (Dec. 1977): 315; Edward S. Herman and Louis Lowenstein, "The Efficiency Effects of Hostile Takeovers," in Coffee, Lowenstein, and Rose-Ackerman, *Knights, Raiders and Targets*, pp. 211–240; Stephen A. Rhoades, *Power, Empire Building, and Mergers* (Lexington, Mass.: Lexington Books, 1983); Mark W. Frankena and Paul A. Pautler, *Antitrust Policy for Declining Industries*, Staff Report, Federal Trade Commission (Washington, D.C.: Federal Trade Commission Oct. 1985); and David L. Birch, "Buyers Beware," *Inc.*, June 1988, pp. 21–22.

32. "Inside A School For Dealmakers," *Business Week*, July 27, 1986, p. 82.

33. "Diversification Blues," *Mergers & Acquisitions*, (May/June 1987), p. 13.

34. "Interview: Peter Drucker," *Forbes*, Jan. 18, 1982, p. 36.

35. Michael E. Porter, "From Competitive Advantage to Corporate Strategy," *Harvard Business Review*, Vol. 65, (May-June 1987), p. 45.

36. Ibid., p. 43. Ironically, by owning and increasingly controlling the diverse firms they buy into, the largest takeover organizations are, in substance, recreating the conglomerate corporate structures of the 1960s—a less than aus-

picious development given the failures of conglomerate mergers just documented. See Carol J. Loomis, "Buyout Kings," *Fortune*, July 4, 1988, p. 53.

37. In the same vein, it is fatuous to argue that because the failed mergers of the 1960s and 1970s are now being undone, corporate deal-mania represents the genius of the market in action. Merely returning back to the status quo ante of the 1960s is scarcely progress in any meaningful sense—especially when the world's most competitive nations (for example, Japan) have forged a two-decade-long lead in the meantime.

38. Henry Ford, *My Life and Work* (New York: Doubleday, 1926), pp. 7, 269.

PART II

ECONOMIC, LEGAL, AND RELATED ISSUES

4

THE ECONOMIC IMPLICATIONS OF THE CHANGING MERGER PROCESS

Edward R. Bruning

The most recent merger activity can be differentiated from previous merger periods by the use of an instrument of unification known as the takeover, particularly the hostile takeover. Takeovers must be viewed within the context of merger activity in general, however, in order to appreciate their significance. Among the many types of mergers, the takeover is the most colorful and awe-inspiring to the general layman. It involves a move by one firm to take over, or seize, another firm against the management's will. It can be friendly (that is, in concurrence with management and the corporate board's wishes), hostile (that is, against either's wishes), or mixed. The key element is that management in the target firm comes immediately under different control. The would-be new owners typically make a tender offer to buy controlling amounts of stock at a price above the current market price (usually 20- to 40-percent higher). This premium reflects their belief that they can manage the company so much better that profits will rise sharply and the stock price will elevate over the takeover price. Takeovers are often done by corporate outsiders, aiming primarily at sluggish firms' substantial market positions. It is believed that current management has failed to fully exploit resources and opportunities, and, as a consequence, that stock prices are artificially low.

External to the fact that immediate gainers and losers are involved in the play for corporate power in a takeover, it is important that a broader issue be kept in perspective. My purpose in this chapter is to focus on the changes that have occurred in the merger process over four merger periods and to assess the impact of the takeover as a technique of corporate unification. The chapter commences with an overview of the trend toward increasing concentration of economic activity and the role mergers have played in this process. Each merger period will be discussed in relation to the resulting economic impacts as well as society's political-regulatory response. The contributions from economic theory in attempting to come to grips with the merger/takeover phenomenon will be assessed. In the final section, various public-policy responses are outlined and evaluated in light of present-day political and economic realities.

MERGER PERIODS

F. M. Scherer makes the point that "any merger among firms competing in the same market is a step toward increased concentration."[1] Although some will argue that this position is extreme, needless to say, mergers have facilitated the tendencies toward concentration of economic power in the United States. We can identify four specific periods that have been characterized by intense merger activity: 1887 through 1904, 1916 through 1929, 1948 through 1973, and from the early 1970s to the present.[2]

The earliest documented merger period began as a recovery from the worldwide depression of the 1880s and continued until the commencement of another major depression in 1904. During this period, significant changes were occurring in technological developments applied to manufacturing, communications, transportation, and various social institutions. An interesting fact is that the initial merger movement began a few years prior to passage of the Sherman Act in 1890. Mergers during this period tended to be horizontal, whereby firms merged with others operating in the same or similar markets. Despite congressional intent and the ensuing legislation of the late nineteenth century, businesses were skilled in locating loopholes in the law and were able to elude many of the sanctions associated with the antitrust laws.

Samuel Reid points out that a total of 2,653 mergers occurred during the period 1898–1902 with capitalizations amounting to $6.3 billion.[3] Seager and Gulick indicated that by 1904, large trusts controlled over 40 percent of the manufacturing capital in the United States.[4] Furthermore, it is generally accepted by many students of the merger movements that concentration was increased considerably during this period and that monopolization was a reality in many markets. It was believed that the dominant focus of merger activities was strictly to obtain a monopoly position in as many markets as possible. J. Moody studied 92 major mergers and found that large firms dominated 80 percent or more of the markets in which they operated.[5]

The second merger period commenced shortly before World War I and continued into the early 1930s as the Great Depression was unfolding. Between 1925 and 1931, 5,846 mergers occurred with asset valuations totalling $9.6 billion. The data dramatize the fact that more than twice as many reported mergers took place over this seven-year period than occurred in the entire first merger wave.[6] The share of total manufacturing assets of the 100 largest firms rose by 8 percent during the seven years. An interesting fact is that the second merger period, far outpacing the first wave in terms of dollar volume as well as asset valuations, commenced shortly after passage of the Clayton Act and the Federal Trade Commission Act in 1914. In similar fashion, the second period ended with a major depression.

The third major movement, the largest and most persistent, began in the post–World War II period and continued throughout the mid–1970s as the OPEC phenomenon wrought havoc in much of the western industrialized world. The number of firms acquired during the period 1955 through 1974 exceeded 20,000, with approximately one-half of acquisitions taking place between 1965 and 1970. During this period, the number of very large firms (assets valued in excess of $10 million) was 1,439, involving nearly $68 billion.[7] In addition, the 200 largest firms acquired or merged with 622 of the large firms with stock valuations totalling close to $40 billion. One particularly distinguishing characteristic of the third merger wave, in addition to its size and longevity, was the breadth of the economic sectors affected. Included in the corporate restructurings were firms from manufacturing, mining, banking, transportation, insurance, and wholesale and retail trade, and firms in the service sectors. The pace of corporate acquisitions increased even though a major antitrust amendment was passed by the Congress (the Cellar-Kefauver amendment to the Clayton Act) and the Supreme Court was applying its "structuralist" interpretations in efforts to stem the tide of corporate giantism.

By the mid–1970s, three merger waves followed legislative efforts to curb concentration tendencies. Each wave commenced during prosperous periods, and, as Scherer points out, "during periods when smaller firms have an environment conducive to growth and entrenchment if left alone."[8] In similar fashion, each wave subsided only after a significant economic recession or depression.

Aside from the relatively high absolute levels of transactions, the third merger wave was quite different from the first two. The Celler-Kefauver Antimonopoly Act of 1950, and subsequent judicial interpretations, discouraged horizontal and vertical mergers entailing sizeable market shifts. Instead, managements chose the conglomerate merger option to build empires. The Federal Trade Commission (FTC) distinguishes between mergers that are horizontal (merging companies sell closely related products in the same geographical market), vertical (where a potential buyer-seller relationship is established), and conglomerate. Conglomerations are of three types. First, the product-extension conglomerate entails joining of noncompeting products with related marketing channels or productive processes. Second, a market-extension conglomerate occurs when a firm acquires another firm with like production facilities in a market it previously had not served. Third, the "pure" conglomerate is a merger involving firms with no clear competitive, potential buyer-seller, or functional relationship between them.

In reality, these delineations are not as distinguishable as implied by the FTC categorization scheme, since actual mergers often involve several dimensions. Mergers in this third period tended to be of the pure conglomerate type, rising from 3.2 percent of total transactions to almost 50 percent during the third merger wave.[9] During the first and second merger periods, antitrust constraints precluded the formation of entities that conferred market dominance either horizontally or vertically. The conglomeration was a means of acquiring size without challenging the established legal precedents of the period. From the legal point of view, conglomerates did not pose significant threats in the marketplace, although dissenting opinions were seriously concerned with the growing overall political/economic/social power amassed by several of the large conglomerations that were forming.

The fourth merger movement is now underway, and appears destined to eclipse all former periods in terms of the number as well as the value of transactions. Recent data point to the fact that the period 1985 through 1987 witnessed the most intense merger activity since the third wave peaked in 1968.[10] Well over 5,000 mergers were tallied, the most in 14 years, with a price tag exceeding $200 billion. The most spectacular feature has been the growth of very large transactions. The number of acquisitions valued at more than $100 billion has grown over tenfold during this period.

Commencement of the fourth merger wave took place with two large diversification acquisitions in the mid–1970s: Mobil's $1.6-billion take-over of Macor, and the bidding war that resulted in International Nickel's acquisition of ESB.[11] These two transactions changed the rules for investment banking by being largely "hostile" and strongly resisted, initially, by the targeted companies. A second unique characteristic was the unprecedented size of the cash premium offered for the target's stock. Third, the acquired target was considered a well-run, blue-chip firm with significant asset growth and profit potential. These characteristics were in direct contrast to either the horizontal or the vertical mergers of the pre–World War II periods and the postwar conglomeration movement where the acquirers tended to be smaller firms that achieved their size and reputation as a result of acquisition. In addition, even though hostile takeovers are not a completely new phenomenon to the merger scene, nonetheless, their use as a means of acquisition in periods prior to the mid–1970s was quite limited.

It is clear that the present merger movement has caused fear in the corporate community. By 1982, more than 1,500 companies had amended their corporate charters or bylaws to provide income protecting golden parachutes for certain managers. More recently, hundreds of companies have adopted fair price or super majority provisions to make takeovers more difficult. Through deliberations within the court system firms have been successful in gaining approval of poison pill securities, and the Federal Reserve Board has invoked a slowdown on junk-bond financing of hostile takeovers.

Initially, large firms appeared in a position to thwart takeover efforts. Mead Corporation and McGraw-Hill were able to withstand encroachments in the late 1970s in part because of having attained a large size. This strategy was not successful in every case, however; Carrier Corporation tried unsuccessfully to avoid a takeover by buying Jenn-Air. Nevertheless, defensive takeovers stimulated growth in merger totals. Firms with liquid assets made rapid acquisitions to avoid takeovers by depleting cash reserves or, as in the case of Bendix Corporation, the target became the aggressor in order to protect itself.

A more direct defensive tactic that developed, however, was the self-tender offer—a bid by the target for its own shares at a price higher than that offered by the acquiring firm. Commonly referred to as the leveraged buyout, this tactic gained acceptance in the business community after successful defenses by Phillips Petroleum, Unocal, CBS, and Union Carbide. Taking firms private is not accomplished without substantial costs to society. In the process, equity is converted into debt. Because interest payments are deductible from corporate profits and dividends are not, the buyer can gain more value on the same cash flow. Employing debt in this way allows the buyer the opportunity of paying a premium over the market price of the targeted stock and a premium to the money lenders and still permits conclusion of the transaction with higher profits because roughly one-half the interest costs are absorbed by taxpayers. More disconcerting than the wealth imbalance occasioned through such financing is the fact that the greater debt subjects the borrowing firms to more cyclical vulnerability in economic downturns. In the long run, the macroeconomic implications could prove costly to society in general.

Another tactic used to acquire firms is the leveraged takeover. Carl Icahn, Sir James Goldsmith, T. Boone Pickens, and others have employed the instrument to acquire public firms. In some cases, use of the leveraged takeover is simply for the purpose of obtaining quick profits either from greenmail for dropping the takeover bid or, after gaining control, from spinning off the individual units of the acquired firm.

There have been increasing numbers of acquisitions of large conglomerate corporations in the fourth merger wave, which is an interesting phenomenon given the headlong rush into conglomerations witnessed in the 1960s and 1970s. The irony is that many of the conglomerates were buttressed with the argument that such unifications would secure synergies for the parent organizations. Obviously, the justification has not been substantiated by market performance if one accepts the logic that many takeovers occur because of undervalued stock. Stock undervaluation is a reflection of less-than-effective management of assets or exploitation of market possibilities. In either event, indications to investors are that greater value could accrue to them if the current management team were replaced and corporate assets were employed in different ways.

The trend away from broad corporate diversification is also reflected in a resurgence of intraindustry acquisitions. Chevron's $13-billion acquisition of Gulf Oil and Texaco's $10-billion acquisition of Getty Oil were significant returns to intense intraindustry concentration. Since the passage of the Celler-Kefauver amendment to the Clayton Act in 1950, mergers of large competitors had all but disappeared. In the late 1970s, however, the process was resurrected. Formation of LTV Steel from Jones & Laughlin and Youngstown Sheet & Tube; the integration of the giant rail systems such as CSX, Conrail, and Norfolk & Southern; unification of the Union, Missouri, and Western Pacific systems; integration of numerous financial institutions; and mergers between leading dishwasher manufacturers, tire makers, soft drink companies, and airlines attest to the fact that market concentration has been seriously altered with many recent mergers. If concern for maintaining competition was the stated objective of merger policy and its enforcement in the years after 1950, the same could not be said of many mergers beginning in the 1980s. Many of these organizations appeared to have relatively few competitors, and a number of these same firms were involved in mergers brought on by actual or perceived threats of corporate takeover of the friendly as well as the hostile varieties.

PRE- AND POST-MERGER PERFORMANCE

It is worthwhile at this point to review the evidence on performance pre- and post-merger for the four periods. Interestingly, a number of researchers employing varying methodologies in different time periods have reached similar conclusions with regard to mergers: No matter what form the acquisition takes, the net effect does not significantly influence efficiency or profitability.[12] Scherer reports that profit perfor-mance during the first three merger periods for merger-prone versus non-merger-prone companies is not significantly different. If anything, merger-prone companies tended to be less profitable in comparison to their non-merger-prone cohorts. In an empirical study conducted by the FTC, it was found that the post-merger profit-sales ratio declined relative to the pre-merger value for 34 acquired entities and rose for 25.[13] R. L. Conn found that the average post-merger profit-assets ratio declined from 6.7 percent pre-merger to 4.2 percent post-merger. His conclusions, after taking into consideration industry effects, indicated that small but significantly negative differences in firm profit rates are evident when comparing pre- versus post-merger performance.[14]

Several summary findings can be gleaned from the evidence presented thus far: (1) mergers throughout the four periods have led to increases in market concentration, (2) the monopoly motive has dissipated as a primary driving force for merger but the speculation motive has risen to take its place, and (3) the expectations of corporate gain that inspire mergers are frequently neither well-formed nor accompanied by com-mensurate benefits to the public. Instead, mergers may merely redis-tribute wealth, intensify product differentiation, provide an illusory growth with no counterpart in macroeconomic improvements, and, as numerous observers of the current wave surmise, pass rents on to ar-bitrageurs and investment bankers. The upshot is that mergers have a tendency in many instances to result in declines in profitability. What explains this result? Some suggest that management's goals are not necessarily stockholders' goals.[15] As sales maximization displaces stock-holders' wealth maximization as the management objective, a tendency exists for profit performance to diminish with increases in the asset base of the organization. At the margin, investments do not bring forth the expected returns, and management, located as it is in the seat of power within the organization, is able to stymie objections from weak boards.[16] Another reason offered for the poor post-merger performance is that acquiring partners unify with a weak mate. Reid, however, reports that only 10 percent of the merging partners during the second and third merger periods were at or near bankruptcy.[17] At the other extreme, almost 50 percent were earning returns in excess of 10 percent after taxes. Furthermore, in assessing the third merger period, Scherer reports that merging firms enjoyed a rate of return equal to the average rate of all corporations over the period.[18] Therefore, if it is true that mergers do not improve profit performance and, at the same time, do lead to increased concentration, then it seems reasonable to question the jus-tification for allowing them to take place.

In contrast to the third merger period, firms appear to be making serious efforts to establish a unified business focus with their acquisitions. For instance, R. J. Reynolds has built its food-related products division of Chun King and Hawaiian Punch with acquisitions of Del Monte, Heublein, and Nabisco. At the same time, it has divested Sea-Land (containerized shipping) and numerous oil and gas interests. To the extent that mergers tend to follow a focused strategy in that partners are chosen that follow a similar line of business in similar markets, a significant role exists for antitrust enforcement. Similarly, if successful companies with significant cash reserves or takeover artists with substantial investment-banking support continue to acquire and spin off companies of which they know little, in the long run mergers are unlikely to benefit shareholders, managers, or the public. Shareholders of unmanageable corporations lose as the value of their stock declines. The public loses as a result of higher costs from strains brought on by the unification as well as from the uncertainties generated with respect to future expectations regarding employment and the tax bases available to communities for the social infrastructure. Managers seeking protection from takeovers by acquiring additional assets or by depleting cash reserves will continue to find their companies under scrutiny as takeover targets. As long as the tax laws favor investments using debt as opposed to equity instruments, and as long as the antitrust agencies choose to approach their enforcement responsibilities in an extremely lax manner, neither large size nor superior performance will offer a safe haven from takeover specialists. For these reasons, antitrust oversight tightening is appropriate, but for a reason altogether different from those put forth in previous periods.

MERGER POLICY

Merger policy is carried out by both the FTC and the Department of Justice. Section 7 of the Clayton Act instructs the agencies to prevent mergers the effects of which "may be substantially to lessen competition, or to tend to create a monopoly." The theoretical developments in economics focus on the possible exercise of market power and have been employed in developing merger guidelines. These guidelines are firmly rooted in oligopoly theory and, furthermore, reflect the sentiments of the traditionalist, structuralist, and Chicago paradigms of industrial organization. An important insight garnered from the theoretical literature is that the more easily a group of sellers can coordinate and police their mutual actions, the more likely they are to approximate a monopoly outcome. From this proposition it is a simple step to seek answers to questions relating to market structure and managerial behavior, and to correlate these findings with observed performance. The merger guidelines offer an organized method for evaluating the competitive effects of a proposed merger.

What is the procedure and what are the factors that the guidelines specifically address? The normal procedure is for the firms planning to merge to contact either the FTC or the Department of Justice for guidance on determining the factors necessary to make the merger application successful. The merger plan is announced and the pre-merger notification requirements of the Hart-Scott-Rodino Act are spelled out. Under these rules, all firms involved in a prospective merger must notify the antitrust enforcement agencies if sales or assets of the acquiring firm exceed $100 million and if sales or assets of the acquired firm exceed $10 million. Other considerations relate to the ownership arrangements on voting securities and the necessary threshold size of the transaction. The notification is followed by a 30-day waiting period (15 days in the case of cash tender offers) before the merger can be consummated. The waiting period can be extended by 20 days if requested by either enforcement agency.

The first issue brought under consideration in a merger proceeding is the definition of the relevant market. In delineating the market boundaries, the analyst is to a significant degree determining the outcome by judging whether market power is present and, more importantly, whether it has been wielded in an unfair way. In past decisions, the regulatory bodies and the courts have evaluated product and geographic substitutability. Due to impracticalities in generating information regarding effective substitution in production and consumption, it is usually the case that the assessment is based on the response a firm's competitors have to a 5-percent increase in market price. If competitive firms incur increased sales, they are presumed to be in the same market as the price-increasing firm. Otherwise, they are out of the relevant market area.

A second consideration is the extent of market concentration. Using the Herfindahl-Hirschman Index (HHI) as the concentration guide, agency staff members evaluate the exact magnitude of market competition. Any merger in a market with a post-merger HHI below 1,000 is unlikely to be challenged; a merger in a relevant market with a post-merger HHI above 1,800 is likely to be challenged if the merging partners cause the HHI to increase by more than 100 points or if entry into the market is found to be easy. Mergers in markets with a post-merger HHI level between 1,000 and 1,800 receive further analysis before a decision is made to challenge the proposal.

If entry conditions are considered easy, virtually any merger will be allowed; with high entry barriers, mergers in the middle and upper HHI regions receive closer scrutiny and additional factors become important.

With promulgation of the guidelines we see that the enforcement agencies perform a crucial role in determining the outcome of a proposed merger. They effectively define the relevant market and, based on this assessment, the specific share of the market affected by the merger. Also, since the other factors in the assessment are not specified as precisely as is market share, significant discretion occurs in assessing the extent to which merger actions impact competition. Thus, it is likely for political ideologies to enter into the determination of the level of enforcement of antitrust violations. At the present time, both the FTC and the DOJ are staffed with personnel whose policies follow very closely the ideological position of the Reagan administration. Active enforcement of the law is quite low, and many companies have been able to merge that either had been unable or had felt it highly unlikely that they would be allowed to unite in earlier periods. This lack of a serious response from the regulators has likely served to encourage mergers that would not necessarily be in the public interest.

SUMMARY STATEMENTS

In this chapter, I have outlined the economic implications of the merger policy that has evolved over time. Obviously, this policy has changed considerably since passage of the initial antitrust legislation in 1890 and 1914 with the Sherman, Clayton, and Federal Trade Commission Acts. The impact of federal legislation has not been to halt the thrust of merger activity nor to reduce its importance to the national economy. On the contrary, it appears that new regulations simply alter the methods by which mergers are consummated. Cyclical changes in economic variables, and not the activities of the Congress or the administration, tend to determine the scope and duration of merger waves.

Four distinct merger periods have been identified. Each is unique and offers different rationales for delineating the motivation for merger. In the initial period, the intention behind a merger was to acquire monopoly control of strategic industrial sectors in the economy. The Sherman Act, originally devised as a way of reducing the import of monopoly elements into society, contained serious shortcomings and failed to limit the rate of industrial concentration. The second wave occurred shortly after passage of the Clayton and Federal Trade Commission acts and is described as the period of oligopoly formation. During this period, industrial concentration intensified.

A lull occurred in merger activity during the Great Depression and World War II; however, after business converted from a war economy, the third merger wave occurred. This was the period of the conglomerate merger. Firms from numerous industrial sectors were brought together because of the synergies that were purported to occur from integration. Finally, the fourth merger period commenced in the late 1970s. It reflects a mixture of motives for unification. Whereas the great majority of mergers in the earlier periods were for market position, a significant number of mergers in the fourth wave appear to be primarily speculative in nature. This is witnessed by the rapid purchase and resale of large blocks of industrial stock by a few well-supported arbitrageurs and investment bankers. The strategy appears to have been to purchase undervalued assets and split them into smaller blocks to maximize the profitability by selling the parts. Many economists applauded this action by the takeover party as instilling an element of discipline into a market that had grown sour. Entrenched management was viewed as being the culprit for undervaluation of a firm's stock. By replacing the management team, the organization would prosper and stakeholders would be assured of maximizing the value of their investments. However, the evidence as to the degree to which poor management actually stimulates a takeover is rather mixed; some obviously poorly managed firms have been absorbed, but a number of well-managed firms have been taken over as well.

A major thesis of this chapter is that antitrust vigilance is called for in this period as much as it has been during any other merger period. With the change in strategy away from conglomerates because of their poor return performance, an increasing number of firms are following a focused strategy that limits the number of different types of businesses brought under the corporate umbrella. More importantly, a growing number of new acquisitions are for firms in the same or a similar line of business. This entails the fact that issues of effective competition will arise frequently as firms unify horizontally and vertically. Even though takeovers are primarily undertaken for capitalizing asset values or to protect against being taken over, nonetheless, the net effect is to lead ultimately to higher degrees of concentration and the loss of effective competition in certain product markets.

With respect to public policy, a final point to be made is that legislative actions have been largely unsuccessful in alleviating the negative features associated with mergers. Merger activity actually intensified after major federal legislation passed, albeit in a different form and with different methods. Thus, proposals to enact state or federal legislation in efforts to limit the abusiveness of takeovers are most likely ill-conceived and will probably serve to harm rather than help those in need of protection. Mergers are extremely idiosyncratic and the stakeholders are quite dissimilar in many cases. To enact one particular law that addresses all takeovers, either at the state or federal level, will surely help some while harming others. We are far from being assured that the greatest good to the greatest number will prevail. While new legislation is not the panacea to the problem, existing legislation does provide a means of minimizing the damages to market processes. Federal and state antitrust laws are designed to maintain effective competition and to identify the factors to evaluate in the event mergers are proposed.

It seems logical to employ these laws to protect the interests of those dependent on unfettered competition.

NOTES

1. F. M. Scherer, *Industrial Market Structure and Economic Performance*, 2d ed. (Boston, Mass.: Houghton Mifflin, 1980), pp. 118–119.

2. This breakdown follows closely but not entirely the delineation presented by Scherer, *Industrial Market Structure*, pp. 119–141.

3. Samuel R. Reid, *The New Industrial Order: Concentration, Regulation and Public Policy* (New York: McGraw-Hill, 1976), p. 67.

4. As reported in ibid., p. 67.

5. J. Moody, *The Truth about Trusts* (New York: Moody Publishing Company, 1904), pp. 453–469.

6. Reid, *The New Industrial Order*, pp. 68–69.

7. Ibid., p. 69.

8. Scherer, *Industrial Market Structure*, p. 128.

9. Ibid., p. 124.

10. Sara G. Zwart, "The New Antitrust: An Aerial View of Joint Ventures and Mergers," *Journal of Business Strategy* 7 (Spring 1987): 68–76.

11. Kenneth M. Davidson, "Do Megamergers Make Sense?" *Journal of Business Strategy* 7 (Winter 1987): 40–48.

12. Scherer, *Industrial Market Structure*, pp. 133–141.

13. See Federal Trade Commission, *Report of the Federal Trade Commission on Rates of Return in Selected Manufacturing Industries 1961–1970* (Washington, D.C.: 1972), pp. 58–65.

14. R. L. Conn, "The Failing Firm/Industry Doctrines in Conglomerate Mergers," *Journal of Industrial Economics* 24 (March 1976): 181–187.

15. Henry G. Mann, "Mergers and the Market for Corporate Control," *Journal of Political Economy* 73 (April 1965): 110–120.

16. Ibid., p. 116.

17. Reid, *The New Industrial Order*, p. 56.

18. Scherer, *Industrial Market Structure*, pp. 138–139.

5

CORPORATE TAKEOVERS AND REGIONAL ECONOMIC DEVELOPMENT: AN OHIO PERSPECTIVE

Brian P. Holly

Among the many factors contributing to changes in the economic geography of the United States is the central role played by large corporate organizations. The decisions made by these institutions profoundly influence the economic health of the regions and communities in which they locate their facilities. Location decisions represent one outcome of investment decisions made by the firm, and they are made manifest in several different ways. As it responds to external forces, the firm can change the scale of output at existing plants, open or close plants, relocate them, or externally acquire productive facilities through merger and acquisition and, increasingly, through joint ventures (Green and Cromley, 1984). This chapter is concerned with the latter form of corporate investment decision, merger and acquisition, and in particular the regional economic implications of external control of locally based acquisition targets.

The chapter examines some of the issues surrounding the recently high levels of merger-and-acquisition activity, especially with respect to external control, regional economic development, and public policy. The recent experience of Ohio-based firms in the takeover wave sweeping the corporate United States is examined, and some conclusions are drawn concerning the economic-development effects of this movement.

EXTERNAL CONTROL

The most spatially important implications of interregional and international transfers of corporate control through merger and acquisition (M & A) concerns core-periphery relationships in regional and national economic development (Lorch, 1981). At a minimum, any corporate acquisition involves a transfer of decision-making power from the acquired to the acquiring firm, thus extending and reinforcing external control (Dicken, 1976). Many large contemporary corporations trace their origins to earlier consolidations that were spatially significant in that they separated administrative and production functions through the absorption of regionally based firms (Pred, 1974).

Recent research on the spatial transfer of control via takeovers indicates a deepening of core-periphery relationships within both the national and the international economic system. A study of 18,000 corporate mergers in the United States between 1955 and 1968 revealed a strong concentration of flows into New York and Illinois, while most other states experienced net outflows (Dicken, 1976). Leigh and North (1978) studied acquisitions in four sectors of British manufacturing for 1973–1974 and found a similar pattern as the southeast core showed a net gain while the more peripheral East Midlands and Scotland suffered net losses. A statewide study of corporate acquisition activity in Nebraska in the early 1960s showed a transfer of corporate decision-making out of the state toward large metropolitan regions of the northeast (Brue, 1975). A study of Canadian merger-and-acquisition activity by North (1981) for the years 1967 to 1976 revealed a complex of core-periphery relationships dominated by transfers of control from the Canadian core to the foreign core (principally the United States and Western Europe) and from the Canadian periphery to the Canadian core (Toronto, Montreal, and Vancouver).

SPATIAL OUTCOMES

These and other studies (for example, Green and Cromley, 1984) suggest that there is an explicit spatial dimension to merger-and-acquisition behavior by corporations involving transfer of corporate control across regional boundaries. This in turn has the effect over time of reinforcing the dominance of core regions and metropolitan areas over more peripheral and rural areas. This has implications for the levels of employment and kinds of jobs that will remain in the facilities and regions subject to external control and ultimately affects the economic-development prospects in such areas.

Green and Cromley (1982) argue that the post-merger period is a time of important spatial adjustment usually involving reorganization of managerial control, changes in product lines, and locational rearrangement of plants and other facilities. Following Watts (1981), they outline a four-point schema of post-merger spatial-rationalization policies that can be enacted by acquiring firms:

1. *Specialization*—a concentration of functions permitting realization of economies of scale.

2. *Concentration and Partial Disinvestment*—a concentration of production at fewer sites, creating savings in services and linkages between facilities.

3. *Complete Disinvestment and Greenfield Site*—the concentration of production at a greenfield site.

4. *Complete Disinvestment and Withdrawal*—as a result of an unsuccessful merger, total removal of the acquired firm's facilities from those of the acquiring firm. This is a common outcome in highly leveraged buyouts (Green and Cromley, 1982, p. 361).

EMPLOYMENT IMPACTS OF TAKEOVERS

Assessing the impact of takeovers on job loss is difficult in view of the lack of hard data and the difficulty of establishing a direct cause-and-effect relationship. In recent congressional hearings on the subject, AFL-CIO spokespersons estimated that "at a minimum, roughly 80,000 jobs of members of unions affiliated with the AFL-CIO were eliminated." Such job loss, it is thought, results directly from the need of the acquirer or the successful resister of a takeover to sell off assets in order to retire part of the debt incurred in the takeover process. Goodyear's divestiture of its Aerospace and Celeron Oil and Gas subsidiaries for a total of $1.24 billion in the wake of the aborted attempt by Sir James Goldsmith to acquire Goodyear serves as Ohio's most visible example.

The literature in both economics and geography gives a mixed picture of the effects of mergers and acquisitions on local employment growth or decline (Erickson, 1981). A recent study of horizontal mergers involving 191 firms during the period 1972–1978 concluded that such mergers maintain or improve employment figures for acquired plants, at least in the short run. Some industrial sectors fare better than others, but no interregional differences seemed to emerge (Green and Cromley, 1982). In a study of post-acquisition employment records of 227 establishments in Wisconsin it was found that 45 percent of the acquired plants had greater employment growth-rates after acquisition than they had experienced before (Udell, 1969). An analysis of post-merger employment in 22 Nebraska manufacturing firms showed that the branches had significantly lower and even negative employment and payroll growth-rates following merger (Brue, 1972, 1975). Erickson (1981) analyzed nonmetropolitan branch plants in Wisconsin and found that 41 percent of the acquired or merged firms experienced negative employment growth-rates after gaining branch-plant status. These studies suggest that, at least at the branch-plant level, post-merger spatial rationalization policies can lead to slower employment growth and even decline. Additionally, external control of companies through takeover invariably results in leakage of higher-level administrative and producer service jobs out of the regions of acquired firms and to the headquarter locations of acquiring corporations.

RECENT M & A ACTIVITY IN OHIO

As reported in *The Cleveland Plain Dealer* (September 26, 1988), W. T. Grimm and Co. announced that the total value of acquisitions in the first six months of 1988 was the highest ever for a six-month period. Over 1,100 acquisitions worth $129.4 billion were completed, compared with the 1,031 deals worth $91.3 billion transacted during the first half of 1987. Other comparisons included 195 deals worth $100 million or more versus 166 in 1987, and 30 acquisitions worth one billion dollars or more in 1988 as opposed to 17 in 1987.

In recent years, firms headquartered in Ohio have figured prominently in the wave of mergers and acquisitions that has swept over the corporate United States. Some of the nation's largest and best-known industrial and retail giants are located in Ohio, and have been acquired or the subject of takeover attempts. The basic questions that arise are: What has been Ohio's experience in the merger-and-acquisition sector in recent years? What trends are evident in terms of size of companies, sectors that are most actively being pursued, and the nature and location of acquiring firms? What evidence is there that recent acquisitions of Ohio-based firms have been either beneficial or harmful to local economic development?

The number of mergers and acquisitions, leveraged buyouts, divestitures, partial acquisitions, and companies going from public to private ownership in recent years has numbered in the thousands, over 7,000 nationally in 1987. Most of these actions involve small firms, valued at less than $1 million, and are considered normal business dealings. It is the hostile mergers, involving hundreds of millions or even billions of dollars, that command the attention of the press, legislators, union leaders, and the corporate world. We will refer to these takeovers as "megamergers" because of their size, complicated nature, and impact. In this analysis, all mergers and acquisitions with a total value of $100 million or more, whether partial or complete, qualify as megamergers.

Several trends are evident in the above-mentioned cases. First, the value of the corporate takeovers has risen sharply in recent years. Second, many companies view takeovers as hostile and increasingly rely on a combination of restructuring and state antitakeover legislation to fend them off. Third, many of the acquiring firms increasingly are based in other countries.

Table 5.1 lists megamergers, acquisitions, or partial buyouts involving Ohio-based corporations from 1982 through 1987 inclusive. A perusal of the table reveals that the number of large acquisitions has been increasing on an annual basis. There were four large mergers in 1984, punctuated by the U.S. Steel takeover of Marathon Oil. The years 1986 and 1987 saw 10 and 24 large mergers, takeovers, or divestitures, respectively. The number of takeovers in 1987 reflects a more thorough review of such activity. Data are derived from the magazine, *Mergers and Acquisitions*, as well as from the popular business press. Only those takeovers involving complete sale or sale of at least 51 percent of a company's assets are included in this analysis.

A second trend noticeable in Table 5.1 is that the value of deals becomes larger with time, no doubt partly due to inflation. Whereas there were three deals valued at $1 billion or more from 1982 through 1986, there were six such transactions in 1987 alone. Several others have been recorded for 1988 and are not included in this analysis. A third trend in the data involves the shift from Ohio-based companies as the primary acquirers in the earlier years to a situation where Ohio companies represent the majority of targets in 1986 and 1987. This trend is also reflected in the value of mergers by the location of the acquiring firm, whether in Ohio or outside Ohio. In 1983 through 1985, the value of acquisitions by Ohio-based firms exceeded that of non–Ohio-based companies. In 1986 and 1987 this trend reversed itself, and in 1987 the ratio of value acquired was about ten to one in favor of non–Ohio firms.

Table 5.2 also reveals that 1987 was an exceptional year for acquisitions by value, with the total value of all megamergers exceeding at 400 percent of the 1986 total. Whether this represents a new trend remains to be seen when the 1988 merger year is completed and evaluated. The reported number and value of megamergers for the first half of 1988 would seem to indicate another busy year.

The year 1987 was selected for further analysis because of the dramatic increase in the number and total value of large mergers and acquisitions. Of the 25 takeovers valued at more than $100 million, only 7 were executed by Ohio-based companies. The remaining 18 involved non-Ohio acquirers. This imbalance is reflected in the total value of such acquisitions, only $2.58 billion for Ohio firms compared with $21.48 billion for non–Ohio firms. The $24,060.2 million in total value for the year accounts for 55 percent of the total value of megamergers since 1982. The fact that most of the large acquisitions in Ohio were made by firms from outside the state suggests that a large component of Ohio's corporate power will soon migrate to other regions and nations.

Table 5.1
Megamergers Involving Ohio Companies, 1982–1987

Year	Acquirer	Acquired	Value[1]
1982	U.S. Steel Corp.	Marathon Oil Co.[2]	$6,150.0
1982	B.F. Goodrich Co.	Diamond Shamrock Plastics Corp.	131.0
1982	Procter & Gamble Co.	Morton-Norwich Products Inc. (Unit)	371.0
1982	The Limited, Inc.	Lane Bryant, Inc.	105.7
1982	Pilkington Bros., Ltd.	Libbey-Owens-Ford Co.	106.0
1983	Kroger Co.	Dillon Cos., Inc.	607.5
1983	Goodyear Tire & Rubber Co.	Celeron Corp.	812.0
1983	Peabody Holding	Armco (WV coal properties)	250.0
1983	Management Group	Taft Broadcasting (three theme parks)	168.0
1983	BancOne Corp.	Winters National Corp.	128.5
1983	MidContinent Telephone Corp.	Allied Telephone Co.	118.3
1984	Standard Oil Co. (SOHIO)	Chevron (service stations and refinery)	690.0
1984	Libbey-Owens-Ford Co.	Sperry Corp. (Division)	265.0
1984	LTV Corp.	Republic Steel Corp.	486.4
1984	National City	BancOhio	297.0
1984	Owens-Illinois, Inc.	Health Care & Retirement Corp. of America	100.0
1985	Procter & Gamble Co.	Richardson Vicks, Inc.	1,245.7
1985	Taft Broadcasting Co.	Gulf Broadcast Co. (five TV and seven radio sta.)	760.0
1985	Chicago Pacific Corp.	Hoover Co.	533.9
1985	Tenneco	Goodyear Tire & Rubber Co. (gas pipelines)	447.0
1985	Owens-Corning-Fiberglass Corp.	Armco, Inc. (Aerospace & strategic materials group)	415.0
1985	The Limited, Inc.	Lerner Stores Corp.	300.0
1986	ANAC Holding Corp.	Revco D.S., Inc.	1,486.2
1986	Cleveland Elec. Ill. Co.	Toledo Edison, Co.	945.8
1986	Electrolux Group	White Consolidated Ind., Inc.	742.7
1986	Sir James Goldsmith	Goodyear Tire & Rubber Co. (11.5%)	500.0
1986	MCA	Gencorp (WOR-TV)	387.0
1986	Mead Corp.	James River (Crown Zellerbach dist. unit)	250.0
1986	Pilkington, PLC	Libbey-Owens-Ford (glass)	249.0
1986	British Petroleum Co., PLC	Owens-Corning-Fiberglass (Hitco subsidiary)	240.0
1986	TVX Broadcasting Group	Taft Broadcasting Co. (five TV stations)	240.0
1986	Singer	Eaton Corp. (cont. div.)	200.0

Table 5.1 (continued)

Year	Acquirer	Acquired	Value[1]
1987	British Petroleum Co., PLC	*Standard Oil Co. (45%)*	$7,564.7
1987	Kohlberg, Kravis, Roberts & Co.	*Owens-Illinois, Inc.*	3,688.0
1987	American Express Co.	*Standard Oil Co. (Ind. Holdings Corp.)*	1,800.0
1987	Chrysler Corp.	*American Motors Corp.*	1,646.0
1987	TFBA LP	*Taft Broadcasting Co.*	1,214.7
1987	Great Northern Nekoosa Corp.	*Owens-Illinois, Inc. (Forest Products Group)*	1,150.0
1987	Continental AG	*General Tire, Inc.*	725.0
1987	Exxon Corp.	*Celeron Oil & Gas Co.*	650.0
1987	*Banner Industries, Inc.*	Rexnord, Inc.	635.0
1987	Loral Corp.	*Goodyear Aerospace Corp.*	588.0
1987	*BancOne Corp.*	American Fletcher Corp.	551.2
1987	Emerson Electric Co.	*Liebert Corp.*	515.9
1987	Leaseway Holdings, Inc.	*Leaseway Trans. Corp.*	494.5
1987	*M.A. Hanna Co.*	Day International Corp.	421.6
1987	*Procter & Gamble Co.*	Blendax Group	400.0
1987	Ecolab	*Chemlawn Corp.*	366.7
1987	Cablevision Systems	*Cablevision of Ohio*	338.0
1987	*Edgell Communications, Inc.*	HBJ Publications, Inc.	334.1
1987	Consolidated Goldfields, PLC	*Am. Aggregates Corp.*	241.8
1987	PON Partners LP	*Ponderosa, Inc.*	233.6
1987	Combustion Engineering	*Accuray Corp.*	213.6
1987	Siebe, PLC	*Ranco Industries*	148.5
1987	*Cole Eyeworks, Inc.*	Eyelab, Inc.	120.0
1987	*Mead Corp.*	Ampho Corp.	117.9
1987	RiteAid Corp.	*SuperX Drugs Corp.*	115.0

Source: Mergers and Acquisitions, Vols. 17–23, 1982–1988.

[1]Value of transactions given in millions of dollars.
[2]Ohio-based companies given in italics.

Finally, Table 5.3 gives a breakdown of mergers by value for nine major Standard Industrial Classification (SIC) Groups for 1987. A total of $27.3 billion was accounted for by 73 transactions reported for the year. Of this total, almost $17-billion-worth involved firms in the two major manufacturing sectors. Coming in third and fourth were Finance, Insurance, and Real Estate (FIRE, $4,824.7 million) and Mining and Construction ($2,972.7 million). Within the FIRE group, banking and financial holding companies were the most active. This breakdown in takeovers most likely mirrors the relative concentration of Ohio companies by sector. One possible implication of the high level of acquisition activity in manufacturing concerns the transfer of control of a substantial portion of industrial activity to other parts of the country and the world. Post-merger spatial rationalization, of the kind mentioned earlier in this chapter, may have the effect of reducing employment in manufacturing

Table 5.2
Value of Megamergers, 1982–1987, Ohio Companies (millions of dollars)

Year	Number	As Acquirers	Acquired	Total
1982	5	607.7	6,256.0	6,863.7
1983	6	1,834.3	250.0	2,084.3
1984	5	1,352.0	486.4	1,838.4
1985	6	2,720.7	980.9	3,701.6
1986	10	1,195.8	4,044.9	5,240.7
1987	25	2,579.8	21,480.4	24,060.2
Totals	57	10,290.3	33,498.6	43,788.9

Source: Mergers and Acquisitions, Vols. 17–23, 1982–1988.

in Ohio over and above what has been lost as a result of economic restructuring.

THE REGULATORY IMPACT

In recent years, many states have enacted legislation designed to frustrate or otherwise delay hostile takeovers, particularly of state-headquartered firms. The primary concern is to preserve local employment and the associated economic development of communities. While little hard evidence exists that links job loss to takeover activity, the connection between jobs, takeovers, and the economic health of areas remains an emotional issue with legislators and labor unions.

A recent U.S. Supreme Court decision (*CTS Corp. v. Dynamics Corp. of America*, 4–21–87) upheld Indiana's antitakeover law, which is designed to place roadblocks in the path of a hostile takeover of any Indiana company. On November 19, 1986, the Ohio Senate passed an antitakeover law that was subsequently passed by the House and signed into law by the governor. This legislation is similar to the Indiana statute in that it is a control share acquisition law. Such laws typically require shareholder approval of an acquisition of a specified threshold·equity interest (usually 20 percent) pursuant to a tender offer, open market purchase, or private transaction. The potential takeover firm's acquisition of stock and/or the ability to vote that stock must await disinterested shareholder approval at a special shareholders' meeting, affording the

Table 5.3
Value of All Mergers and Acquisitions in Ohio by SIC Code Groups, 1987*
(millions of dollars)

SIC Code	SIC Group	Total Value
01-09	Agriculture, Forestry, Fisheries	$366.7
10-19	Mining and Construction	2,972.7
20-29	Manufacturing (food, apparel, lumber, furniture, paper, chemicals, petroleum)	9,919.1
30-39	Manufacturing (rubber. glass, metals, machinery, electronics, instruments)	6,958.2
40-49	Transportation and Utilities	1,610.9
50-59	Wholesale and Retail Trade	467.6
60-69	Finance, Insurance and Real Estate	4,824.7
70-79	Services (personal, business, recreation)	166.6
80-89	Services (health, legal, educational, social)	13.9
Total		**$27,300.4**

Source: Mergers and Acquisitions, Vols. 22 and 23, 1987 and 1988.

*Based on 73 transactions for which terms were reported. Takeovers involving at least 51 percent of target firm are included.

target company time to formulate a strategy designed to fend off the acquirer. Possible responses by the target company's management might include seeking a white knight with a higher bid, executing a management-led leveraged buyout, or launching a recapitalization/restructuring program to increase shareholder value (Tannon and Stewart, 1987).

Since passage of the Ohio law, the number and value of large takeovers of Ohio firms by outside acquirers has increased dramatically in 1987 and 1988, thus calling into question the effectiveness of such legislation. Another questionable outcome of the Ohio statute is its effects on the share prices of target companies. A study by the Office of the Chief Economist of the Securities and Exchange Commission detailed abnormal declines in shareholder value of Ohio companies immediately before and during the time of the law's passage (Tannon and Stewart, 1987).

CONCLUSIONS

Mergers and acquisitions, as manifestations of investment decisions by corporate organizations, have both intended and unintended spatial manifestations. If the acquiring and acquired firms are not located in the same state, region, or nation, then the result is a transfer of control, to varying degrees, out of the locale of the acquired firm. Generally, this process of external control strengthens the region of the acquiring organization at the expense of the regional base of the target firm. In the aggregate, high levels of merger-and-acquisition activity result in a further deepening of core-periphery relationships with its consequent effect of engendering greater economic instability in the peripheral areas. Post-merger spatial-rationalization policies of acquiring firms suggest that increasing levels of external control by distant corporations would lead, at best, to specialization of functions in target-firm regions, making such regions more vulnerable during periods of economic decline.

Recent high levels of takeover activity involving Ohio-headquartered companies raise some questions about the effects of major transfers of control to other regions. Recent takeovers of major firms in petroleum, steel, rubber, energy, and consumer products by non-local corporations invite speculation about possible rationalization in these important industries in the Ohio economy. The implications of this takeover activity require further study, particularly concerning effects on employment, economic diversification, and the potential for reversing the decline in the state's industrial base in recent decades.

6

RESTRUCTURING THE FORTUNE 500: THE VIEW FROM OHIO

R. D. Norton

As the nineteenth-century homeland of John D. Rockefeller, Ohio offers a good vantage point for observing corporate restructuring today. A case in point is the 1987 acquisition of Standard Oil of Ohio by British Petroleum. In the 1880's, Rockefeller operated out of Cleveland to consolidate the U.S. petroleum industry. A century later, the Ohio branch of Rockefeller's creation finds itself named BP America, a British outpost. The urge to merge remains—but the players, the boundaries, and the rules of the game have changed.

This chapter provides an overview of corporate restructuring and then surveys the record for Ohio-headquartered firms. The overview compares the Fortune 500 list for 1965 and 1987. A majority of the class of 1965 were gone by 1987, mainly because of takeovers. In addition, however, the geography of the 500 has changed because newcomers to the list are more likely to be headquartered in the South and West. The dual context of takeovers and regional change sets the stage for the Ohio survey, which is based mainly on the fates of the 41 Ohio-based firms in the 1965 Fortune 500 class. The purpose of this chapter is thus to document what has happened to Ohio's largest companies since 1965 in light of the national pace and pattern of corporate restructuring.

WHAT HAPPENED TO THE FORTUNE 500 CLASS OF 1965?

Fewer than half the firms on the Fortune 500 list for 1965 remained there in 1987. Indeed, at first count, the list looks even shorter than it is because well over 50 of the survivors appear under new names. After allowing for name changes, however, 246 of the firms on the May 1966 Fortune 500 list also appear in the April 1988 list. A slight majority, 254, disappeared from the list. Of the 254 disappearances, only 52 reflected firms that fell off the list as their relative size decreased. A handful (4) met a more extreme fate and were liquidated. A larger number, 21, became "non-industrial" (earning less than 50 percent of their income from manufacturing operations) through diversification into service activities.

Thus, as subtotals, 56 of the initial 254 disappearers fell off the list due to shrinkage or liquidation, and 21 more diversified out. That leaves 177 losses to be explained. If they did not shrink away, and did remain industrial, what happened? The answer is that more than one third of the initial 500 disappeared via mergers or leveraged buyouts. Of these, mergers eliminated 158 firms. Going private via a leveraged buyout accounted for most of the remaining 19.

Here, then, is the explanation of the high turnover rate in the Fortune 500 list: Over a third disappeared as a result of mergers or leveraged buyouts. What happened to the U.S. corporate elite in 1965 was not a gradual replacement of slower-growing companies but rather a process through which some firms on the initial list absorbed others. In sum, the wholesale replacement of firms on the list was not mainly a result of faster-growing firms overtaking slower-growing ones; it was not, in other words, a gradual process in which some firms fell off the list as their growth lagged. Instead, roughly one third of all the firms on the 1965 list disappeared via takeovers or (in a few cases) leveraged buyouts—creating vacancies on the list for initially smaller firms to fill.

Most of the takeover activity fell within two periods: the late 1960s and the 1980s. A brief comparison reveals that these two bursts of merger activity were opposite in a sense. The hallmark of the diversifying mergers of the 1960s was something called "synergy." In the name of synergy conglomerates like LTV and Gulf & Western took over companies in industries unrelated to their own activities. Synergy, as the corporate advertising of that day put it, meant that somehow $1 + 1 = 3$: The whole was said to be greater than the sum of its parts. Diversifying mergers were well within antitrust guidelines because they did not increase industry concentration ratios.

Unfortunately, however, their contribution to corporate profits was disappointing. Synergy is a relic of the high-flying 1960s bull market;

when the market tumbled in the early 1970s, synergy lost its lustre. This fall from grace sheds light on the 1980s in two ways. First, diversifying mergers are opposite from the divestiture activity we associate with leveraged buyouts (LBOs) today. A hallmark of LBO is the stripping off of corporate divisions for sale to private bidders. The premise behind LBOs is that less is more, or that the sum of the parts is worth more than the whole. (As a byproduct, a quirk in the Fortune 500 data in the 1980s is that a number of companies show diminishing assets over the decade. In other words, some of their divisions have been stripped off and sold.)

Second, in their day conglomerate mergers were claimed by their authors to be the wave of the future. The skeptics, it was said, failed to grasp a powerful new logic. Eventually, however, a rejection of synergism became No. 6 of the 8 basic tenets of *In Search of Excellence*. The new rule: "Stick to the knitting" (Peters and Waterman, 1983, Ch. 10).

What is the lesson? Just because sophisticated financiers claim their mergers are done in the spirit of Adam Smith does not make it true. When claims are made today that LBOs and debt-financed takeovers strengthen the nation's corporate system, history may yield a different judgment. In particular, the durability of debt-burdened takeover targets has not yet been tested by a recession. Critics contend that when the next recession comes, falling revenues will make it much harder for highly leveraged firms to pay the interest on their debt. That is, just as the conglomerate mergers of the 1960s were undone by events, today's debt-financed takeovers could be discredited by a wave of recession-bred bankruptcies.

GROWTH INDUSTRIES AND THE TILT SOUTH AND WEST

Between 1965 and 1987, the North's count of 500 headquarter cities fell by 81—from 406 in 1965 to 325 in 1987. This redistribution to the South and West was less due to outright moves by firms remaining on the list than from the new regional locations of newcomer firms. In fact, the net gain to the South and West resulting from moves by survivor firms was only 14.

The lion's share of the 81 new South and West 500 listings came about because newcomer firms were much less concentrated in the North than the original 1965 class. Specifically, 114 or 45 percent of the 254 newcomers were from the South and West. The South and West share for newcomers was thus more than double the share for "starters" on the initial 1965 list.

Headquarters of Growth Industries in the South and West

Why were newcomer firms so much more likely to be headquartered outside the Manufacturing Belt? The answer, in outline, is that the industries that were on the rise in this period were more likely to originate in decentralized locations. What were these "growth industries?" They were activities linked to population growth, such as building materials and food. They were resource-tied industries like petroleum refining and mining and crude-oil production in the post-OPEC era of soaring commodity prices. Finally, they were the stereotypical high-tech sectors, computers and electronics.

In each of these growth industries, a majority of the firms entering the Fortune 500 list were headquartered outside the North. Thus the shift of production activity in manufacturing away from the North since the mid–1960s has taken place not only through branch-plant placement by firms with headquarters in the North, but the decentralization of production to the "periphery" has also occurred in part because rising firms in rising industries were headquartered outside the North.

Traditional Northern Mainstays

On the other hand, even the newcomers in a number of industries continued to have corporate headquarters in the North; nor were all these industries "basic" or "old-line." To be sure, apparel and metal products were among the activities whose newcomer firms were almost entirely from the North, but so were scientific and photographic equipment and chemicals.

These and other traditional Northern mainstays were the reason that a majority of the newcomer firms were headquartered in the North. Despite the tendency for growth industries to have newcomer headquarters in the South and West, other industries also had large numbers of newcomers—typically with Northern locations. The balance for newcomer firms thus remained slightly in the North's favor, 55 percent to 45 percent.

To sum up the national picture, roughly half of the largest U.S. companies in 1965 are no longer in business today. The principal reason for firm disappearances is mergers, whether hostile or (more often) relatively friendly. In addition, the regional array of 500 headquarters is no longer dominated by the Manufacturing Belt. A tendency for firms in growth industries to be headquartered in the South and West has altered the balance.

OHIO: THE VIEW FROM THE HEARTLAND

Ohio's experience displays the restructuring of the corporate United States in more vivid terms. As a pillar of the industrial heartland, the

Table 6.1
Ohio-headquartered Firms on the 1965 Fortune 500 List

1965 RANK	COMPANY	LOCATION	1987 RANK OR FATE
20	GOODYEAR TIRE	AKRON	#35 FOR 1987
23	PROCTER & GAMBLE	CINCINNATI	#17
31	FIRESTONE TIRE	AKRON	#102, CHICAGO
41	REPUBLIC STEEL	CLEVELAND	TAKEOVER (1984), LTV DALLAS
51	ARMCO STEEL	MIDDLETOWN	#143, PARSIPPANY,N.J.
64	B.F. GOODRICH	AKRON	#180
69	GENERAL TIRE	AKRON	#139/TKO 1987 CONTI.AG (GER.)
82	OWENS-ILLINOIS	TOLEDO	#116 BUT LBO'D 1987 BY KKR
85	YOUNGSTOWN SH.&TUBE	YOUNGSTOWN	TKOS, LYKES (1969),LTV (1979)
92	NATIONAL CASH REG.	DAYTON	#74 AS NCR
100	EATON YALE & TOWNE	CLEVELAND	#110 AS EATON
107	TRW	CLEVELAND	#61
109	WHITE MOTOR	CLEVELAND	TKO ELECTROLUX (SWEDEN) 1986
116	STANDARD OIL (OHIO)	CLEVELAND	#22, BP AMERICA (1987 TKO,BP)
123	MARATHON OIL	FINDLAY	TKO U.S. STEEL (USX) 1982
124	MEAD	DAYTON	#102
164	CHAMPION PAPERS	HAMILTON	TKO (1967) U.S.PLYW.(CH.INT.)
170	DANA	TOLEDO	#107
180	TIMKEN ROLLER BRG.	CANTON	#280
197	SHERWIN-WILLIAMS	CLEVELAND	#185
206	OWENS-CORNING FBRGL.	TOLEDO	#144
227	GLIDDEN	CLEVELAND	TKO (1967) SCM (U.K.)
234	MIDLAND-ROSS	CLEVELAND	PRIVATE (LBO?) 1986
248	LIBBEY-OWENS-FORD G.	TOLEDO	TKO (1986) PILKINGTON (U.K.)
256	ADDRESSOGRAPH-MULTI.	CLEVELAND	#293 (CHICAGO) AS AM INTER.
279	HOOVER	N.CANTON	TKO (1985) CHICAGO PACIFIC
309	DIAMOND ALKALI	CLEVELAND	MOVED (D.SH.); TKO (1982) B.F.G.
318	CINCI.MILL.MACHINE	CINCINNATI	#357 AS CINCINNATI MILACRON
334	HUPP	CLEVELAND	TKO (1967 WHITE (OF OHIO)
357	ANCHOR HOCKING GL.	LANCASTER	TKO (1987) NEWELL (ILL.)
364	EAGLE-PICHER INDS.	CINCINNATI	#399
396	HANNA MINING	CLEVELAND	#500
427	CHAMPION SPARK PLUG	TOLEDO	#329
437	E.W. BLISS	CANTON	TKO (1969) GULF&WESTERN N.Y.
442	HARRIS-INTERTYPE	CLEVELAND	#187 HARRIS, MELBOURNE, FLA.
456	HOBART MFG.	TROY	TKO (1981) KRAFT (ILL.)
477	COOPER INDUSTRIES	MT. VERNON	#118 MOVED TO HOUSTON
480	CLEVITE	CLEVELAND	TKOS GOULD (1969), PULLMAN (1987)
483	U.S. SHOE	CINCINNATI	NO LONGER INDUSTRIAL (1976)
484	WARNER & SWASEY	CLEVELAND	DISPLACED 1970
500	ISLAND CREEK COAL	CLEVELAND	TKO (1968) OCCI.PETR. (L.A.)

Buckeye State had 41 of its firms listed as part of the class of 1965 (see Table 6.1). By 1987, it still had 35 listings—a seemingly mild decrease over the period. However, 5 of the 35 "Ohio companies" in 1987 were in fact owned by foreign firms (and another was about to go private in a Kohlberg, Kravis, Roberts LBO). By this more accurate count, then, the 41 Ohio-owned firms in 1965 had fallen to 30 in 1987—the same rate of loss as for the North as a region.

Pillars and Newcomers

Not everything changed over the 22 years. Some 15 firms from the 1965 Ohio contingent remained freestanding (that is, not owned by another company) and still had their headquarters in the same city in 1987. As Table 6.2 reveals, most of these 15 "pillars of the community" even had the same name: Goodyear Tire, Procter & Gamble, Mead, Dana, and Champion Spark Plug are familiar examples.

Table 6.2
Pillars of the Community: Freestanding Survivors Who Stayed

1965 RANK	COMPANY	LOCATION	1987 RANK
20	GOODYEAR TIRE	AKRON	#35 FOR 1987
23	PROCTER & GAMBLE	CINCINNATI	#17
64	B.F. GOODRICH	AKRON	#180
92	NATIONAL CASH REG.	DAYTON	#74 AS NCR
100	EATON YALE & TOWNE	CLEVELAND	#110 AS EATON
107	TRW	CLEVELAND	#61
124	MEAD	DAYTON	#102
170	DANA	TOLEDO	#107
180	TIMKEN ROLLER BRG.	CANTON	#280 AS TIMKEN
197	SHERWIN-WILLIAMS	CLEVELAND	#185
206	OWENS-CORNING FBRGL.	TOLEDO	#144
318	CINCI.MILL.MACHINE	CINCINNATI	#357 AS C.MILACRON
364	EAGLE-PICHER INDS.	CINCINNATI	#399
396	HANNA MINING	CLEVELAND	#500
427	CHAMPION SPARK PLUG	TOLEDO	#329

Table 6.3
Newcomers: 1987 Fortune 500 Firms in Ohio, Not on 1965 List

1987 RANK	COMPANY	HEADQUARTERS	INDUSTRY
131	UNITED BRANDS	CINCINNATI	FOOD
203	PARKER HANNIFIN	CLEVELAND	AEROSPACE
216	TRINOVA	MAUMEE	EQUIPMENT
242	PENN CENTRAL	CINCINNATI	METALS
245	RELIANCE ELECTRIC	CLEVELAND	ELECTRONICS
298	AMERICAN GREETINGS	CLEVELAND	PRINTING
323	RUBBERMAID	WOOSTER	RUBBER
324	LUBRIZOL	WICKLIFFE	CHEMICALS
349	FERRO	CLEVELAND	CHEMICALS
362	WORTHINGTON INDS.	COLUMBUS	METALS
402	COOPER TIRE	FINDLAY	RUBBER
405	STANDARD REGISTER	DAYTON	PRINTING
429	OHIO MATTRESS	CLEVELAND	FURNITURE
432	PHILIPS INDUSTRIES	DAYTON	METAL PRODS.
447	REYNOLDS & REYNOLDS	DAYTON	PRINTING
460	CARLISLE	CINCINNATI	RUBBER
496	CLEVELAND-CLIFFS	CLEVELAND	MINING, OIL
497	STANDARD PRODUCTS	CLEVELAND	RUBBER
498	A.SCHULMAN	AKRON	CHEMICALS

Ohio also had its share of newcomers to the list, as Table 6.3 shows. Just as for the North as a region, the state's newcomers tended to represent traditional industries: rubber (including tires), chemicals, metals, and metal products. The newcomer count was aided by the lower dollar.

Several Ohio newcomers climbed onto the bottom of the 500 list for 1987. Four of the 500's bottom five were Ohio firms, and three of the bottom five were Ohio companies that had not been on the list the previous year. The reason seems to be the improvement in the midwest's industrial performance in response to the lower dollar. As Ohio-based manufacturers fared better, their growing sales boosted them onto the 500 list (which is based on sales revenues).

Movers...

A handful of the 1965 Ohio contingent are still on the list for 1987 but are headquartered elsewhere. Thus Firestone moved from Akron, the tire capital, to Chicago (see Table 6.1). Armco Steel, in Middletown in 1965, now has its headquarters in New Jersey. The former Addressograph-Multigraph of Cleveland is now AM International of Chicago.

Then there were the Frostbelt-Sunbelt moves. In a twist, Diamond Alkali of Cleveland became Diamond Shamrock of Dallas, only to be taken over by Ohio-based B. F. Goodrich and thus disappear from the list. Harris-Intertype of Cleveland became Harris of Melbourne, Florida. In another interregional shift, Cooper Industries of Mt. Vernon moved to Houston.

...And Shakers

As Table 6.4 reveals, takeovers of Ohio firms since 1965 can be grouped into three distinct phases. The first is typified by the conglomerate or diversifying mergers of the late 1960s. Part of their rationale was to avoid antitrust sanctions; by crossing industry lines, acquiring firms would not increase concentration ratios or reduce price competition within an industry. A variant was the merger designed to enhance vertical integration, whereby a company at one stage of the production process merges with a company at another stage so as to bring supply, production, and distribution under a single management.

Both diversification and vertical integration motivated the takeovers of Ohio firms in this first, late–1960s phase. The conglomerate takeover is illustrated by Gulf & Western's 1969 acquisition of E. W. Bliss. A resource-based diversification was Occidental Petroleum's takeover of Island Creek Coal (1969). An example of vertical integration was U.S. Plywood's merger with Champion Papers, the scion of which is now Champion International of Stamford, Connecticut. The second and third phases have occurred in the 1980s. The second is the resurgence in takeovers of Ohio companies by U.S. firms, including LBOs by private buyers. The third is the beginning of a long-term rise in takeovers by foreign buyers.

Table 6.4
Takeover Targets: The 1960s, the 1980s, and Foreign Buyers

1965 RANK	COMPANY	LOCATION	ACQUIRER
	A. THE 1960S		
85	YOUNGSTOWN SH.&TUBE	YOUNGSTOWN	LYKES (1969) AND LTV (1979)
164	CHAMPION PAPERS	HAMILTON	U.S.PLYWOOD (1967)NOW CH.INT.
334	HUPP	CLEVELAND	WHITE (1967) OF OHIO
437	E.W. BLISS	CANTON	GULF & WESTERN (1969)
480	CLEVITE	CLEVELAND	GOULD (1969); GULF& WEST.(1979)
500	ISLAND CREEK COAL	CLEVELAND	OCCIDENTAL PETR. (1968)
	B. THE 1980S		
41	REPUBLIC STEEL	CLEVELAND	LTV (1984)
82	OWENS-ILLINOIS	TOLEDO	#116 BUT LBO'D 1987 BY KKR
123	MARATHON OIL	FINDLAY	U.S. STEEL (USX) (1982)
279	HOOVER	N.CANTON	CHICAGO PACIFIC (1985)
357	ANCHOR HOCKING GL.	LANCASTER	NEWELL (1987)
456	HOBART MFG.	TROY	KRAFT (1981)
	C. TAKEOVERS BY FOREIGN FIRMS		
69	GENERAL TIRE	AKRON	#139/TKO 1987 CONTI.AG.(GER.)
109	WHITE MOTOR	CLEVELAND	ELECTROLUX (SWEDEN) (1986)
116	STANDARD OIL (OHIO)	CLEVELAND	BP (U.K.) (1987)
227	GLIDDEN	CLEVELAND	SCM (U.K.) (1967)
248	LIBBEY-OWENS-FORD G.	TOLEDO	PILKINGTON (U.K.) (1986)
	D. APPARENT BUT UNTRACED TAKEOVERS		
234	MIDLAND-ROSS	CLEVELAND	PRIVATE (LBO?) 1986
484	WARNER & SWASEY	CLEVELAND	DISPLACED 1970

MERGERS AND FOREIGN TAKEOVERS IN OHIO IN THE 1980s

The second phase is the 1980s wave of mergers and leveraged buyouts or LBOs. In 1982, the world gasped when U.S. Steel (now USX) bought the Ohio-based Marathon Oil for the then unheard-of sum of $6 billion. Since then, several additional Ohio members of the class of 1965 have been taken over by U.S. firms. Among them are Hoover (by Chicago Pacific) and Republic Steel (by LTV).

Leveraged Buyouts in Ohio

A hallmark of the U.S. activity of the 1980s, of course, has been the LBO, as symbolized by the financial house of Kohlberg, Kravis, Roberts. In 1987 Kohlberg, Kravis, Roberts & Co. financed the private purchase of Toledo-based Owens Illinois for $3.7 billion. The usual practice in such LBOs is that the buyers, having taken a (formerly publicly held) corporation private, then split up some or all of the company's divisions and resell them, either as privately held entities or as new public offerings.

As Brian Holly suggests (in Chapter 5 of this volume), the pace of this sort of LBO and division-splitting activity in Ohio during the 1980s has been fast and furious. Not all of it registers on the Fortune 500 list, since parts of existing (and surviving) companies can be stripped and sold while the original corporation remains intact and on the list. When LBOs do occur they may be difficult to trace, because when companies go private (as they do after an LBO), they typically disappear from the list.

This is apparently what happened, for example, to Midland-Ross of Cleveland, which was ranked at 369 in 1985 but was taken off the list for the following year.

As a sidelight on these issues, a recent *Wall Street Journal* story provides a vivid case study of an Ohio-based division of ITT that was purchased and restructured under a leveraged buyout at the end of 1986 (Anders, 1988). The account tells how O. M. Scott & Sons, a manufacturer of lawn fertilizer and grass seed, was purchased with debt. The result saddled the new company with immediate and sizeable interest payments that in turn required rapid cost cutting, layoffs, and streamlining. Viewed as a success story (in contrast to some LBOs), this case also illustrates the severe dislocations that accompany an LBO.

Phase 3: Foreign Buyers

For Ohio and for the United States the mid–1980s have witnessed the first act of a drama that is just now beginning, the large-scale purchase of major U.S. companies by foreign owners. As noted at the outset, British Petroleum's purchase of 45 percent of Standard Oil of Ohio for $7.6 billion in 1987 symbolizes the expansion of the takeover game to a global scale. In light of the continued large U.S. trade deficit and the prospect of further downward pressure on the dollar, U.S. companies are likely to look attractive to foreign buyers for the foreseeable future.

Table 6.4 shows that three other members of the Ohio class of 1965 have been bought by foreigners since 1986. Electrolux of Sweden purchased White Motors; Pilkington, a British firm bought Libby-Owens-Ford Glass; and Continental AG of Germany bought General Tire. Thus Ohio companies in traditional manufacturing lines are attractive not only to LBO purchasers, but to foreign buyers as well.

CONCLUSION: RESTRUCTURING, CONTINUED

The acceleration of foreign purchases of Ohio firms in the mid–1980s serves as a reminder that we are only mid-stream in the present round of historical restructuring, as played out now not only on a regional but also on a global scale.

Economists tend to view the prospect of stepped-up direct foreign investment calmly, pointing out that it confers benefits not rendered by the more volatile purchase by foreigners of U.S. financial assets (Little, 1988). But it clearly signals a new phase in the process of restructuring, the political ramifications of which are as yet only partly understood Tolchin and Tolchin, 1988).

By the same token, the results reported here must be considered only an interim tally, in effect a half-time score. The restructuring of Ohio's and the nation's industrial base is far from complete. Whether the result will be to weaken or to enhance the state and the nation's economic competitiveness is an open question, one debated by other contributors to this volume.

REFERENCES

George Anders. "Leveraged Buy-Outs Make Some Companies Tougher Competitors." *Wall Street Journal*. 15 September 1988.

Jane Sneddon Little. "Foreign Investment in the United States: A Cause for Concern?" *New England Economic Review* (Federal Reserve Bank of Boston), July/August 1988, pp. 51–58.

Thomas J. Peters and Robert H. Waterman, Jr. *In Search of Excellence: Lessons from America's Best-Run Companies*. New York: Warner Books, 1983.

Martin Tolchin and Susan Tolchin. *Buying into America*. New York: Times Books, 1988.

7

ETHICAL CONSIDERATIONS IN TAKEOVERS

Gordon E. Heffern

DEFINITION

Ethics is defined as a set of standards or code of values; it is a system by which free human actions are determined as ultimately right or wrong, good or evil. How does one evaluate the rightness or wrongness of a takeover? There are a number of "publics" that must be considered in arriving at an ethical judgment. Another key consideration in making such an evaluation is the type of takeover, whether friendly or unfriendly. The various publics will be considered from both an unfriendly or hostile and a friendly basis for both the short and the long term.

THE VARIOUS PUBLICS

Shareholders

In general there are two types of shareholders, institutional and individual. There are different subgroups within the two broad categories, each having somewhat different interests. However, the overriding purpose of the shareholder, regardless of particular focus, is to maximize the return on investment. By definition this means increasing the price of the shares or increasing the dividend paid on the shares in the shortest possible time frame.

1. *Institutional Investors*: This group tends to have the shortest time horizon. At the same time, there are different expectations or levels of tolerance among the various groups.

117-4771

a. *Arbitrageurs*: The least tolerant are the arbitrageurs, who operate on a minute-by-minute basis. They are truly opportunists and have absolutely no concern about what or who is moving the stock and why, but only care that there is an opportunity to take advantage of price differentials before other investors catch on to the potential for gain.

The arbitrageurs' interests are served only on a short-term time horizon. In general they care little about long-term effects, good or bad, on the enterprise and the remaining publics. Their role is to supply liquidity and to arouse the interests of other potential shareholders. In general, they are not concerned with ethical considerations.

b. *Takeover Entrepreneurs*, sometimes called takeover artists, are almost always short-term opportunists somewhat like lions stalking their prey. They seek out companies whose performance has not been up to standard and try to entice shareholders to sell by offering a substantial premium above the going market price. Frequently a large number of shares can be accumulated because some shareholders have become impatient waiting for something good to happen to their investment. This technique is usually of the unfriendly or hostile variety, and is certainly hostile insofar as the entrenched management group is concerned.

Frequently, after the hostile takeover investor has accumulated a substantial position (on the order of 25 percent of the shares outstanding), an attempt will be made by management to buy the shares at a substantial premium to the hostile investor's price. Valuable resources are usually needed to make the funds available for the purchase. They may be in the form of the sale of parts of the business in order to service the debt incurred to buy the shares. The resulting company will shrink in size and will probably be less viable than before. Management's attention is also diverted from day-to-day operations, and the firm's competitive position may be weakened. Ethical considerations are usually not important, although takeover artists will usually claim concern for the long-term investor as the basis for their actions.

c. *Takeover Companies and Leveraged Buyouts*: During the last several years, a new game has arisen wherein relatively small and sometimes weak companies have taken over larger, stronger enterprises by leveraging the resources of the acquired company to serve the debt. The resulting company is leveraged and sometimes put at risk as the debt-to-equity ratios are increased considerably. In future periods of stress in the economy, such as during recessions or times of high interest rates, many of the highly leveraged businesses will not survive. These buyouts may be ethical especially if the venture is at risk of failing and the employees are willing to forgo wage and benefits in order to enhance the value of their investment.

d. *Money Managers*: Included in this group are mutual fund managers, pension fund managers, trust fund managers, and other institutional investors such as insurance companies. Some of them are quite oriented toward short-term results, while others take the longer view. Frequently institutional managers are given at least one business cycle for which to perform better than the Dow Jones averages or the Standard & Poor's 500 Index. This would last for approximately five years. Generally corporation executives favor these investors because they are more patient and are interested in strategic issues. The fund managers want to understand the business they are buying into and most visit with management on a regular basis. Corporate managers would place fund managers on a fairly high ethical rung in the ladder. Takeovers are all right if the price is right.

2. *Individual Investors*: As a group, individuals tend to be the most loyal of all categories of investors. They have a very real interest in the affairs of the company, frequently buy the product, and are goodwill ambassadors for the company and its products and services. They take the longest view and therefore tend to be the most ethical. They want good things to happen and expect the management to be highly ethical. Usually they do not like takeovers, unfriendly or friendly.

MANAGEMENT

The chief executive officer (CEO) of a corporation spends a good deal of his time plotting and implementing defensive and offensive takeover strategies. Most CEOs would state that they prefer to acquire rather than to be acquired. When making an acquisition, the preferred method is to have a firsthand meeting with the management of the company to be acquired and try to arrange a friendly merger. A second method is to have a third party such as an investment banker make the approach. If all else fails, the CEO will make a tender offer which is usually regarded as unfriendly and in some quarters unethical.

The senior management group generally is interested in running the new company or having similar positions in the corporate structure, or, at worst, to be bought out by the new management group. This process may take many forms but is usually a matter of survival. The buyout is the shortest-term approach, usually the least desirable, and the least ethical. The senior management group's interests under these circumstances are not necessarily the same as the other publics' interests and therefore may cause friction and stress.

NON-MANAGEMENT EMPLOYEES

When a merger or takeover, whether friendly or unfriendly, is announced, there is great concern on the part of all employees, both white-collar and blue-collar. Will the office or plant close or cut back employment? Will I lose my job? Will I have a new boss? Will I be transferred? These are only a partial list of questions that will arise among the group. Management owes a full disclosure to its employees as soon as possible in order to quiet such fears. Honesty and forthrightness are always the best policy when there is uncertainty. Communication with employees is extremely important. It should be undertaken at every level and as clearly articulated as possible. Information should be updated frequently in order to dispel fears and concerns.

If terminations are required, they should be handled with honesty, concern, and assistance in securing new employment opportunities as soon as possible.

CUSTOMERS

Will the customer receive the same quality product and service in the future that has been provided in the past? The new senior management team should make known to the customer group their new programs and policies immediately in order to dispel any concern the customers may have and to provide as much lead time as necessary for the customer to secure new suppliers.

THE COMMUNITY AT LARGE

How might the economy of the community be affected? Are there community resources that might be available for changes that are being contemplated? (This could apply to expansions as well as contractions that are planned.) Resources in the community are limited, and full disclosure of any major changes will permit maximization of help and support. If offices or plants are closed or moved away, what impact will it have on the local economy? If expansions are planned, how will the expansions impact the community?

Hostile takeovers frequently result in contraction of the enterprise due to the short-term focus for near-term gains. Therefore, hostile arrangements may frequently result in a negative perception, while friendly mergers may have a favorable impact on the community.

THE GOVERNMENT

Local governments are usually adversely affected in unfriendly or hostile takeovers due to the short-term emphasis, while taxes, revenues, and employment may be increased by friendly mergers. If large expansions are planned, the result may present an immediate problem if additional schools and community services are required. This is the kind of "problem" most communities and local governments desire, as it results in greater well-being in the long run. The state and federal governments are usually not adversely affected immediately but may suffer in the long run if contractions in businesses result in more goods and services being imported from abroad.

The ethical solution is for closely working private-public partnerships wherein both parties are as fully informed as possible and a spirit of cooperation and openness prevails.

THE SHORT TERM AND THE LONG TERM

Hostile and unfriendly takeovers are driven by short-term rewards. The aggressor usually wants to maximize his or her return, and is frequently driven by greed and an attitude of "take no prisoners." Friendly mergers and takeovers, on the other hand, are planned with a longer view, and the drive for immediate riches is frequently subservient to the goal for results to flow more solidly over future years.

Hostile takeovers usually result in a contraction of the enterprise, while the friendly takeover frequently produces expansion of the business with attendant increased employment and more production at lower costs.

HOW HAVE TAKEOVERS BEEN FACILITATED?

Federal Reserve Easy-Money Policy

During most of the decade of the 1980s, the Federal Reserve has found it necessary to pursue a course of easy money. This has been due in large measure to huge domestic and international deficits. The money had to be borrowed in part from the banks, and stability was a requirement in the money markets of the United States in order to attract investments from abroad, which also helped underwrite the domestic deficits. The resulting liquidity in the banking system permitted takeover specialists to set up huge credit lines to back their investment efforts. This is one of the few times, if not the only time in modern banking, when the economy has expanded for a very long period of time and money and credit have been freely available. Of course, the large U.S. trade deficits have provided huge amounts of liquidity throughout the western world, which might be characterized as being awash with liquidity during most of the decade of the 1980s.

The Stock Market

From the early 1980s until October 19, 1987, the market moved ever higher. Thus, a speculator in an equity of a good, strong company had little risk in borrowing money and taking a large position in the company's common equity. Even the correction of October 1987 only gave up the gains of the first ten months. The market closed the year higher than on January 1, 1987; this was hardly a crash as characterized by most of the media.

The combination of steadily rising equity prices and no limit on the amount of available credit provided an unbeatable opportunity for those who wanted to play the game. Unfortunately, their game will not last forever, and the consequence is likely to be a rapid increase in the inflation rate at some time in the future. When that occurs, there will certainly be "weeping and gnashing of teeth." The excesses of the 1980s will come home to roost one day in the not too distant future. The ethical implications of these developments are very serious: We have not been good stewards of our limited capital resources.

SUMMARY

The ethical implication of takeovers is not a simple matter. Questions arise as to whom is benefitted in the short and long term. Is the combination of business enterprises, either friendly or hostile, the best way to serve the public interest? Is bigness good or bad? How does the takeover game affect international trade? Is merger-mania a passing fancy facilitated by an easy-money policy for a long period of time? What will happen to leveraged buyouts when recession strikes or higher inflation rates with attendant higher interest rates descend on us?

There are no simple answers to these questions. However, it appears that long-term strategic plans produce the greatest benefits. The Japanese have such a model, and U.S. enterprises have been criticized for too much emphasis on short-term results that sometimes come at the expense of long-term well-being. One solution to the problem is the discipline of the marketplace for both money and equities, with the maxim, "no pain, no gain."

8

THE CORPORATE TAKEOVER REGULATORY ARENA

Lois J. Yoder

The emergence of legislation to control corporate takeovers began in the 1960s to fill a void in the federal securities laws regarding cash tender offers. The Securities Acts of 1933 and 1934, which regulate stock tender offers, contain no provision for cash transactions.[1] As knowledge of this regulatory void spread, cash tender offers developed as a means of acquiring firms. Hostile cash tender offers were accomplished inexpensively, swiftly, and neatly, with no government intervention. This lack of regulation caused states to begin implementing legislation designed to control these cash tender offers. Virginia adopted the first state tender-offer law in 1968, the Virginia Takeover Bid Disclosure Act to meet an emergency takeover attempt in its state.[2]

The federal government also entered the field in 1968, a few months after Virginia had enacted its statute, by passing the Williams Act.[3] While the Williams Act regulated cash tender-offer transactions at the federal level by including detailed disclosure requirements, it did not expressly preempt this area of regulation. Hence, dual regulation of cash tender offers, at both the federal and state levels, was permissible. This dual regulatory aspect set the stage for the two primary constitutionality challenges to state takeover laws.

One such challenge is based on the Supremacy Clause of the U.S. Constitution, which maintains that state laws that either conflict with federal statutes on a topic or that attempt to regulate an area that is exclusively within the province of the federal government are null and void, since the federal law is the supreme law of the land. The second

86   HOSTILE TAKEOVERS

federal constitutionality challenge common to state takeover laws is a Commerce Clause argument wherein a state law is deemed to be unconstitutional if it places an undue burden on interstate commerce. Both these arguments have been used repeatedly in court challenges to state takeover laws at both the federal and state court levels.

The U.S. Supreme Court has addressed the constitutionality of state takeover laws in two recent cases, in 1982 and 1987. These decisions have served as important benchmarks in the evolutionary process as states have reviewed, revised, repealed, or adopted legislation in an effort to develop laws that could withstand constitutionality attacks.

The first Supreme Court decision, *Edgar v. Mite Corporation*[4] on June 23, 1982, reviewed and struck down Illinois's takeover statute, the Illinois Business Takeover Act.[5] This decision marked the end of the first-generation period of state takeover legislation and began the second-generation period. The second-generation period lasted until April 21, 1987, when the Supreme Court upheld Indiana's takeover legislation, the Indiana Control Share Acquisitions Act,[6] in *CTS Corporation v. Dynamics Corporation of America.*[7] This decision breathed new life into state takeover legislation from a legal perspective and began the third-generation period. Hence, the 20-year evolution of state tender-offer regulations can be categorized into three generational periods benchmarked by the two U.S. Supreme Court decisions. April 22, 1987, began the third-generation period. The following portions of this chapter review state tender-offer activity during each generational period, with a section highlighting the role played by the Midwestern states in all three periods.

The first-generation period, which began in 1968 and lasted until June 23, 1982, was a period of exploration, creativity, and experimentation as many states devised provisions to regulate corporate takeover activity.

Since in 1968 the federal Williams Act did not expressly preempt the area, many states followed Virginia's lead by adopting protective measures designed specifically to meet hostile cash tender-offer "emergencies" occurring within their borders. Most of these regulations were included as part of state securities laws. Provisions of many state regulations mirrored those of the Williams Act, while some states included even greater disclosure, notice, and hearing requirements. A majority of these regulations, being tailored to meet a specific emergency situation in the state, were drafted quickly and narrowly, and sometimes contained sunset provisions and unique clauses.

During the first-generation period, 37 states entered this regulatory area. While most state regulations took the form of legislatively enacted statutes in some states such as Texas, rules and regulations were issued by state administrative agencies. Table 8.1 indicates each state's takeover-regulation status as of June 23, 1982, the date of the *Edgar v. Mite Corporation* decision that ended the first-generation period. Al-

Table 8.1
State Hostile-Tender-Offer Provisions as of 6–23–82

STATE	NO PROVISIONS	ADOPTION YEAR OF PROVISION
ALABAMA	X	
ALASKA		1976
ARIZONA	X	
ARKANSAS		1977
CALIFORNIA	X	
COLORADO		1975
CONNECTICUT		1976
DELAWARE		1976
FLORIDA	X	
GEORGIA		1977
HAWAII		1974
IDAHO		1975
ILLINOIS		1977
INDIANA		1975
IOWA	X	
KANSAS		1974
KENTUCKY		1976
LOUISIANA		1976
MAINE		1978
MARYLAND		1976
MASSACHUSETTS		1976
MICHIGAN		1976
MINNESOTA		1973
MISSISSIPPI		1980
MISSOURI		1979
MONTANA	X	
NEBRASKA		1977
NEVADA		1969
NEW HAMPSHIRE		1977
NEW JERSEY		1977
NEW MEXICO	X	
NEW YORK		1976
NORTH CAROLINA		1977
NORTH DAKOTA	X	
OHIO		1969
OKLAHOMA		1981
OREGON	X	
PENNSYLVANIA		1976
RHODE ISLAND	X	
SOUTH CAROLINA		1978
SOUTH DAKOTA		1975
TENNESSEE		1976
TEXAS		1977
UTAH		1976
VERMONT	X	
VIRGINIA		1968
WASHINGTON	X	
WEST VIRGINIA	X	
WISCONSIN		1972
WYOMING	X	

Source: Commerce Clearing House, Inc., *Blue Sky Law Reporter*, Chicago, IL (1984).

though Florida initially enacted antitakeover legislation in 1977, it repealed its law in 1979 and had no new provisions on its books as of the end of the first-generation period.

During this experimental first-generation period, various state laws were challenged in the state and federal courts as being unconstitutional under the Supremacy Clause and/or the Commerce Clause. When the U.S. Supreme Court first reviewed a state takeover statute in the 1982 case of *Edgar v. Mite Corporation*, the Court struck down the Illinois Business Takeover Act on the grounds that it violated the Commerce Clause of the U.S. Constitution by unduly burdening interstate commerce. The Court determined that the state's interests in protecting its shareholders and other investors and in regulating the internal affairs of Illinois corporations did not justify or outweigh the burden that the act placed on interstate commerce. By its language, the Court noted, the act regulated not only companies incorporated in Illinois but some out-of-state corporations as well. Likewise, the act's provisions, protecting corporate shareholders and investors, affected not only Illinois investors but also investors of other states. Additionally, the Court questioned whether the act actually accomplished its alleged purpose of aiding shareholders in view of similar provisions contained in the Williams Act. While the *Mite* decision struck down the Illinois statute, the decision did not prohibit state regulation in this area. This decision ended the first-generation period of state takeover legislation and began the second-generation period.

The second-generation period was filled with regulatory activity as states scrambled to review their statutes, revising them to avoid the pitfalls outlined in *Edgar v. Mite Corporation*. Most of these second-generation statutes were included as part of a state's general corporation laws rather than as part of the securities laws. Several basic types of statutes emerged during this second-generation period.[8]

1. *Control Share Acquisition Laws* (The Ohio Approach): This type of statute was initially developed and adopted by the State of Ohio, with Indiana also following this approach. The Ohio statute is a typical example of this type of provision. Under this type of law, an entity acquiring "control shares" in a corporation subject to this law obtains voting power of those shares only when a majority of all shareholders, excluding the "interested shares," grants this voting power at a shareholders' meeting specially called by the board of directors after the corporation receives an "acquiring person statement" from the acquirer. If voting rights are not granted, the corporation may redeem the acquirer's shares.

2. *Fair Price Laws* (The Maryland Approach): Developed by the State of Maryland, its statute is a typical example of this type. Under this type of statute, any business combination involving a resident corporation and a shareholder

owning a minimum percentage (for example; 10 or 20 percent) of the resident corporation stock must be recommended by the board of directors and approved by a high percentage (for example; 80 or 95 percent) of the owners of outstanding shares, unless the minority shareholders are to receive, in the business combination, an amount of compensation for their shares that satisfies the fair-price provision of the statute.

3. *Heightened Appraisal Rights, also known as Control-Share Cash-Out-Laws* (Pennsylvania and Maine Approaches): Both Pennsylvania and Maine were on the forefront in developing and adopting this type of regulation, and their statutes are good examples of this type. Under this type of statute, an entity acquiring a certain percentage of the stock of a corporation (for example; 25 or 30 percent) must notify remaining shareholders, who then have a right for a reasonable period of time thereafter, to demand cash payment for their shares at a fair-value amount prescribed by the statute.

4. *Five Year Moratorium Laws* (The New York Approach): Developed and adopted in New York, its statute is typical of this type. This type of statute prohibits an interested shareholder (one who obtains 10 or 20 percent of the corporate stock, for example) from participating in a business combination with the corporation for the five-year period following achievement of the interested shareholder status unless the board of directors approves either of the following prior to the acquirer becoming an interested shareholder:

   a. the business combination; or

   b. the stock purchase that created the interested shareholder status.

5. *Expanded Constituency Laws* (Illinois Approach): Adopted by Illinois initially, its statute is a typical example of this type of provision. These permissive statutes give the board of directors the power to consider both short-term and long-term effects, not only on corporate shareholders, but also on corporate employees, customers, communities, and suppliers, in determining the best interests of the corporation in any action taken.

6. *Heightened Disclosure Statutes* (Minnesota Approach): Developed and initially adopted by Minnesota, its statute is typical of this type of provision. This disclosure type of statute requires, for effective offers, that potential acquirers file a registration statement with the State Commissioner of Securities. If the filing is insufficient, the commissioner is empowered to suspend the takeover, with a hearing and final determination occurring rapidly thereafter.

Several states adopted statutes containing various combinations of the foregoing types of provisions during the second-generation period. Some states followed a certain basic type of statute but modified its provisions somewhat to meet their specific needs. Thus, classification of these second-generation statutes is somewhat overlapping and complex.

The lower courts again addressed constitutionality attacks on these statutes during the second-generation period. This period ended on April 21, 1987, when the U.S. Supreme Court reviewed another state takeover statute, the Indiana Control Share Acquisition statute, in the case of *CTS Corporation v. Dynamics Corporation of America*. In this case, the Court upheld the Indiana statute, thus breathing new life into this type of regulation, and thereby beginning the third-generation period.

In *CTS*, the Court ruled that the Indiana statute's provisions were not in conflict with the federal Williams Act, nor did the Indiana statute impermissibly burden interstate commerce. Although recognizing that the Indiana statute did have an effect on interstate commerce, the Court noted that it affected interstate commerce only to a "limited extent."[9] The Court further recognized Indiana's legitimate state interests in enacting such legislation, since the Indiana statute applied only to corporations chartered in Indiana.

In effect, the Court viewed this legislation as a natural extension of a state's general corporation laws which allow states to create corporations, and, hence, should allow states to regulate their structural changes. In contrast, in *Mite* the Court had expressed the view that states should not interfere with the interstate market for corporate control and that takeovers promote efficiency. In *CTS*, the Court noted that "the Constitution does not require the States to subscribe to any particular economic theory."[10] Noting the conflicting views expressed in various studies, the Court in *CTS* placed little emphasis on financial and economic theories regarding the effectiveness of tender offers. Thus, the Indiana statute survived the traditional constitutionality attacks under both the Commerce Clause and the Supremacy Clause.

As of the end of the second-generation period, 17 states had no provisions regulating hostile cash tender offers.[11] Additionally, although 6 states continued to have first-generation statutes on their books, these statutes were ineffective as of April 21, 1987, generally because their enforcement had been enjoined as a result of their lack of constitutionality in view of the 1982 *Mite* decision.[12] Of the remaining 27 states with hostile tender-offer provisions in effect as of April 21, 1987, 7 states continued to have enforceable first-generation statutes only.[13]

Table 8.2 lists the remaining 20 states that had second-generation hostile-takeover regulations in effect as of April 21, 1987, categorizing the regulations as to their various types of provisions.

In view of the positive impact on state takeover legislation created by the April 1987, *CTS* decision, many states have again ventured into this regulatory arena during the third-generation period. While some states have repealed their statutes in view of the *CTS* decision, most states have enacted legislation containing provisions mirroring those in the Indiana statute. Because of the favorable *CTS* decision, the experimental and exploratory attitude toward state takeover legislation is reemerging during the third-generation period. Table 8.3 lists those states that have, to date, experienced changes during this third-generation period.

During all three generational periods, ten states have never ventured

Table 8.2
State Hostile-Tender-Offer Provisions as of 4–21–87

STATE	I.	II.	III.	IV.	V.	VI.
GEORGIA			X			
IDAHO						X
ILLINOIS						X
INDIANA	X			X		
KENTUCKY			X	X		
MAINE				X		X
MARYLAND		X				
MICHIGAN		X				
MINNESOTA						X
MISSISSIPPI		X				
MISSOURI	X					
NEBRASKA						X
NEW YORK				X		X
OHIO	X				X	
OKLAHOMA						X
PENNSYLVANIA			X			
TENNESSEE						X
UTAH				X		X
VIRGINIA		X				
WISCONSIN	X		X			X

TABLE KEY:

TYPE	I.	Control Share Acquisition Laws (IN-Type)
TYPE	II.	Fair Price Laws (MD-Type)
TYPE	III.	Heightened Appraisal Rights Laws, a.k.a. Control Share Cash-Out Laws
TYPE	IV.	Five-Year Moratorium Laws (NY-Type)
TYPE	V.	Expanded Constituency Laws
TYPE	VI.	Heightened Disclosures Statutes

into this regulatory arena.[14] A study of state officials reveals that the most common reason cited by officials of these ten states for not regulating in this area is their lack of need for this type of regulation, since corporate activity is slight in their states. In California, where corporate activity abounds however, the reason cited by California officials is the state's strong conviction that this area of regulation should exist at the federal level only. Hence, California officials strongly favor federal

Table 8.3
Third-Generation-Period State Regulatory Changes

State	Year of Change
Arizona	1987
Connecticut	1988
Delaware	1988
Florida	1987
Kansas	1987
Louisiana	1987
Massachusetts	1987
Minnesota	1987
Missouri	1987
Nevada	1987
New Jersey	1987
North Carolina	1987
Oklahoma	1987
Oregon	1987
Washington	1987

preemption of this entire area and are active proponents of such legislation in Congress. Although West Virginia has never entered this regulatory arena, it is currently considering doing so for the first time, with legislation on this issue currently pending.

Several other states, along with West Virginia, may experience future changes in their hostile tender offer regulations, since these states currently have hostile-tender-offer legislation pending.[15] Various additional states also indicate that their regulations are currently under review during this third-generation period in view of the *CTS* decision.

During all three generational periods, the Midwestern states have been actively involved in all aspects of the legal controversy.[16] Such continual involvement by these states has placed them at the forefront of many of these issues, thereby establishing them as leaders in this legislative area. As the data in Table 8.4 indicate, 10 of the 12 Midwestern states enacted takeover legislation during the first-generation period beginning with Ohio's statute passed in 1969, only a year after Virginia's.[17]

Constitutionality attacks on several Midwestern statutes abounded during the second-generation period, beginning with the U.S. Supreme Court striking down Illinois's statute in 1982 and culminating with the Court's upholding Indiana's statute in 1987. This active involvement and exposure to the constitutional attacks on their legislation during the second-generation period caused many Midwestern states to respond by amending their statutes to avoid the Illinois problem.

Table 8.4
State Takeover Laws in the Midwest

	First Generation 3/5/68- 6/23/82	Second Generation 6/24/82- 4/21/87	Third Generation 4/22/87- Present
Illinois	1977	1986	No Change
Indiana	1975	1983	No Change
Iowa	None	None	None
Kansas	1974	1983	No Change
Michigan	1976	No Change	No Change
Minnesota	1973	No Change	1987
Missouri	1979	1986	1987
Nebraska	1977	No Change	No Change
North Dakota	None	None	None
Ohio	1969	1982	No Change
South Dakota	1975	1983	No Change
Wisconsin	1972	1984	No Change

Source: Commerce Clearing House, Inc., *Blue Sky Law Reporter*, Chicago, IL (1984).

Seven of these Midwestern states rapidly revised their legislation to meet the constitutionality mandates set forth in *Edgar v. Mite Corporation*, with Ohio being the first of any state in the nation to do so.[18] Continued exposure to the progress and developments in these cases during the second-generation period caused the Midwestern states to develop unique, creative provisions. Many of these positions became models for legislation in other states.

The close proximity of the Indiana situation enabled the Midwestern states to follow its progress continually and intimately. In anticipation of Indiana's treatment, many of the Midwestern states patterned their statutes after Indiana's and, in some instances, developed legislation simultaneously with Indiana. This foresight by many Midwestern states has created little need for further amendments by these states during the third-generation period. However, the myriad of corporate takeover attempts within these states' borders has caused them to continue their leadership role into the third-generation period by actively reviewing, applying, and testing their state takeover laws in a variety of situations.

Ohio enacted its first tender-offer law in 1969.[19] It was the third state nationally to do so, preceded only by Virginia[20] and Nevada.[21] The Ohio statute allowed management of the target company to delay a hostile takeover attempt for up to 60 days, pending the outcome of a hearing determining the adequacy of disclosure given to shareholders of the target company.[22] Most of the provisions of this first-generation statute have been preempted by the federal Williams Act as well as by SEC Rule 14d–2(b) under the Securities Act of 1934. The Ohio statute was also determined unconstitutional under the Commerce Clause, since it placed an undue burden on interstate commerce. This statute was attacked in three federal district court cases in 1979,[23] 1981,[24] and 1982.[25] The *Hanna Mining Co.* case was decided only two weeks prior to the U.S. Supreme Court decision in *Edgar v. Mite Corporation*, which struck the final blow to Ohio's statute.

Thereafter, Ohio scrambled rapidly in the early part of the second-generation period to revise its tender-offer statute. In 1982, Ohio enacted its Control Share Acquisition Act with an effective date of November 18, 1982.[26] This was the first state statute enacted during the second-generation period and appeared as part of Ohio's General Corporation Laws rather than as part of its Securities Laws as the first-generation statute had been. This innovative approach with unique provisions was designed to avoid the pitfalls of the first-generation statutes. Many states, including Indiana, followed Ohio's lead, patterning provisions of their statutes after Ohio's.

The constitutionality of Ohio's second-generation statute was challenged in the federal courts in the case of *Fleet Aerospace Corporation v. Holderman*.[27] The federal district court in this case found, in its 1986 decision, that the Ohio statute violated the federal Williams Act and, hence, was unconstitutional. The U.S. Sixth Circuit Court of Appeals reviewed the decision in 1986 and affirmed that trial court's decision. An appeal to the U.S. Supreme Court resulted, on April 27, 1987, in the Court vacating the Sixth Circuit Court of Appeal's decision and remanding the case to the trial court for reconsideration in view of the U.S. Supreme Court's April 21, 1987, opinion in *CTS Corporation v. Dynamics Corporation of America*. The *CTS* decision, which upheld Indiana's statute, was key to the constitutionality of Ohio's statute, since the Indiana statute, which was reviewed by the Court, contained a control-share-acquisition provision patterned after Ohio's. Thus, Ohio's second-generation statute appears constitutional.

During the third-generation period, Ohio has enacted several additional tender-offer provisions designed to protect directors from liability in formulating and approving tender-offer defenses.[28] These provisions are also contained as part of Ohio's General Corporation Law. Thus, it is evident that Ohio has taken a very active leadership role over the past 20 years in devising, implementing, defending, and revising state tender-offer laws.

A review of the past 20 years of tender-offer regulation generates several observations and recommendations regarding current shortcomings in this regulatory area.

1. The dual regulation aspect of tender offers, at both the federal and

state levels, has created a very nonuniform area of law, thereby causing great compliance difficulties and consequential legal expense for corporations and acquirers. Several solutions have been suggested, including federal preemption, to create one uniform body of law. The legal debate surrounding this preemption issue, however, involves two opposing schools of thought. Those favoring federal preemption feel that regulating corporate takeover activity is a natural extension of the federal government's current regulation of corporate securities activities through the Securities and Exchange Commission. Those opposed to federal preemption argue that regulation of corporate takeovers belongs at the state level as part of states' general corporate laws, which traditionally have exclusively controlled all aspects of internal corporate organization, including corporate formation and termination.

Recent legislation introduced in Congress illustrates federal legislative attempts to settle the preemption issue. The likelihood of passage of this or any federal legislation, however, appears slim at the current time. Another attempt at creating uniformity in this area is state adoption of a model state takeover statute. However, initial reaction to the North American Securities Administrators Association (NASAA)/American Bar Association (ABA) model statute, introduced in the spring of 1988, appears far from uniform. Still others have suggested having the SEC control this area. However, from a practical standpoint, budgetary and staffing limitations make this undesirable. Hence, uniformity in this area, although highly desirable, seems unlikely in the near future.

2. States, in legislating in this area, are reluctant to do so unless faced with an actual emergency within their state. Thus legislation in this area is often drafted and passed quickly to meet specific limited circumstances when an emergency situation arises. Such legislation, since it is haphazardly passed, tends to lack prior cost-benefit analyses and other research, and also tends to result in inconsistent, conflicting, or duplicating provisions within a state's body of laws. Some provisions appear under a state's corporate code provisions, while others appear in the securities code provisions. Still others may appear in special code areas such as banking, insurance or oil and gas, with no guidance or overview as to the priority or practical interaction of all sections in the event of an actual takeover attempt. This patchwork legislation also creates administrative inconsistencies. State officials themselves often disagree as to which state administrative agency is responsible for policing and administering these regulations. The lack of uniformity and chaotic administration, needless to say, create a compliance nightmare for corporations.

3. An additional compliance difficulty arises due to the differing jurisdiction provisions in various state statutes. While some states attempt only to regulate corporations chartered in their state, other states' pro-

visions may apply to out-of-state as well as domestic corporations. Some state regulations apply to corporations that are chartered or headquartered in the state. Still other jurisdictional provisions make state tender-offer laws applicable to corporations having a certain minimum percentage of shareholders residing in the state regardless of the state in which the affected corporation is chartered or headquartered. For example, during this third-generation period, North Carolina has enacted a statute with broad jurisdictional applicability.[29] Accordingly, a corporation involved in a hostile tender offer may concurrently be under the jurisdiction of several states' tender-offer provisions. If these states' provisions lack uniformity, a conflict-of-laws problem results, with compliance impossibilities.

4. In enacting regulations to meet an isolated emergency, states create very limited, unique provisions with limited time durations. These drafting limitations may cause these regulations to be inequitably applied in all situations within a state. Often the provisions are so narrowly drafted that they conceivably could apply only to the specific corporate emergency necessitating the said legislation. For example, Missouri, in response to a takeover attempt of TWA a few years ago, limited the language in its statute so that the provisions of the statute were applicable only to common carriers having 50 gates at Logan Airport. Examples in other states would include Ohio's limited language in its December 1986 legislation in response to the hostile takeover attempt of the Goodyear Tire and Rubber Company; Washington's limited language to protect Boeing from being taken over; Oklahoma in the Phillips Petroleum situation; and North Carolina in the Burlington Industries hostile takeover. Such narrow provisions cannot withstand constitutionality challenges, and they demonstrate a lack of foresight and planning on the part of government legislators in regulating in this area. The narrow applicability of a state tender-offer statute also makes planning for hostile takeover threats difficult for corporate management, since it causes uncertainty as to what the existing state tender offer law is. Hence, much corporate time, effort, and resources must be spent lobbying for legislation when the emergency arises, since appropriate regulations may not already be in place.

5. Constitutional due-process requirements mandate that persons affected by pending legislation be given public notice of said regulations so that they have an opportunity to respond either in favor of or against the legislation prior to its enactment. It is for this reason that the traditional legislative process is a slow, methodical interchange of ideas with ultimate legislative adoption occurring after a substantial period following the initial introduction.

The method of enactment of state tender-offer laws, however, deviates drastically from the normal legislative process. Designed to thwart on-going or contemplated hostile takeovers in the state, most of these statutes are passed quickly in emergency legislative sessions. Many of these proposed takeovers promise to pay a substantial premium to shareholders of the target corporation. Unfortunately, these shareholders, who may be denied this property premium when the tender-offer law goes into effect, are given little or no notice of the pending legislation nor any opportunity to respond prior to its adoption. Thus, the basic emergency legislative procedure used in enacting these tender-offer statutes appears to deny certain potential property rights to shareholders without affording them due process of law. The right of the government to protect managerial interests over shareholder interests by enacting these statutes in such a nontraditional, rapid manner has also been challenged in the legal literature.[30]

6. In enacting this emergency legislation, states justify doing so on their presumption that adverse effects on the state's economy will result if the takeover is successful. The validity of this presumption, however, has never been tested. While studies have been conducted to determine the effect state tender-offer laws may have on the market value of the target company's stock, to date no studies have been conducted to determine the overall, long-term economic effects these laws or hostile takeovers in general may produce. The lack of studies to support this underlying presumption, on which so much emphasis is placed, causes one to question the soundness of such reliance.

Controversy regarding the viability and effectiveness of state tender-offer laws has enshrouded this legal area ever since their introduction 20 years ago. During the ensuing two decades, 40 states have ventured into this field at one time or another. As previously outlined, debates in the legal community abound regarding the constitutionality of state takeover laws. While much time, money, and energy have been expended over the past 20 years in enacting, revising, enforcing, and attacking such laws, the effectiveness of the regulation is presently unknown. The legal, financial, management, and economic literature present contrasting views regarding the viability of state tender-offer regulation. However, to date no studies have been conducted to determine the actual economic impact, if any, of this type of regulation. The foregoing review of the three generational periods of state tender-offer regulation suggests the possibility that these laws may not be achieving the goals their legislative authors assumed. Perhaps this, the 20th year since a state first enacted takeover legislation, may be a most appropriate moment at which to carefully examine the effectiveness of such regulation at the state and federal levels in an effort to avoid wasting time and resources in an exercise that may, in the end, prove to be futile.

NOTES

1. The Securities Act of 1933, 15 U.S.C. Sec. 77a–77bbbb (1982), and the Securities Exchange Act of 1934, 15 U.S.C. Sec. 78a–78kk (1982).

2. Virginia Takeover Bid Disclosure Act, Virginia Code Sec. 13.1–528 to 541 (1978 Supp. 1981).

3. The Williams Act, 15 U.S.C. Sec. 78m(d)-(e), 78n(d)-(f), 1982.

4. *Edgar v. Mite Corporation*, 457 U.S. 624 (1982).

5. Illinois Business Takeover Act, Illinois Ann. Stat. Ch. 121–1/2, Sec. 137.52–10 (Smith-Hurd Supp. 1983–1984).

6. Indiana Control Shares Acquisitions Act, Indiana Code Annotated Sec. 23–1–42–4(a), (Supp. 1986).

7. *CTS Corporation v. Dynamics Corporation of America*, 107 S. Ct. 1637 (1987).

8. Stephen M. Shapiro and Jeffrey M. Strause, "Breathing New Life into State Takeover Statutes," *Practicing Law Institute's Nineteenth Annual Institute on Securities Regulation*, September 21, 1987 (New York: Practicing Law Institute), pp. 457–512.

9. *CTS Corporation v. Dynamics Corporation of America*, 107 S. Ct. 1637 at 1652 (1987).

10. *CTS Corporation v. Dynamics Corporation of America*, 107 S. Ct. 1637 at 1651 (1987).

11. The 17 states are as follow: Alabama, Arizona, California, Colorado, Florida, Hawaii, Iowa, Montana, New Mexico, North Dakota, Oregon, Rhode Island, Texas, Vermont, Washington, West Virginia, and Wyoming.

12. The six states are Arkansas, Connecticut, Kansas, Massachusetts, New Jersey, and South Dakota.

13. These seven states are Alaska, Delaware, Louisiana, Nevada, New Hampshire, North Carolina, and South Carolina.

14. The ten states are Alaska, California, Iowa, Montana, New Mexico, North Dakota, Rhode Island, Vermont, West Virginia, and Wyoming.

15. These states include Idaho, Kansas, Kentucky, Michigan, Nebraska, Pennsylvania, Tennessee, Texas, and West Virginia.

16. For purposes of this chapter, the Midwestern states consist of the following 12 states: Illinois, Indiana, Iowa, Kansas, Michigan, Minnesota, Missouri, Nebraska, North Dakota, Ohio, South Dakota, and Wisconsin.

17. Ohio Takeover Act, Ohio Revised Code Sec. 1707.041.

18. Ohio Takeover Act, Ohio Revised Code Sec. 1701.831–832 and Sec. 1707.042.

19. 133 Laws of Ohio 352 (1969).

20. 1968 Laws of Virginia 167.

21. 1969 Laws of Nevada 120.

22. ORC Section 1707.041.

23. *AMCA International Corporation v. Krouse*, 482 F. Supp. 929 (SD Ohio 1979).

24. *Canadian Pacific Enterprises (U.S.), Inc. v. Krouse*, 506 F. Supp. 1192 (SD Ohio 1981).

25. *Hanna Mining Company v. Noreen Energy Resources, Ltd.* (ND Ohio 1982).

26. 1982 H. 822. ORC Section 1701.831.

27. *Fleet Aerospace Corporation v. Holderman*, 637 F Supp. 742 (SD Ohio, 1986), affirmed by 796 F 2d 135 (6th Cir. 1986), vacated and remanded sub nom *Ohio v. Fleet Aerospace Corporation*, 107 S Ct. 1949 (1987).

28. 1986 H. 902, eff. 11–27–86; 1987 H 50, eff. 2–26–87.

29. North Carolina Control Share Acquisition Act, NC Gen. Stat. Section 55–90 through 55–98, eff. 5–13–87.

30. Henry N. Butler, "Corporation-Specific Anti-Takeover Statutes and the Market for Corporate Charters," *Wisconsin Law Review* 3 (1988): 365.

PART III

FOREIGN DIRECT INVESTMENT, FEDERAL TAX POLICY, AND CORPORATE CONTROL

9

FOREIGN DIRECT INVESTMENT IN THE UNITED STATES: IMPLICATIONS FOR CORPORATE CONTROL

William D. Gunther

In 1986, the total dollar value of all merger-and-acquisition activity in the United States was estimated to be $204 billion. Of this total, an estimated $25.2 billion or 12.4 percent was foreign-based activity.[1] While the dollar amount of merger-and-acquisition activity declined to $167 billion in 1987, the proportion accounted for by foreign-based firms increased from 12.4 to 24.9 percent. Clearly, foreign direct investment plays an important role in the corporate takeover arena.

Foreign direct investment (FDI) can be defined as "investment for the purpose of establishing lasting economic relations with an undertaking such as, in particular, investments which give the possibility of exercising an effective influence on the management thereof."[2] Effective influence is defined by the U.S. Department of Commerce's International Trade Administration as "the direct or indirect ownership of 10 percent or more of the voting securities of an incorporated business."[3] What is clear is that FDI is defined as investment by a foreign nation for the purpose of exercising corporate control. What is often not clear are the implications of that foreign corporate ownership and its short- and long-run impacts on the domestic economy. Articles in the popular press that lament the "foreign invasion," the "gobbling up" of U.S. firms, and the "loss of control," add much heat to the debate but shed little light on the issue of foreign direct investment. This chapter seeks to clarify some of these issues by reviewing recent trends of FDI in the United States, the reasons for rapid increase in FDI, and some of its costs and benefits.

FDI IN THE UNITED STATES

The data that exists on FDI in the United States is unfortunately limited and scattered across different federal agencies. A uniform reporting requirement for all transactions that meet the Commerce Department's definition of FDI does not exist, and many transactions often go unreported or understated. Moreover, there is often a general confusion between FDI annual flows and FDI positions (total assets), which has appeared in the popular press. In this chapter I shall generally rely on the annual FDI flows reported in the International Trade Administration's annual report, *Foreign Direct Investment in the United States.*[4]

Following World War I, the United States was a net exporter of capital. During the 1960s, the United States received only about 10 percent of the world's flow of total foreign direct investment. Since the United States was experiencing a growing domestic economy with adequate employment opportunities for most residents, little concern was expressed over the relatively small and slow-growing role of FDI. By the 1980s, however, approximately 60 percent of all foreign direct investments generated outside of the United States was finding its way into U.S. financial markets. The country's rapid shift from net exporter to net importer of capital is the result of a number of factors.

An important factor associated with the rapid increase in FDI is the overvaluation of the dollar in the early 1980s and its subsequent significant decline. The dollar lost 37 percent of its value between 1985 and the second quarter of 1988 when compared to the ten major industrialized countries, creating a buyer's market for dollar-denominated assets. The failure of the United States to effectively deal with its domestic budget deficit and the resulting trade deficit assumes a significant role in the explanation of this decline.

A second important factor explaining the rapid rise of FDI, particularly acquisitions, is the availability of companies for sale as a consequence of industrial restructuring. A rather convincing argument can be made that U.S. firms made a strategic mistake when they went on an acquisition binge to diversify. This diversification produced some very large, and consequently inflexible, organizations with a limited knowledge of the markets in which they operated. Competition from firms whose managerial expertise was more concentrated quickly made the point that diversification is no substitute for knowledge of your markets and the flexibility to respond quickly to market demands. Firms that failed to recognize the limitations of their diversification found themselves the target of corporate takeover activity by both domestic and foreign interests.

The Tax Reform Act of 1986 is the third factor explaining the rapid increase in FDI. Under the pre–1986 tax law, capital gains from FDI were taxed at the 40-percent capital gains tax rate. Effective January 1, 1987, capital gains were taxed as ordinary income and the appreciated value of properties included in any exchange were now made subject to tax. In order to avoid the new tax liabilities, many firms worked hard to complete agreements in 1986.

A final factor explaining why a large portion of the world's FDI finds its way to the United States is a relatively simple one. The political stability of the United States has always made it an attractive place for foreign investments. There is little probability that foreign investments will be expropriated; inflation is relatively mild; and interest rates are relatively stable by world standards. A growing world economy that produces an increased supply of savings tends to find these characteristics attractive.

Collectively, these forces produced dramatic increases in the frequency of transactions and the dollar amount of foreign direct investment in the United States. As Table 9.1 shows, FDI increased from $14.8 billion in 1980 to $35.8 billion in 1986, a 143.5-percent increase in six years. Between 1985 and 1986 alone, FDI increased by slightly more than 71.6 percent, and there appears to be little reason to expect significant changes in these flows during the 1986–1989 period.

While the total dollar amount of FDI has been increasing rapidly, there have also been important shifts in the home country of FDI and in the type of investment placed (see Table 9.2). During 1980, the largest investor in the United States was Canada (31.04 percent), followed by the United Kingdom (23.75 percent), then the Netherlands (9.56 percent), West Germany (6.67 percent), France (6.38 percent), Japan (5.98 percent), and Switzerland (2.53 percent). All other countries amounted to 14.09 percent. By 1986 Japan had jumped to first place, accounting for almost 26 percent of a much larger total FDI.

An even more dramatic change occurred during this time in the type of investments. In 1980, real estate investment accounted for 36.63 percent of all FDI dollars, and 58.5 percent of all real estate investments were made by Canadian investors (See Table 9.3). Merger-and-acquisition investments accounted for another 36 percent of 1980 FDI dollars. By 1986, real estate investments had dropped to slightly more than 17 percent of the total, and the major player in real estate was Japan, with 67.8 percent of the total. Merger-and-acquisition investments jumped from 36 percent to 63 percent of total FDI, and almost 82 percent of the $21-billion increase in FDI between 1980 and 1986 was in merger-and-acquisition investments.

Shifts in the type of investments made by individual home countries were also dramatic. Canada, for example, increased its investments in mergers and acquisitions from 23 percent in 1980 to 81 percent in 1986. Japan shifted away from investments in new plants and expansions in

Table 9.1

Foreign Direct Investment into the United States, 1980 and 1986 (in millions of dollars, by home country and investment type)

Country	Year	Total	Mergers & Acquisitions	Equity Increases	New Plants & Plant Expansions	Real Estate	Other
All Countries	1980	$14,797.6	$ 5,419.2	$1,056.3	$1,233.8	$5,379.3	$1,705.8
	1986	35,806.0	22,597.2	2,513.6	2,252.2	6,298.3	2,144.8
Canada	1980	4,592.5	1,062.7	57.4	85.4	3,148.6	288.8
	1986	6,763.3	5,497.2	821.0	63.6	280.0	100.8
France	1980	943.6	542.5	94.3	1.2	209.5	19.8
	1986	2,807.5	2,467.5	71.8	43.2	65.1	160.0
Germany*	1980	987.7	356.1	15.7	328.5	175.2	112.1
	1986	1,659.3	936.5	354.4	247.7	39.9	80.4
Japan	1980	884.9	186.2	--	342.4	80.7	275.4
	1986	9,274.9	2,048.8	261.5	1,621.2	4,274.8	1,069.4
Netherlands	1980	1,414.5	386.4	--	18.8	260.9	698.0
	1986	1,395.7	1,280.7	--	49.9	65.0	--
Switzerland	1980	374.1	169.2	120.6	29.1	49.3	5.8
	1986	955.0	454.2	.1	40.7	460.0	--
United Kingdom	1980	3,515.1	2,116.8	630.6	215.5	535.3	16.8
	1986	8,073.7	6,910.2	732.3	8.0	50.8	371.4
Other Countries	1980	2,085.2	599.7	62.3	163.1	920.2	229.1
	1986	4,876.6	3,001.5	273.1	177.5	1,063.1	360.9

Source: United States Department of Commerce, *Foreign Direct Investment in the United States: Transactions* (Washington, D.C.: U.S. Government Printing Office). 1980 and 1986 issues.

*Federal Republic

Table 9.2
Foreign Direct Investment into the United States, 1980 and 1986 (percent by country)

Country	Year	Transactions Known Value Mil $	Percent	Mergers & Acquisitions	Equity Increases	New Plants & Plant Expansions	Real Estate	Other
All Countries	1980	$14,797.6	100.00%	100.00%	100.00%	100.00%	100.00%	100.00%
	1986	35,806.0	100.00%	100.00	100.00	100.00	100.00	100.00
Canada	1980	4,592.5	31.04	19.61	5.42	6.90	58.52	13.98
	1986	6,763.3	18.89	24.33	32.66	2.82	4.45	4.72
France	1980	943.6	6.38	10.01	16.13	.10	3.90	1.16
	1986	2,807.5	7.84	10.92	2.86	1.92	1.03	7.46
Germany*	1980	987.7	6.67	6.57	1.49	26.62	3.26	6.57
	1986	1,659.3	4.63	4.14	14.10	11.00	.63	3.76
Japan	1980	884.9	5.98	3.44	--	27.75	1.50	16.15
	1986	9,274.9	25.90	9.07	10.39	71.98	67.86	49.88
Netherlands	1980	1,414.5	9.56	7.13	--	5.59	4.85	40.91
	1986	1,395.7	3.90	5.67	--	2.22	1.03	--
Switzerland	1980	374.1	2.53	3.12	11.42	2.36	.92	.34
	1986	955.0	2.67	2.01	--	1.81	7.30	--
United Kingdom	1980	3,515.1	23.75	39.06	59.65	17.46	9.95	.98
	1986	8,073.7	22.55	30.58	29.13	.36	.81	17.36
Other Countries	1980	2,085.2	14.09	11.07	5.90	13.22	17.10	13.43
	1986	4,876.6	13.62	13.28	10.86	7.89	16.88	16.83

Source: Table 9.1.

*Federal Republic

Table 9.3
Foreign Direct Investment into the United States, 1980 and 1986 (percent by investment type)

| Country | Year | Transactions Known | | Mergers & Acquisitions | Equity Increases | New Plants & Plant Expansions | Real Estate | Other |
		Value in Mil $	Percent					
All Countries	1980	$14,797.6	100.00%	36.63%	7.14%	8.34%	36.36%	11.53%
	1986	35,806.0	100.00	63.11	7.02	6.29	17.59	5.99
Canada	1980	4,592.5	100.00	23.14	1.25	1.86	68.56	5.20
	1986	6,763.3	100.00	81.28	12.14	.94	4.14	1.49
France	1980	943.6	100.00	57.49	9.99	.13	22.21	2.10
	1986	2,807.5	100.00	87.89	2.56	1.54	2.32	5.70
Germany*	1980	987.7	100.00	36.06	1.59	33.26	17.74	11.35
	1986	1,659.3	100.00	56.44	21.36	14.93	2.41	4.85
Japan	1980	884.9	100.00	21.05	--	38.69	9.12	31.13
	1986	9,274.9	100.00	22.09	2.82	17.48	46.09	11.53
Netherlands	1980	1,414.5	100.00	27.32	--	4.88	18.45	49.35
	1986	1,395.7	100.00	91.76	--	3.58	4.66	--
Switzerland	1980	374.1	100.00	45.23	32.26	7.78	13.18	1.55
	1986	955.0	100.00	47.56	.01	4.26	48.17	--
United Kingdom	1980	3,515.1	100.00	60.22	17.94	6.13	15.23	.48
	1986	8,073.7	100.00	85.59	9.07	.10	.63	4.60
Other Countries	1980	2,085.2	100.00	28.76	2.99	7.82	44.13	10.99
	1986	4,876.6	100.00	61.55	5.60	3.64	21.80	7.40

Source: Table 9.1.

1980 to a heavy concentration in real estate investments in 1986, while the Netherlands increased from a 27-percent commitment in mergers and acquisitions to almost 92 percent by 1986.

The dramatic increase in FDI in the United States from 1980 to 1986 was largely in the form of acquisition of firms either directly or through mergers, and this shift is not country-specific. Of the total increase in merger-and-acquisition dollars between 1980 and 1986 ($17.178 billion), Japanese merger-and-acquisition investments accounted for only 11.4 percent, while the United Kingdom and Canada accounted for 27.9 percent and 25.8 percent respectively.

In Ohio in 1986 there were 30 separate FDI transactions with a known value of $1.2 billion dollars, or about 3.4 percent of the known value of all FDI in the U.S.[5] Of the 30 transactions, 15 were either acquisitions, mergers, or equity increases. These 15 transactions, however, accounted for 93.4 percent of all FDI in Ohio in 1986. Japan represented 56.7 percent of all FDI transactions in Ohio but accounted for only 4 of the 15 mergers, acquisitions, or equity increases. In terms of dollar impact, Japan accounted for only 1.8 percent of the known value of acquisition, merger, and equity-increase activity in Ohio in 1986, and only 8.1 percent of all dollar FDI activity. Switzerland accounted for 61.7 percent of all FDI in Ohio, with Canada accounting for an additional 24.4 percent.

There is no argument against the observations that there have been dramatic increases in the dollar amount of FDI in the United States and that much of this new investment is in the form of mergers and acquisitions of U.S. firms. The perception that much of this activity is in the form of Japanese investments was not the case in 1986 for the United States nor was it true for Ohio. Widespread fear of corporate takeovers by cultures that do not understand the United States were unwarranted in 1986 since 53.6 percent of the increase in merger-and-acquisition activity between 1980 and 1986 was from Canada and the United Kingdom.

THE GEOGRAPHIC IMPACT OF FDI IN THE UNITED STATES

Another common misconception regarding FDI in the United States is that it tends to be geographically concentrated in areas of low labor costs. In 1986, however, 67 percent of all FDI dollars were accounted for by six states (New York, Texas, California, Hawaii, Illinois, and Kentucky), states that are not typically associated with low labor costs. However, since most of these states have relatively large shares of population and employment, it would be surprising if the distribution of FDI in the United States were not skewed to these areas.

In a recently published study, Norman Glickman and Douglas Woodward examined the locational determinants of FDI investments over the 1974–1983 period, holding the effects of size constant.[6] They found that rather than being cost-driven, FDI is positively related to the degree of urbanization, the availability of skilled and semiskilled labor, the existence of an innovative capacity, and access to markets. Regions are therefore not at a comparative disadvantage simply because of relatively high labor costs.

Glickman and Woodward also examined the geographic preferences of three different nations of investors (Canadian, European, and Japanese) using a "state attractiveness index." They found that the geographic pattern of FDI varies significantly according to country, with Japanese investors having a preference for California, New Jersey, Tennessee, Washington, Alabama, Georgia, New York, Vermont, and Illinois. European investors have a preference for New York, California, Texas, Pennsylvania, Maine, and North and South Carolina. Canadian investors preferred West Virginia, Maine, Vermont, Iowa, and North Carolina. This data suggests that there does not appear to be a single geographic preference for all FDI, nor does any country appear to have a single geographic preference.

DEINDUSTRIALIZATION AND FDI

There is perhaps no more threatening a word to the industrialized countries than "deindustrialization." It immediately brings visions of a wasteland of empty factories, decaying cities, and vast unemployment. Deindustrialization is viewed by many workers as the major threat to the American dream, and many associate deindustrialization with foreign direct investment.

It is probably not a worthwhile exercise to debate the definition of deindustrialization, but it is important to note that while manufacturing employment as a percent of total employment has been declining, the manufacturing sector's share of total output in the United States has been relatively constant. Barry Bluestone and Bennett Harrison argue that the decline in employment is the result of misguided corporate policy blindly seeking to restore corporation profits,[7] while Robert Reich argues that the problem is more fundamental and is related to a production mentality of U.S. managers in combination with conflicting social and economic policies.[8] Neither suggest that deindustrialization is a foreign plot to take over the productive assets of the United States. Nonetheless, there continues to be a great deal of finger pointing between special interest groups in the United States. As Richard McKenzie notes:

Labor blames management, management blames labor, the people in the North blame the people in the South and West, while the South and West ask the North to look at its own policies as a source of its problems. Perhaps it is only natural for people to want to blame anybody but themselves.[9]

To a large extent, our own economic policies, both public and private, are providing the opportunities for increased foreign direct investment. Much of the industrial restructuring that is occurring in the United States and is providing opportunities for the acquisitions of plants is the direct result of increased global competition forcing U.S. firms to become competitive. Certainly the federal budget deficits that produced a falling dollar provide even greater opportunities for the acquiring firms. However, it would be counterproductive to ignore the fact that some part of the merger-and-acquisition portion of FDI are the direct result of U.S. firms failing to remain competitive. It is difficult to understand how the buyer of these manufacturing plants is somehow responsible for deindustrialization. In fact, exactly the opposite may be true. Between 1977 and 1986, manufacturing employment in firms with 10 percent or more of their stock owned by a foreign parent grew from 3.8 percent to 7.8 percent of all manufacturing employment. Although the manufacturing sector's share of employment in such firms is higher than the all-industry average of 3.5 percent, it does not appear to be sufficiently high to justify the fear of losing control of employment in the United States.

The share of sales and assets within the manufacturing sector that is associated with foreign-owned firms is also not as high as one would believe based on media attention devoted to the subject. In 1986, only 9.9 percent of all manufacturing sales and 12.3 percent of manufacturing assets were owned by these foreign firms.

There are some sector-specific concentrations that are above the all-manufacturing average. The sector with the largest shares in 1986 was the chemical sector, with 32.5 percent of all assets and 29.5 percent of sales. Stone, clay, and glass was second with 22.8 percent of assets and 20.2 percent of sales, followed by primary metals with 20.5 percent of assets and 19 percent of sales. Access to markets and raw materials are important reasons for these concentrations (petroleum for the chemical industry, and U.S. quotas on imports for the primary metals sector).

Additional evidence of the share of manufacturing employment associated with FDI was recently presented by Glickman and Woodward, who compared employment shares between foreign and domestic manufacturing activities from 1974 through 1983. The Great Lakes region had the largest share of domestic manufacturing employment in 1974, but was replaced by the Southeast in 1983. While the Great Lakes region lost 1,320,000 manufacturing jobs and the Southeast added 206,000 jobs, over 700,000 manufacturing jobs were generated by FDI. According to Glickman and Woodward, foreign-based manufacturing employment increased in every region of the United States over this period. The evidence presented suggests that FDI has done more to slow down deindustrialization than to cause it. As Glickman and Woodward suggest, lagging regions "need to redouble their efforts to attract this new found source of industrial growth."[10] In 1986, 43.4 percent of total FDI was made in the manufacturing sector, providing employment opportunities for hundreds of thousands of U.S. workers. It would be very difficult to argue that FDI is the cause of the decline in manufacturing employment or deindustrialization in the United States.

MATTERS OF CORPORATE CONTROL

Since the 1930s, economists have studied the impact of the separation of management from ownership. The basic hypothesis has been that non-owners do not have the same motivation to maximize the value of the firm as the owners. To the extent that such differences have existed in the past, the losers have been stockholders (owners) and society, while management gained in perks or a more relaxed management style.

When differences exist between the optimal value of the firm and its current value, one may say that the firm is put into play with respect to the possibility of a takeover. This does not mean that all takeover attempts are the result of misguided management, but it does suggest that a major explanation for such activity may be the failure of existing management to maximize the value of the firm to its stockholders.

Other factors that are important in explaining recent takeover activity include (1) relaxed antitrust restrictions, (2) deregulation, and (3) changing technology in financial services.[11] Collectively these forces require that firms reexamine existing corporate strategy and in many cases sell assets that are not consistent with maximizing the value of the firm. Failure to do so may result in a takeover attempt by those who perceive the possible increase in value and are more willing to undertake the necessary changes. Since 63 percent of FDI in 1986 was in the area of mergers and acquisitions, foreign investors are recognizing some of these opportunities.

The fact is that takeover attempts make life uncomfortable for existing management. Management has thus developed a number of tactics to forestall such efforts, including greenmail, golden parachutes, and poison pills. Injured and potentially injured economic groups (namely management) have exerted political pressure to increase the difficulty of corporate takeovers by legitimizing these new tools. As Michael Jensen notes, however,

This political activity is another example of special interests using the democratic political system to change the rules of the game to benefit themselves at the expense of society as a whole.[12]

THE BENEFITS AND COSTS OF FDI

In the rush to criticize FDI and cite specific examples of employment impacts, the benefits of FDI are often overlooked. However, the benefits are as real as the costs, and should be explicitly recognized in any debate regarding FDI.

First, FDI is a net infusion of capital into the economy of the United States. The Department of Commerce estimated that in 1981, foreign investment was responsible for generating 2,343,115 direct jobs[13] While this estimate surely overstates the marginal impact of a dollar of 1988 foreign direct investment, it does suggest that FDI plays an important role in providing jobs for U.S. citizens.

A second benefit of FDI is that it provides a buyer for the assets of U.S. firms when these assets are released as part of a restructuring process. The alternative to selling to a foreign-based parent may be to liquidate the asset through bankruptcy proceedings or to sell excess capacity to a domestic competitor.

A third benefit is the new technology and management skills that are often introduced into a market as the result of FDI. One has only to read Tom Peters and Nancy Austin's *A Passion for Excellence* to be familiar with the stimulus that foreign-based firms have provided to shaking loose traditional managerial philosophies.[14]

A fourth benefit accrues to the many state and local communities that are able to restore employment opportunities and hence their tax bases as a result of new FDI. FDI has become such a visible source of new investment that some 40 states now have development offices overseas. While much of this competition results in negative fiscal impacts on the competing communities, it has the potential to play a positive role in community development.

Finally, focusing on only the investment and not on the end result of that investment tends to obscure some important facts. It is a fact that many of the firms created with FDI are export-oriented and compete in international markets against other international firms, not domestic ones. In 1984, for example, it was estimated that one quarter of all U.S. exports were accounted for by foreign firms. Another important fact is that within the manufacturing sector, foreign-based firms paid an average 9-percent wage premium relative to domestic firms.[15] These are indeed benefits that have accompanied FDI and are derived by the host country, and when FDI involves a takeover, the benefits to stockholders that are generally believed to accompany such events are not limited to domestically financed takeovers.

Are there no costs to FDI? Of course, there are costs, but they must be weighted against the benefits. Certainly there have been jobs lost in the process of restructurings and takeovers. In some cases the employment losses were inevitable if the firm was to survive. Salary and fringe-benefit concessions have also been common, forcing a reduction in the accustomed standard of living for many workers. However, these adjustments are not fundamentally due to FDI, but rather to the economic conditions that make FDI profitable.

One often hears the argument that we should not lose control of our own companies to foreigners. This fear is difficult to counter when expressed in this way, but it seems to imply that the source of a nation's economic power is somehow related to the ownership of the company. A mere change in ownership of a physical asset does not normally imply a negative change in that asset's productivity. If poor management accompanies a change in ownership that then results in a decrease in the value of the firm, that should be a concern to stockholders. It is illogical to suggest that FDI will injure a country because the new owners are likely to intentionally decrease the value of the firm (which of course is now owned by the foreign parent).

A second argument is that foreign firms tend to utilize foreign rather than domestic suppliers in the production process. This argument has led some developing countries to institute local content laws. To some extent, these laws can be viewed as a form of indirect private foreign aid to the developing country. It is a strange argument to make for the United States, however, where the problem is not a lack of infrastructure. The decision to purchase inputs from another country should be recognized as a statement about the input markets in the United States and not about the desirability of FDI.

A third argument is that FDI provides opportunities for foreign governments to influence U.S. economic and foreign policy. This familiar national-interests argument has some merit when the FDI is made in sensitive areas. However, the case, like the "Petition of the Candle makers", which seeks protection from the unfair rays of the sun, is very much overstated. There are regulations already in place that prevent the takeover of defense-related firms by foreign-based parents. Even in the field of strategic resources such as coal or oil, ownership does not guarantee access to the resource if the host country determines that such access is not in the national interest.

CONCLUSIONS

The world is changing very rapidly and history is a poor guide to the future. Global competition and integrated world financial markets are the present, not the future, and the impact of forces on the international capital flows must be recognized. Foreign direct investment must be recognized as part of the process of globalization and increasing world interdependence, and should not be analyzed with the paradigm of nineteenth-century colonialism.

NOTES

1. Reported in *Mergers and Acquisitions* 22, no. 6 (May–June 1988).
2. Organization for Economic Cooperation and Development, *Controls and Impediments Affecting Inward Direct Investments* (Paris: OECD 1987), p. 7.
3. U.S. Department of Commerce, International Trade Administration, *Foreign Direct Investment in the United States* (September 1987), p. 1.
4. Ibid.
5. Ibid., p. 97.
6. Norman J. Glickman and Douglas P. Woodward, *Regional Patterns of Manufacturing Foreign Direct Investment in the United States* (Austin, Tex: Lyndon B. Johnson School of Public Affairs, University of Texas at Austin, 1987).
7. Barry Bluestone and Bennett Harrison, *The Deindustrialization of America* (New York: Basic Books, 1982).
8. Robert Reich, *The Next American Frontier* (New York: Time/Life Books, 1983).
9. Richard B. McKenzie, *Fugitive Industry: The Economies of Politics and Deindustrialization* (San Francisco: Pacific Institute for Public Policy Research, 1984), p. 3.
10. Glickman and Woodward, *Regional Patterns*, p. 24.
11. Michael C. Jensen, "Takeovers: Their Cause and Consequences," *Journal of Economic Perspective* 2, no. 1 (Winter 1988): 24.
12. Jensen, "Takeovers," p. 45.
13. As reported in Martin Tolchin and Susan Tolchin, *Buying into America* (New York: Times Books, 1988), p. 312.
14. Tom Peters and Nancy Austin, *A Passion for Excellence* (New York: Warner Books, 1985).
15. Glickman and Woodward, *Regional Patterns*, p. 3.

10

FEDERAL TAX POLICY AND THE MARKET FOR CORPORATE CONTROL: RELATIONSHIPS AND CONSEQUENCES

Robert P. Strauss

ECONOMIC DARWINISM AND CORPORATE CONTROL

A fundamental premise of a market economy is that competition enhances the overall efficiency in that economy, generates economic growth, and expands the number of job opportunities and income available to all market participants. Since the mid-nineteenth century, the corporate form in the United States has been the principal vehicle through which large-scale capital investments have been made to exploit new, capital-intensive technologies in manufacturing and, among other things, to create a transportation network that has allowed the exploitation of natural resources and agricultural products. In Ohio and Pennsylvania, the growth in primary metals, rail transportation, and energy could not have occurred without the corporate form to raise and expend the necessary capital, which in turn led to the growth in the cities and a long-term increase in the country's general standard of living.

The public corporation is a creature of the state in which it is incorporated pursuant to state statutes governing the right to incorporate. Through the corporate form, shareholders delegate significant discretion and latitude to management to organize the internal affairs of the business, and to market the goods and services such businesses create. The corporate form provides a number of distinct benefits to shareholders: perpetuity of the corporation from generation to generation, a separate identity that results in limited liability for shareholders and management so that they are not directly liable for each of the actions of the corporation itself, and easy transfer of share ownership.

A consequence of the public trading of shares in public corporations is that stockholders may readily alter their investments based on their analysis and expectations of the relative profitability of each business that competes for shareholder capital. The ultimate reward for each shareholder investing in a corporation is the periodic receipt of dividends paid by the corporation along with any increase in share value that represents expected increases in the future income stream of the company.

Over the business cycle, the prospects and profitability of any firm will vary, and its stock price will accordingly reflect such fortunes; in turn, shareholders will be positively or adversely affected as their wealth holdings in various businesses change with market-share prices. For any number of ordinary business reasons, a particular company or person will expand or contract its business as it adjusts to changes in market tastes for its goods and services, the presence of competitors in the market in which such goods and services sell, its own cost circumstances (labor, capital, and materials), and changes in technology. Economic efficiency is served when such business activities occur at arms-length prices, and when business assets are redeployed to their most profitable use.

This process of economic change, which necessarily involves the purchase and sale of assets owned by businesses, or of the businesses themselves, is generally healthy; and it may be viewed as an organic part of the economic process. However, this impersonal description of the Darwinian process of economic competition understates the drama, if not the trauma, that a change in business ownership can create for current employees, their families, and their communities. In the abstract it would seem generally beneficial to allow the just described process to work itself out, but when it involves a major employer and prospects of plant closings and permanent layoffs, this theoretical justification for competition becomes less acceptable, and the circumstances of changes in corporate ownership become a matter of public policy.

Public Concerns: The Level of Acquisition Activity and Its Motivation

The issue of the desirability of changes in ownership and control has become increasingly pronounced as the pace of merger-and-acquisition activity has increased in the 1980s. In 1987, better than $167.5 billion of corporate assets changed ownership as a result of mergers, acquisitions, and leveraged buyouts (LBOs).[1] By contrast, in 1979, mergers, acquisi-

Figure 10.1
Merger and Acquisition Activity, 1979–1987

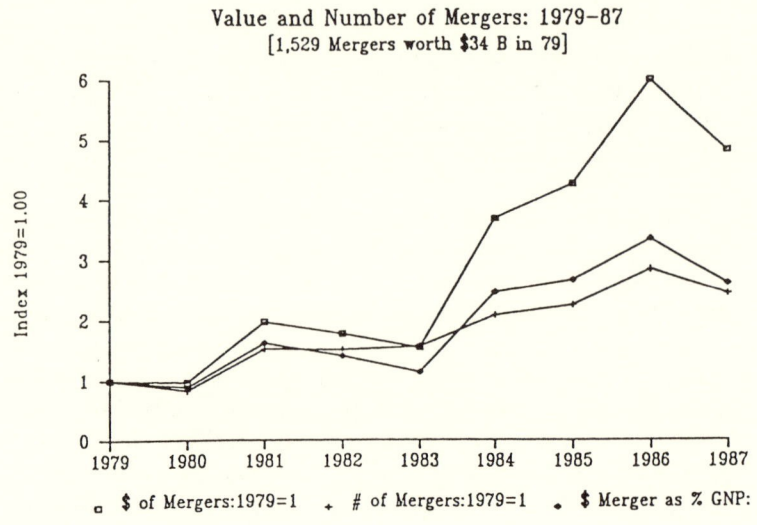

Value and Number of Mergers: 1979–87
[1,529 Mergers worth $34 B in 79]

Index 1979=1.00

□ $ of Mergers:1979=1   ╋ # of Mergers:1979=1   ◆ $ Merger as % GNP:

tions, and leveraged buyouts amounted to only $34.2 billion. Equally troubling to some is the fact that foreign participation has increased dramatically over this nine-year period as well: In 1986, 12 percent of the transactions, measured by value, were made by non-U.S.-firms acquiring U.S. firms; while in 1987, 25 percent of the transactions were made by non-U.S. firms acquiring U.S. firms.[2]

Figure 10.1 displays recent mergers and acquisitions from 1979 through 1987. Using 1979 as the base year, we see that merger activity increased fivefold in that nine-year period; GNP by contrast did not quite double. In 1986, the peak year for merger-and-acquisition activity, better than $204 billion in assets changed hands, or 4.6% of GNP. Scherer (1970) observed three earlier merger-and-acquisition waves in the U.S. industrial economy: 1887–1904, 1916–1929, and 1948–1970; it is evident that we are experiencing a fourth wave of merger activity in the mid–1980s.

Elsewhere in this volume experts discuss the social desirability of such widespread changes in corporate ownership and control. Whether shareholder and societal wealth are enhanced by such transactions is also an important matter. Here I shall concentrate on the more technical but nonetheless important question of whether such merger-and-acquisition activity artificially results from provisions in our federal tax laws. In particular I shall examine the question of whether the Internal Revenue Code unwittingly (and wittingly) provides incentives for such changes in corporate ownership and control by encouraging profitable firms to take over unprofitable firms in order to acquire the favorable tax attributes of the target corporation.

The answer to this apparently simple question involves examining some of the most complex parts of the U.S. tax system. Moreover, the answer to the question has changed with the Tax Reform Act of 1986, which sought to substantially reduce, if not eliminate, what had become "trafficking" in corporate tax losses and unused tax credits, and sought to limit a number of indirect takeover strategies. For example, it is often conjectured that some takeover attempts are motivated by the excess assets of the target's qualified pension plan. In this circumstance, either the target firm or the buyer will seek to use the excess assets to finance the acquisition or to buy back shares from the market or from the buyer (so-called greenmail). The complex manner in which the Internal Revenue Code encourages such activities and recent actions by the Congress to limit such incentives are important aspects to consider.

My purpose here is thus severalfold:

1. To provide a background on how corporations and their pension funds are generally organized and affected by the Internal Revenue Code;
2. To discuss the historical tax-planning methods by which corporations have been able to lessen their tax burden and that of their shareholders, with particular attention to the importance of the *General Utilities* Doctrine;
3. To discuss the mechanics of mergers and acquisitions as they are affected by the federal Internal Revenue Code;
4. To underscore how net operating loss, unused investment tax and foreign tax credits, the deductibility of interest costs, and the tax-exempt nature of qualified pension plans affect the attractiveness of the target company; and,
5. To appraise the various tax incentives and tax considerations for mergers and acquisitions as they exist post-Tax Reform Act of 1986.

The reader should be forewarned that some of this discussion is complex; it is my hope that some numerical examples will simplify and help explain the importance of various federal tax considerations as they impact on the merger and acquisition process.

KEY PROVISIONS OF THE INTERNAL REVENUE CODE AFFECTING THE MERGER-AND-ACQUISITION DECISION

The effect of the Internal Revenue Code on the acquisition-and-merger decision can be analyzed directly in terms of:

1. The federal corporate income tax; and
2. The federal individual income tax.[3]

Also, the federal tax treatment of certain pension plans creates several indirect incentives for merger and acquisition. The general structure of these direct effects is discussed below, along with the important matter of liquidations.

The Federal Corporate and Individual Income Taxes: Two Tiers and Double Taxation

Historically, income earned by a corporation has been taxed at a rate approximating 46 percent and, since World War II, after-tax income paid to shareholders in the form of dividends has been taxed at a tax rate as high as 70 percent. This system of taxation of corporate source income plus taxation of distributions at the individual level has been criticized as constituting double taxation and imposing a much higher tax than had the shareholder earned the income directly.[4]

An example makes this textbook argument clear: Assume that the corporation has pre-tax profits of $100 and faces a corporate tax rate of 46 percent; further, assume that the shareholder is in the 50-percent tax bracket for earned and unearned income. Now let us compare the overall taxation of $100 of corporate source income to $100 of wage (or sole proprietorship) income. Were the shareholder to be taxed on $100 of wage income at a marginal tax rate of 50 percent, then $50 of total taxes would be due. On the other hand, if we begin with $100 of corporate source income which is taxed first at the corporate level ($46 of tax with a tax rate of 46 percent), and then at the shareholder level on the presumed $54 of dividends, we arrive at a total tax burden of $73 ($46 of corporate tax plus $27 of personal tax). Thus, the two tier taxation of corporate source income gives rise to a tax differential of 23 percentage points.[5]

For a considerable period of time, the tax rate on dividend income was above that for wage income, for example, 70 percent versus 50 percent, so the above example was even more extreme. Clearly, unless shareholders had a peculiar willingness to finance the costs of government through voluntarily higher taxes, they had a clear incentive to find ways to work with the corporation to move toward Case 2 and away from the tax consequences of Case 1 (see Table 10.1). To the extent that shareholders could forgo current dividends, and to the extent that the corporation used its after-tax income for reinvestments in itself, the stock market simply capitalized the forgone dividends, and shareholders looked for periods when their own tax circumstances favored selling the appreciated stock and realizing the forgone income.

Table 10.1
The Extra Burden of Corporate and Individual Income Taxes

Case 1: $100 of Corporate Income			Case 2: $100 of Personal Income
Corporate Income	$100		
Corporate Tax	- 46	46	
After Tax Income	$54		
Dividends Recvd	54		$100
Personal Tax	-27	27	-50
After Tax Income	$27		$50
Total Tax		$73	$50
Effective Tax Rate		.73	.50

Tax Treatment of Long-Term Capital Gains

The next important structural feature of the U.S. federal tax system that needs to be understood in conjunction with the merger-and-acquisition decision involves the historically preferential tax treatment accorded to capital gains on assets held more than one year. Technically, the difference between the net sales price of the stock and the original cost or "basis" in the stock historically constituted a capital gain, as contrasted to ordinary income of individuals and corporations. The preferential treatment has been accorded by excluding part of the gain from tax so that the application of the taxpayer's marginal tax rate would result in a lower effective tax rate. For example, up until 1986, individuals had been able to exclude as much as 60 percent of long-term gain from tax, resulting in a maximum effective rate of 20 percent on long-term capital gains.[6]

With such preferential tax treatment of capital gains compared to ordinary income, our taxpayer and corporation have an incentive to not only forgo payment of dividends to the individual shareholder, but in general to structure transactions at the corporate and individual level so that the ordinary income is viewed as long-term capital gains by the tax system. Not only is 20 percent a considerably lower tax rate than 50 percent, by carefully timing the date of realization and receiving the proceeds of the sale over time as an installment sale, the shareholder could easily be in a tax bracket well below 20 percent. It should also be noted that if the shares are not disposed of prior to death but rather are transmitted through an estate to the next generation, the basis of the shares will be "stepped-up" to market value without any tax consequence to either the estate or the beneficiary. As a consequence, the next generation could then dispose of the shares at market value with no personal tax whatsoever. If there were appreciation after receiving the bequest, the tax would only be on that portion of the appreciation that was at capital gains tax rates.

The *General Utilities* Doctrine

Between 1935 and 1986, as a result of a U.S. Supreme Court decision and subsequent ratification by the Congress in Sections 311, 336, and 337 of the Internal Revenue Code, the impact of the above-mentioned two-tiered structure of the corporate and individual income tax (Case 1) was substantially mitigated in certain important circumstances.[7] Under the *General Utilities* rule, the distribution by a corporation of certain appreciated property to shareholders on the liquidation of the appreciated property resulted in non-recognition (for corporate tax purposes) of the gain at the corporate level, and tax at only capital gains rates at the shareholder level. The history of the *General Utilities* case underlines the importance of this mechanism.

In 1927, General Utilities purchased 50 percent of the shares of Island Edison Company for $2,000. In 1928, a prospective buyer offered to buy all of General Utilities' holdings in Island Edison, which apparently had a fair market value of more than $1 million. If General Utilities had sold the shares directly it would have been forced to pay significant corporate tax on the difference between $1 million and $2,000. Instead, General Utilities offered to distribute the Island Edison stock to its shareholders with the understanding that the shareholders would in turn sell their stock to the prospective buyer. However, the shareholders were under no obligation to sell the shares under the terms of the distribution.

General Utilities declared a dividend in an amount equal to the value of the Island Edison stock to be payable in shares of that stock. General Utilities distributed the Island Edison shares, and four days later the shareholders sold the Island Edison shares to the buyer on the terms previously negotiated by the General Utilities officers. The IRS held that the distribution of the Island Edison shares in the amount of $1 million was a taxable transaction to General Utilities. The Supreme Court held that the distribution was not taxable income at the corporate level. Thus, the shareholders in the General Utilities case simply paid long-term capital gains taxes on the differences between the $2,000 purchase price that the corporation made on their behalf and the $1 million that the shareholders realized upon sale of their shares.[8] In a number of subsequent related cases, the Court generally upheld its original decision with the general effect that from 1935 through 1985, no gain at the corporate level (and thus no corporate tax) was realized on corporate distributions of appreciated property to shareholders.

In 1954, Congress enacted Section 311(a) of the Internal Revenue Code, which essentially provided that a corporation recognized no gain or loss on a non-liquidating distribution of property with respect to its stock. Section 336 was also enacted to provide for non-recognition of gain or loss to a corporation on distributions of property in partial or complete liquidations. Also, in the 1954 Act, Section 337 of the code stated that if a corporation adopted a plan of complete liquidation and distributed all its assets to its shareholders within 12 months, there were no corporate-level tax consequences of the gain or loss on the sale of such property.

In effect, the *General Utilities* Doctrine, which became codified and refined over the period of 1935 through 1986, provided a method of relieving the double taxation of corporate source income described above. Equally beneficial, of course, is the fact that such a transformation of corporate source income to the shareholder level was taxed during this period at long-term capital gains rates rather than as ordinary income; for example, compare a tax rate of 73 percent in Case 1 with a tax rate of 20 percent, which is the maximum tax rate on long-term capital gains realized by individuals in the 1980s.

In effect, the *General Utilities* Doctrine created a vehicle for individuals to utilize the corporate form to acquire assets, hold them until they appreciated, shield them from personal risk during the appreciation period, and then turn over effective ownership at the shareholder level for disposition at long-term capital gains tax rates. As such, it created an incentive for corporations to acquire other corporations and then liquidate them in a specific fashion. Alternatively, it created the incentive for a corporation to form an entity within the corporation that could be spun off for shareholders to sell at long-term capital gains rates.[9]

Federal Tax Implications of Debt versus Equity Financing

As noted earlier, dividend payments are paid out of after-tax income. On the other hand, interest payments to bondholders are paid out of before-tax income, and are an ordinary cost of doing business. Since both equity and debt are sources of capital to the firm, the ability to deduct the cost of debt capital as contrasted to the inability of deducting

Table 10.2
Effect of Debt Financing on Yield to Shareholder

Item	All Equity Firm	50% Debt Financed Firm
Balance Sheet		
Total assets	$1,000	$1,000
Debt	0	500
Shareholders Equity	1,000	500
Income Statement		
Operating Income	200	200
Interest Expense	0	70
Taxable Income	200	130
Corporate Tax [46%]	92	59.80
After-Tax Income	$108	$70.20
Return on Equity :		
Income/Equity	10.8%	14.04%

the cost of equity capital provides a powerful incentive to favor debt financing. An example will make this more clear.[10]

Consider two corporations each with $1,000 of total assets and each experiencing $200 operating income; Corporation A is an all-equity corporation while Corporation B is financed half by equity and half by debt. Let us assume that the debt was borrowed at 14 percent, and that the corporate tax rate is 46 percent. The question we wish to answer is how shareholders of each firm fare in terms of the after-tax return on their equity.

Table 10.2 lays out the analysis. The all-equity firm has no interest expenses to deduct, pays $92 on its $200 of operating income, and provides an after-tax return to its shareholders of 10.8 percent ($108 of after-tax income divided by $1,000 of shareholder equity). The half-equity, half-debt financed firm, by contrast, has only $130 of taxable income by virtue of paying $70 of interest expenses, and pays $59.80 in taxes. Its after-tax return is 14.04 percent ($70.20 of after-tax income divided by $500 of shareholder equity). Thus, the leveraged (or indebted) firm provides a rate of return to shareholders that is 40 percent greater than the return of the firm that relies on just equity for its capital. To the extent that a firm eschews debt to raise additional capital, it may be short-changing its shareholders.

Alternatively, one may view firms that are not leveraged as targets for takeover, since a change in the composition of the target's balance sheet can immediately benefit the remaining shareholders. A leveraged buyout (LBO) is really an acquisition of an economically profitable, "under-leveraged" firm by another firm that is willing to buy it on a highly leveraged basis. For example, it has historically been common practice for a buyer to contribute 20 percent of the purchase price as equity and borrow the remaining 80 percent through the issuance of short-term bonds reflecting the high degree of risk; these so-called junk bonds are secured, at best, by pledges of the target's future profits, and typically pay high rates of interest. Typically such bonds are unsecured, and accordingly pay very high rates of interest to reflect the high level of risk. The increased interest payments of the new firm are paid for by the increased cash flow to the target that results from the interest deductions that reduce taxable income.

Some Implications of Corporate Losses and Unutilized Tax Credits

When a business' costs exceed its receipts, we characterize the business as "losing money," and, if this circumstance persists over any appreciable period of time, we would not view the firm as being particularly attractive for investment or acquisition purposes. However, the commonsense characterization of the economic position of the firm is often quite distant from the realities of corporate tax and financial reporting, and the firm indeed may be quite healthy at least from a financial reporting perspective. In turn, it may be an attractive takeover target.

In order to appreciate how this may come about, it is important first to understand how a corporate loss can be generated for tax-reporting purposes while profits may be reported for financial-reporting purposes. Second, we must understand how such federal tax attributes persist over time, and how they create incentives for acquisitions.

Generating Federal Tax Loses

Two types of disparities between tax-accounting and financial-accounting rules can generate tax losses: general differences between these rules, and specific provisions of the Internal Revenue Code that provide special considerations to particular industries. By far the most important general difference between the two rules involves the measurement of depreciation. In the abstract, it is appropriate for a business to deduct as a cost of doing business the loss in value of machinery and equipment that results from their usage. Space limitations prevent a historical description of how our tax-depreciation rules have evolved; however, the more generous depreciation allowances accorded under the Economic Recovery Act highlight how disparate tax- and financial-accounting rules can become. Prior to 1981, taxpayers were depreciating apartment buildings on average over 32 years, while bank buildings were depreciated over 43 years. As a result of the Economic Recovery Act of 1981, useful lives were dramatically shortened. In the case of real property such as apartment buildings, the tax life was shortened to 16 years. For financial-reporting purposes the longer time period has generally remained in effect.

Essentially, cutting in half the time period across which one may deduct the value of the asset means that the present value of the deductions will increase geometrically since all deductions are increasing much earlier than before. In turn, such earlier deductions reduce gross receipts and taxable income, and in a wide array of circumstances create expenses in excess of receipts for tax-reporting purposes, for example, losses for tax purposes as contrasted to profits reported using the depreciation rules required for financial-reporting purposes.[11]

The matter of generous depreciation deductions creating artificial tax losses becomes more important in acquisitions that are debt-financed, since the base for calculating depreciation depends on the purchase price. If the buyer pays a very high price for the target firm, it will enjoy very large depreciation deductions at the outset. Using debt financing with balloon forms of debt, the buyer can further increase the apparent excess of costs over revenues, which will create a shielding from taxation cash flow generated from other activities.

Beyond this general difference in tax- and financial-reporting rules, there have historically been a large number of specific provisions of the Internal Revenue Code that accord particular businesses cost deductions that are larger than allowed under financial-reporting rules. For example, commercial banks have been historically allowed to deduct as bad debt reserves a percentage (.6 percent) of certain loans without regard to actual bad-debt experience. As a result, banks have historically paid little federal corporate income tax.

Historically, firms that constructed long-lived assets over a period of time, for example, manufacturers of commercial aircraft, have been able to forestall recognizing the income received from the sale of such aircraft until the entire fleet of assets (aircraft) constructed for a customer has been delivered, but have been able to recognize the costs of construction of each component delivered on essentially a current basis. Under financial-accounting rules, this completed-contract method of accounting is not permitted, and the costs and income of each element of a long-term contract must be simultaneously recognized. Again, this sort of difference between tax-accounting and financial-accounting rules can lead to a firm reporting tax losses to the Internal Revenue Service while reporting profits and paying dividends to shareholders. With such a significant divergence in the way costs are measured between the tax system and financial reporting standards, it follows that a firm can report a net operating loss (NOL) for tax purposes while still paying dividends and issuing healthy financial reports to shareholders.

The Value of Corporate Tax Attributes over Time

It is generally agreed that 12 months is an arbitrary period over which to record income and impose taxes. As a consequence, the Internal Revenue Code has allowed corporate taxpayers to carry forward losses created in one year to subsequent years to offset future income and thereby lower future taxes. Also, carrybacks of such losses to prior, profitable years' returns have been allowed. With carrybacks, firms recompute their taxes and obtain a refund check from the IRS. Such forward and backward averaging has been accorded in recognition of the arbitrary nature of the 12-month taxable year. In addition to the ability to carry forward and carry back tax losses, firms have similarly been able to carry forward and carry back tax credits earned from making certain investments in equipment that they are currently not able to use.

To the extent that a firm has such tax losses or tax credits on its books, they represent an opportunity for firms with positive taxes, through careful merger, to reduce their joint taxes upon combination. Firms with unused NOLs may find themselves unable to use them within a few years, while other, profitable and taxable firms may be able to use them immediately.[12] For example, if firm A is in the 46 percent-marginal tax bracket, and another firm, B, has losses, firm B's tax losses are of value to firm A since it can reduce its tax liabilities and increase its cash flow, holding all else constant. Firm A should be willing to pay up to the value of the tax shield that would result to it were the losses applied to reduce its tax liabilities, for example, $.46 for each $1.00 of loss firm B has on its books.

It is argued by some (see especially Gilson, Scholes, and Wolfson, 1988), that the price of A's shares in the stock market should perfectly reflect the capitalization of this tax attribute. This presumes that the stock market is perfectly informed about A's tax return. In fact, Section 6103 of the Internal Revenue Code makes it a criminal offense for anyone in the IRS to disclose such tax-return information, so it is unlikely that the stock market would be perfectly informed. On the other hand, when firms look for suitors, they will voluntarily disclose such information to help market the business.

It should also be noted that the entity represented on a firm's filings to the Security and Exchange Commission under Regulation 10-k is often rather different than the entity reported to the Internal Revenue Service. Not only does the 10-k utilize financial- as contrasted with tax-accounting methods, in addition, the entity reported to the SEC is the worldwide entity, and includes subsidiaries of which 50 percent or more are owned.

By contrast, the entity for U.S. tax purposes is the domestic portion of a multinational corporation, which may or may not reflect the foreign activities of the firm depending on the choices made by the firm, and includes subsidiaries owned at 80 percent or more. For these reasons it is unlikely that the value of unutilized tax credits and NOLs will be accurately capitalized by the stock market's valuation of the firm.[13]

Pre–1986 Limitations on the Purchase of Tax Attributes

The history of the federal corporate income tax can be characterized in aggregate terms as a game of chess between the IRS, the Congress, the courts, and taxpayers. At one extreme, the IRS has sought, through the regulatory process and litigation, to narrow access to the various incentives discussed above. The service has generally sought to limit the extent to which corporations can avoid the double-tier tax structure described at the outset of this chapter. At the other extreme, corporations, taxpayers, and their advisors have constantly sought new, innovative mechanisms to generate corporate source income tax-free at the corporate level, transmit it to the shareholder level, and transform such income into long-term capital gains.[14]

The Congress has, through amendments to the Internal Revenue Code, periodically reacted to reports of the worst abuse situations. The courts have played an uncertain role in refereeing the ingenuity of taxpayers, the reactions of the IRS, and periodic legislative attempts to plug the leaks (or chasms) in the fiscal dikes. Below, some of the limitations that have evolved up to 1986 are noted so that the reader does not simply conclude that the various tax-reduction mechanisms discussed above have gone completely unchecked.

Section 269: Acquisition for Tax Avoidance Prohibited

The federal tax attributes of a corporation continue from year to year, so that at any point in time a corporation has a tax history that may be attractive, as noted above. Section 269 was enacted in 1943 to deny the acquiring corporation or its shareholders the benefits, deductions, or credits to reduce its taxes if the principal purpose of the acquisition was the evasion or avoidance of income tax. As might be expected, substantial litigation ensued following the enactment of Section 269, as taxpayers and the service sought to demonstrate that the purpose of various corporate acquisitions was or was not tax avoidance.[15]

Section 382: Restrictions on Use of Target's NOLs by the Acquiring Corporation

In 1954, Congress added Sections 382(a) and 382(b) to the service's arsenal of weapons to defend against purely tax-motivated acquisitions.

Under Section 382(a), NOLs were denied entirely to the acquiring corporation if ten or fewer shareholders increased their holdings of the target firm by 50 percent or more over a 12-month period, if the stock purchase was from an unrelated person or from a decrease in the amount of stock outstanding, and if the target corporation did not continue to carry on the trade or business in substantially the same manner. NOLs were also denied to the acquiring corporation, under Section 382(b), if the shareholders of the target corporation (with NOLs) received less than 20 percent of the stock of the merged corporation.[16]

The enactment of Section 382 did not exhaust the available avenues for the ingenious to acquire tax-loss corporations and benefit from them, and until 1976 Congress struggled to find a legislative solution. As a part of the Tax Reform Act of 1976. Congress imposed a series of additional limitations that would have had the effect of eliminating many of the remaining incentives for so-called "trafficking" in tax losses that Section 382 failed to reach.[17] However, the effective date of the 1976 revisions to Section 382 was delayed repeatedly until passage of the Tax Reform Act of 1986.[18]

IRS Regs Section 1.1502–21: Rules Governing NOL Computations and Consolidated Returns

In general, when a group of affiliated corporations files their federal tax return on a consolidated basis, operating losses may be used to offset operating income from other members of the affiliated group. As subsidiaries report losses or profits, the balance sheet of each subsidiary is adjusted with upward-basis adjustments to reflect positive earnings and profits and downward adjustments to reflect losses.

A major thrust of these regulations has been to limit the availability of pre-acquisition losses of the target firm to the parent or group in subsequent time periods when the target firm has become part of the affiliated group. The losses incurred in the (prior) separate return limitation year (SRLY) can only be used to offset future income of the subsidiary once it has become part of the affiliated group. In effect, such prior losses are traced to income of the subsidiary once in the affiliated group, and allowed to offset such current income. Losses incurred by the subsidiary once within the affiliated group can, however, be used to offset income of other members of the consolidated group within the entire consolidated group to the extent that it has been a member of the group on a day-by-day basis.[19]

Federal Tax Characteristics of Pension Plans

Pension plans are generally of two types: defined-contribution or defined-benefit plans. Under a defined-contribution plan, the employer (and sometimes the employee) makes contributions into a pension trust in stated amounts. Subsequent retirement benefits depend on the success of such investments over time. Under a defined-benefit plan, the employer promises to make certain retirement payments to the employee in recognition for years of service and pattern of wages, and sets aside through pension contributions funds that actuarially should allow these obligations to be met. Typically, defined-benefit plans are not indexed for inflation; however, such benefits are often adjusted upward for the retirees in recognition of increases in the cost of living.

Such pension plans, if they meet a number of requirements of the Internal Revenue Code, are tax-exempt entities. This means that contributions by employers, which are a cost of doing business, and contributions by employees, which may be in the form of wage reductions, will grow in value in the pension trust without regard to taxation of such interest, dividend, or capital-gain income. This tax-free accumulation is typically called "tax deferral," since pension payments to retirees are taxable income.

This mechanism of tax deferral is of major consequence as the following example demonstrates. Consider a firm with $100 of pre-tax profits. If it wishes to reinvest the after-tax profits, and if the corporate tax rate is 46 percent, then it will be able to invest $54. Suppose that the market rate of interest is 10 percent. Since the interest income is taxable each year, the net annual yield is 5.4 percent. After 20 years, the firm will have accumulated $154.60 ($54 compounded at 5.4 percent for 20 years). Instead, let us suppose that the firm made an initial $100 payment into the pension plan. The firm would have no taxes due, since the pension payment is made as a corporate expense. Suppose now that in turn the pension plan invests the $100. Now the $100 will compound at 10 percent, since the pension fund is tax-exempt. In this instance, the firm through its pension plan will have accumulated $672.75 ($100 compounded at 10 percent for 20 years). These accumulations will continue to be tax-exempt as long as they remain in the plan. Were the pension fund to pay the firm the $672.75, the $672.75 would be taxed at the corporate tax rate of 46 percent. The firm would find itself with $363.28 in after-tax income. By contrast, had it invested after-tax dollars that were taxed each year, it would have earned only $154.60. The mechanism of tax deferral thus created a 240 percent increase in net, after-tax accumulation over the 20-year period.

In order for a pension plan to meet its legal obligations, contributions must be put into the trust and invested so that sufficient capital is available in income thereof to make retirement payments later on. Each year, the trustees of the pension trust must calculate whether the assets on hand are sufficient to meet the future obligations of the trust. However, in periods of rapid economic growth and boom periods in the stock market, a pension trust may find itself overfunded. If a firm is extremely conservative in its actuarial assumptions, it may in effect engage in a tax-free savings plan that may ultimately rebound to its advantage when it reverts the excess assets back to the firm. The extent of this advantage depends on: (1) the period of time over which such excess funding occurs, (2) when excess assets are put aside, and (3) the rate of interest that is earned in the pension trust.[20]

Until 1981, there was considerable uncertainty among business taxpayers whether such reversions could occur without serious consequences to current employees. In particular, it was not clear that an employer could:

1. Terminate its defined benefit plan;
2. Use the proceeds to buy annuity contracts for the existing retirees;
3. Set up a new, qualified pension trust for existing employees that was actuarially sound but not overfunded; and
4. Realize the excess assets as ordinary income.

At issue was whether an employer could set up a new pension plan that would be a qualified plan and thus tax-exempt under the Internal Revenue Code. However, in a suit involving LTV and one of its subsidiaries, the courts held in 1981 that such a process did not endanger the tax-exempt status of the new pension trust. In such circumstances, especially in the case of defined-benefit plans, which are more clearly the prerogative of the employer, it is within the legal right of the employer to terminate the plan and create a new plan with assets adequate to pay current and expected benefits. The excess profits from such a transaction are, however, ordinary income. To the extent that the termination and reversion of excess assets to the employer occur at times when the corporation may have tax losses or unused tax credits, the reversion may have no tax consequences to the employer.[21] Since the corporation controls the timing of the reversion, it may be able to plan it to coincide with a period of tax losses and excess tax credits.

The aggregate data on terminations and reversions available from the Pension Benefit Guarantee Corporation, which insures qualified private pension plans, indicate a dramatic increase in termination-and-reversion activity in the 1980s. In 1980, there were 9 terminations involving reversions; the total value of reversions was $18.5 million. In 1985, the high point of terminations in terms of numbers and amount of reversions, there were 580 terminations with reversions worth $6.67 billion. Figure 10.2 displays this information graphically with 1980 serving as the base year. Over the period 1980 through 1987, better than 1,600 plans terminated, with reversions totalling $18.1 billion.[22]

Figure 10.2
Terminations and Reversions of Single-Employer Pension Plans, 1980–1987

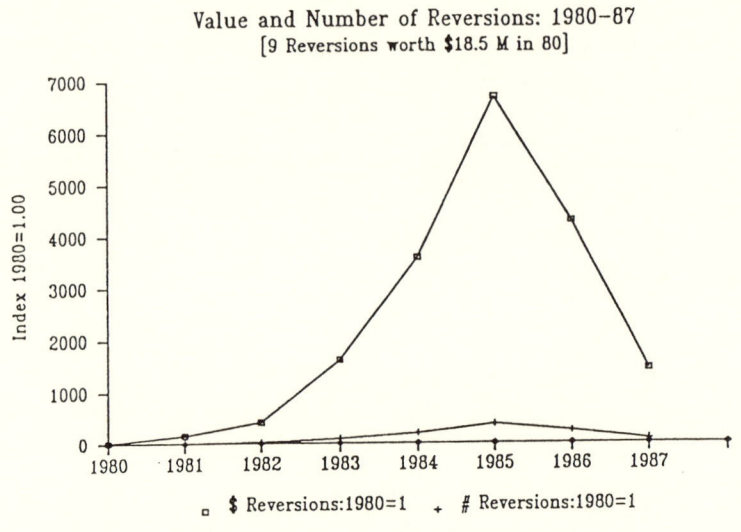

Value and Number of Reversions: 1980–87
[9 Reversions worth $18.5 M in 80]

□ $ Reversions:1980=1   + # Reversions:1980=1

THE FUTURE OF FEDERAL TAX INCENTIVES FOR MERGERS AND ACQUISITIONS

There are many reasons why the Tax Reform Act of 1986 is generally viewed as a watershed in the development of federal tax policy. The wave of tax-motivated mergers of the 1980s mobilized Congress to face up to a wide variety of structural corporate tax issues that had been festering for many years. In order to understand how and why mergers and acquisitions may occur in the future, it is important to examine those features of the 1986 act (implicitly juxtaposed against the above discussion) that affect the merger decision. This section concludes with speculations about the future course of mergers and acquisitions.

Major Provisions of the Tax Reform Act of 1986

Elimination of the Capital Gains Exclusion

As of 1987, the historical exclusion of 60 percent of long-term capital gains from taxable income was eliminated by the Tax Reform Act of 1986 for individuals and corporations. As a consequence, the incentive to use the corporation as an intermediary in the acquisition of assets, or to transmit long-term gains to shareholders, was eliminated. It is likely that this will have several long-term effects: It will create greater interest in receiving current dividends on the part of shareholders, and will penalize or reward firms in terms of their share prices in the capital market to the extent that they pay or fail to pay competitive dividends.[23]

Lowering of Corporate and Personal Tax Rates

The top corporate rate was lowered to 34 percent from (46 percent), and the top marginal personal tax rate, after certain income-conditioned phase-outs are complete, will be lowered to 28 percent (from 50 percent) effective in 1988.[24] Both rates are about 45 percent lower than before the 1986 Act; however, note that the top corporate tax rate is now noticeably less than the top personal tax rate. This differential of six percentage points has led some closely held corporations to become Subchapter-S corporations whose economic characteristics flow through entirely to each shareholder. This lower tax rate means that the value of various types of deductions and tax shields has fallen by 44 percent for corporations and individuals. In effect, the government is sharing far less in the financing of debt-financed acquisitions, and the risk associated with such leveraging lies increasingly with the buyer.

In terms of the double taxation issue, under the new rate schedule, $100 of corporate source income will be taxed $34 at the corporate level (34 percent times $100), and $18.48 at the individual level (28 percent times $66 of dividends) for a combined tax of $52.48. This contrasts with a tax of $28 were the $100 earned at the personal level under the new tax rates. Recall that under pre–1986 law, the potential difference in effective tax rates was 23 percentage points; under the new rate structure it will be slightly larger, at 24.48 percentage points. On the other hand, because the capital gains exclusion was eliminated, the worst-case differential under pre–1986 law of 53 percentage points has been considerably narrowed to 28 percentage points or 25 percent.[25]

The elimination of the long-term capital gains exclusion coupled with the lowering of the corporate and personal tax rates reduces the incentive to try to find ways to exempt corporate source income at the corporate level and transform it to long-term capital gains at the individual level. In turn, this should reduce the interest on the part of shareholders to use the corporation as a surrogate investment shield. Also, lower personal tax rates mean that shareholders will be more anxious for current dividends than in the past; the elimination of long-term capital gains magnifies this.

Repeal of General Utilities *Doctrine*

Effective in 1987, Section 336 of the Internal Revenue Code was amended to require that, in general, gain or loss is to be recognized to a corporation on a distribution of its property in a complete liquidation. This, in effect, repeals the *General Utilities* Doctrine, and eliminates in turn a major tax incentive for corporations to acquire and dispose of other corporations. Hereafter such activities will have tax consequences at the corporate level, albeit at a lower, 34 percent marginal tax rate, and will not be subject to long-term capital gains treatment.

Revised Depreciation Rules

The highly accelerated depreciation schedules of 1981 were revised several times in the 1980s (1982 and 1984) and again in the Tax Reform Act of 1986. As a consequence, plant and equipment put in place in the future will not generate such large, early deductions for depreciation as in the past; however, investments put in place in the early 1980s will continue to benefit from the more generous treatment.

Trafficking in NOLs: Reform of Section 382

Space limitations preclude a systematic overview of the extent to which the revisions to Sections 381 and 382 have eliminated opportunities for a profitable firm acquiring a target firm's unused tax credits and operating losses. After an ownership change, annual limitations are imposed on the ability of the acquired corporation to benefit from pre-acquisition NOLs. The limitation is equal to a specified interest rate times the value of the target corporation's stock on the date of acquisition. Further, NOL carryforwards are disallowed unless the target firm maintains continuity of business for two years after the ownership change and certain ownership requirements are met. The practical effect of this rewrite of Section 382, in the view of Borris Bittker and James Eustice, is to "virtually eliminate any significant loss carry-over possibilities, except in those cases where the acquired company's losses are relatively incidental to its business enterprise."[26]

Classification of Income: The Passive Loss Rules

In order to stop the trafficking in depreciation deductions that resulted from the very generous depreciation rules of the 1981 Economic Recovery Act through the syndication of various types of real estate and other tax shelters, the 1986 act created a complex and perhaps unworkable system of limitations on the losses that individuals can recognize for tax purposes. For the first time, income is classified into three different types: active income, portfolio income, and passive income. Passive losses, which are losses incurred where the investor is essentially not actively involved in the management of the investment (for example, real estate tax shelters), are severely limited in the extent that they can offset positive, active income. In general, no more than $25,000 per year of such passive losses can offset positive, active income and portfolio income;

however, this is phased out in cases of adjusted gross income between $100,000 and $200,000. This limitation becomes fully effective in 1991 for investments in pre–1986 tax shelters, and effective in 1987 for post–1986 tax shelters.

In addition, rules that limit personal interest deductions to the extent that an investor is economically at risk were extended to include real estate investments. Historically, interest deductions for non-recourse loans were permitted without limitation in the case of real estate investments; however, this opportunity to mismatch cash interest payments and accrued interest payments to generate current tax losses was eliminated in the 1986 Tax Reform Act. Also, the $10,000 pre–1986 allowance for personal interest deductions, available for those who itemized their individual tax returns, was eliminated.

Ten-Percent Excise Tax on Pension Fund Reversions

As noted, the termination of single-employer defined-benefit plans and reversions of the excess assets to employers became quite pronounced after 1981. In recognition of the growth in this tax-deferral technique, Congress enacted a new, non-deductible, 10-percent excise tax on the amount of reversion an employer may realize on termination of a qualified plan. Note that the excise tax is imposed on the amount of the fair market value of cash and property that the plan transfers to the employer. To the extent that the business is taxable, it must also treat receipt of transfers as ordinary income, although such transfers would be taxed at a 34-percent tax rate; in effect, such marginal income will thus be taxed at a combined tax rate of 44 percent, and for firms in a loss position at a minimum tax rate of 10 percent.

Whether this new excise tax adequately removes prior incentives depends on a number of factors, the most important of which is the market rate of interest compared to the rate of return incurred when the plans were formed. Also, the general lowering of the corporate rate reduces the value of deferral. However, were interest rates and the stock market to again rise generally, these plans could look substantially overfunded as they did in the early 1980s, and it is conceivable that the excise tax of 10 percent combined with the use of NOLs to offset the income being returned to the employers will be insufficient to encourage further plan terminations and reversions.

Federal Tax Incentives and the Merger-and-Acquisition Decision: Some Forecasts

It is instructive now to examine where our federal tax system stands vis à vis the various incentives discussed earlier along with the Internal Revenue Code of 1986. Let us first examine the taxation of $100 of corporate source income compared to the taxation of $100 personal income in a post–1986 world: Under the two-tier system, a tax of $34 will be levied at the corporate level, and the $66 of dividends will be taxed at a top marginal rate of 28 percent or $18.48 of tax, for a combined tax of $52.48; this contrasts with a levy of $28 on $100 of personal income under the individual income tax. Thus, the effective tax rate of the two-tier system is 52.48 percent, while the effective tax rate of the single tax system is 28 percent, with a differential of 24.8 percent in place. This is somewhat larger than under prior law, when the differential was 23 percent.

While the overall level of tax rates is lower, the differential between the double-tax system and the single-tax system is about the same. Before, as I have shown, there were additional opportunities to take the double tax and reduce it below the single-tax system by virtue of taking advantage of the *General Utilities* Doctrine and the favorable treatment of long-term capital gains. It would appear, however, that currently such opportunities to avoid the double tax have been effectively eliminated, and the incentive to use corporations as a mechanism to translate ordinary income into long-term capital gains is now gone. As such, one set of incentives for mergers and acquisitions in federal tax law is now gone.

This does not mean, however, that incentives do not remain. Since interest remains deductible while dividends are not, the analysis of the tax advantage of debt financing remains intact. If we return to the example showing the effect of debt financing on the after-tax yield to shareholders in the previous section, we find that both after-tax returns have increased as a result of the corporate tax rate having dropped from 46 to 34 percent. Since the new rate is the same for both firms, it follows that the differential in after-tax returns remains the same in percentage terms, although it has widened in absolute terms. With a corporate rate of 34 percent, the all-equity firm will pay $68 of tax on $200 of operating income, and report an after-tax return to its shareholders of 13.2 percent ($132 of after-tax income divided by $1,000 of shareholder equity). Our 50-percent debt-financed firm will now pay $44.20 of tax on $130 of operating income, and report an after-tax return to its shareholders of 17.16 percent ($85.80 of after-tax income divided by $500 of shareholder equity). The difference in rate of returns is now larger than before (compare an absolute difference of 3.24 percentage points under the prior law to an absolute difference of 3.96 percentage points under the new regime), but the differential in relative terms remains at 30 percent.

This suggests that highly debt-financed takeovers will continue as in the past, especially takeovers of those firms that are not already highly leveraged. Firms with unutilized NOLs and tax credit carryforwards will be less attractive as takeover candidates because the Tax Reform Act of 1986 increased the neutrality of the tax system with regard to those classes of businesses. Firms with overfunded pension plans will not be as attractive as before, although whether a 10-percent excise tax is enough to dissuade interest for this reason remains to be proven. In view of the fact that the Congress now has before it proposals to raise the rate to 60 percent, it may be that firms with such characteristics will remain attractive. Since the current amount of overfunding may still be in excess of $200 billion, one should not rule out the possibility that the searchlight for takeover firms will focus increasingly on pension trusts, if for no other reason than the fact that other opportunities for quick cash flow have diminished as a result of the 1986 legislation.

I should like to close with a prediction that does not have a strong analytical base but that may nonetheless prove correct. As we have seen, prior to 1986 the double taxing of corporate source income created, through the courts and through legislation, a wide variety of vehicles for escape. We have also seen that the 1986 act seems to have closed down all the historically known ways to escape the double tax, and indirectly has reduced if not eliminated many of the raw federal tax incentives for mergers and acquisitions. It is my conjecture that, through a combination of pressures (ingenuity of the tax professionals, eccentricities of our courts, and even future action by Congress if replacement revenues can be estimated to be found) relief from the double taxation of corporate source income will be found again. If this conjecture is correct, it is reasonable to surmise that the corporate veil will be increasingly used again for tax-motivated mergers and acquisitions.

NOTES

1. This figure is reported by the publication *Mergers and Acquisitions* (May/ June 1988): 45, and represents 3,701 transactions that involved a U.S. company valued at $1,000,000 or more.

2. Undoubtedly this increase in overseas interest in domestic firms mirrors the drop in the value of the dollar relative to other major currencies, and has had the beneficial effect of helping to finance our enormous balance-of-trade deficit since investments into the United States are measured as exports of capital and offset our adverse merchandise trade deficit.

3. Throughout this section, reference is made to the "historical" provisions of the Internal Revenue Code. In general, this means provisions prior to the results of the 1986 Tax Reform Act taking effect.

4. See Pechman (1987), Appendix A, for a useful historical table of statutory personal and business tax rates, 1913–1987.

5. The reader may object to the realism of this example, since historically many firms have not faced effective tax rates of 46 percent, and dividend recipients have had access to small but nonetheless important dividend exclusions of $100 for single taxpayers and $200 for married taxpayers filing jointly. However, in order to understand taxpayer behavior, it is crucial to understand that

the fundamental double taxation of corporate source income is the starting point for tax-planning decisions.

Whether such potential double taxation is appropriate raises a number of essentially philosophical issues. Since the corporation is legally a separate "person," it may be argued that it has a separate ability to pay. Irrespective of having a separate ability to pay, it may be further argued that the corporation enjoys a number of public services for which it has an obligation to pay, irrespective of whether there is a corporate "veil" between the corporation and the shareholder. On the other hand, the taxation of intangible corporate wealth at the shareholder level could, arguably, be viewed as adequate payment for such public services. Furthermore, in a competitive world economy, it may be argued that such double taxation drives domestic corporate investment overseas where it may be more favorably taxed.

6. That is, a top rate of 50 percent times the residual of 40 percent which was taxable amounted to a top tax rate of 20 percent; the corresponding rate for corporations prior to 1986 was 28 percent.

7. *General Utilities & Operating Co. v. Helvering*, 296 U.S. 200 (1935).

8. Thus, when the shareholders sold the stock for $1 million to the prospective buyer, the transaction was regarded as a wash transaction at the corporate level.

9. Gulf Oil's failure to create and then spin off a separate trust to hold its substantial oil reserves led one raider to unsuccessfully attempt to take over the company. He promised that he would sell off the trust, owning such property through a liquidation in such a manner that would result in taxation at the shareholder level only at long-term capital gains rates, and none at the corporate level.

10. This example is drawn from U.S. Congress (1985), pp. 11–12.

11. This is not to suggest that there was no economic rationale for such a change in depreciation rules, especially in light of the rapid inflation of the 1970s which eroded the real value of depreciation deductions from earlier investments. However, the radical change in depreciation rules significantly affected the size of the federal corporate tax base for a number of years, and resulted in a complete revision again in 1986. This enormous increase in depreciation deductions for real property had the predictable effect of creating a commercial-property construction boom and the creation of widely syndicated partnerships in such buildings so individuals could share in these tax shields at the individual income tax level.

12. The incentives are much more complex than this as the Congress and the courts have been mindful that such losses can readily allow sizeable tax reductions for taxable firms. Some of the limitations on such tax-motivated mergers will be discussed, as well as the restrictions put in place by the Tax Reform Act of 1986.

13. These observations may explain the general lack of statistical relationship between the merger-and-acquisition decision and tax considerations found by Auerbach and Reishus (1988a, 1988b).

14. Given wide disparities in marginal tax rates between the corporate and individual levels, and the aforementioned two-tier structure of taxation for cor-

porate source income, this sort of effort can only be viewed as rational, tax-minimizing behavior.

15. See Bittker and Eustice (1987), pp. 16–42 through 16–46.

16. The 20 percent floor explains the nature of the LBO example used above, and why up to 80 percent of the purchase can be borrowed without endangering the ability of the acquiring corporation to obtain the NOLs of the target firm.

17. For example, Sections 269 and 382 failed to reach the loss corporation, which acquired a profitable corporation so that the profitable target could then reduce its taxes by virtue of becoming a part of the loss corporation—the so-called "minnow swallowing the whale" strategy.

18. See Bittker and Eustice (1987), pp. 16–60 through 16–70, for the legislative history of the 1986 provisions of Section 382 as well as a lucid discussion of it. See also, Bacon and Tomasulo (1983) for an appraisal of various proposals to limit trafficking in NOLs in the 1970s as well as their own suggestion to reform Section 382.

19. The issue of how one computes profits and losses of members of an affiliated group is not, however, without its own difficulties. Since many trans-actions within a corporation take place at prices and costs that it sets for itself, there are opportunities for the creation of certain types of accounting losses that may circumvent the aforementioned limitations. On the other hand, the Con-gress, Treasury, and IRS have been mindful of such tactics, and Section 482 of the code, which deals with the pricing of such intracompany transactions, seeks to impose arms-length standards for such pricing calculations to thwart tax avoidance. Where market prices are not available for comparison or audit pur-poses, the development of reasonable pricing rules is inherently problematical, and is the source of continuing conflict between the IRS and business taxpayers.

20. See Ippolito (1985), chapter 13, and Ippolito (1986) for instructive calcu-lations on the value of deferral to employers and the federal government.

21. It should be remembered that such termination and reversion of excess assets is only available for single-employer plans and is not available under multi-employer plans, which are covered under the Taft Hartley Act.

22. Pension Benefit Guarantee Corporation, *Annual Report to the Congress, Fiscal Year 1987*, p. 12.

23. While the elimination of the apparatus of capital gains was one of the major features of the 1986 act, and perhaps justified the renaming of the Internal Revenue Code of 1954 to the Internal Revenue Code of 1986, the Congress was sufficiently unsure of itself that it left all provisions of pre–1986 law in the new code, simply rendering them inoperative. Restoration of the capital gains exclu-sion was an important presidential campaign issue in 1988.

24. Recall that in 1987 a transitional set of personal tax rates were in effect with the top marginal rate being 38.5 percent.

25. That is, compare the combined rate of 73 percent from Table 10.1 to just the long-term personal capital gains rate of 20 percent.

26. Bittker and Eustice (1987), p. 16–68.

PART IV

CONCLUSION

11

THE EVIDENCE AND PUBLIC POLICY

Walter Adams
and James W. Brock

In the face of continuing declines in the international competitiveness of U.S. firms, with the nation confronting a succession of record foreign trade deficits, and in an intellectual atmosphere animated by a recrudescent economic Darwinism, U.S. antitrust is under renewed fire. Cast as an economic anachronism in a new age of global competition, it is attacked by critics along the political spectrum—critics who clamor for the "modernization" of the antimerger law so as to facilitate the restructuring of U.S industry. This, they believe, is imperative if the United States is to regain its erstwhile competitiveness in international markets.

Some of the attacks emanate from the very highest levels of government. Cabinet members in the Reagan administration, for example, have stated that antitrust can no longer be based "on economic theories with no relation to the present and future." The claim that:

The world economy has changed, trade patterns have changed, but the antitrust laws have not. It is not just that some parts of those laws are irrelevant today; it is the fact that they place additional and unnecessary burdens on the ability of U.S. firms to compete.[1]

The administration's bête noire is Section 7 of the Clayton Act, which prohibits mergers and acquisitions that may substantially lessen competition or tend to create monopolies. To reduce the effectiveness of the statute, the administration promulgated new enforcement guidelines— first in 1982, and once again in 1984. Later, it proposed a package of legislative amendments that, if enacted by Congress, would effectively repeal Section 7 and emasculate its proscriptions against anticompetitive mergers. The avowed objective was to promote the kinds of efficiency-creating mergers the United States needs to be internationally competitive and also to safeguard employment in U.S. manufacturing industries.

The theory behind this policy was candidly articulated: Corporate giantism is the touchstone of production efficiency, technological advance, and international competitiveness in the modern era. Bigness, especially when induced by mergers and acquisitions, marks the path to world-class economic performance. It promotes efficiency and economies of scale in production. It fosters technological invention and innovation. Moreover, centralized administrative planning in the private sector eliminates wasteful "transaction costs" and, therefore, produces better economic results than does decentralized decision making in competitively structured capital and product markets. Above all, since it is "obvious" (as Robert Bork claims) that "larger size shows greater efficiency,"[2] we must rely on corporate giantism and megamergers as the central building blocks in any blueprint for revitalizing U.S. industries. This theory, we contend, does not survive dispassionate empirical examination, nor does it provide a sound foundation for public policy.

THE EVIDENCE

First, merger-mania has not promoted operating efficiency. In the case of conglomerate mergers, for example, the most exhaustive review of the evidence to date reports "a surprisingly consistent picture. Whatever the stated or unstated goals of managers are, the [conglomerate] mergers they have consummated have on average . . . *not* resulted in increased economic efficiency."[3] An impressive body of studies of all varieties of mergers—horizontal and vertical, as well as conglomerate—reach similar conclusions.[4] Moreover, the high post-merger divorce rate—up to 40 percent of the 1970s acquisitions—is further evidence that the efficiency-through-merger strategy is a dubious basis for formulating public policy. (A recent study of diversification by 33 large U.S. companies puts the failure rate at more than 50 percent—a track record the investigators characterized as "dismal.")[5]

Furthermore, such evidence is not new. For example, Livermore's analysis of the turn-of-the century merger movement in the United States revealed that nearly one half the consolidations between 1888 and 1905 subsequently failed; if success attributable to patents or monopoly power is excluded, the failure rate exceeded 50 percent.[6]

Second, the disabilities of merger-induced giantism are no longer a secret. Giant firms like ITT and Gulf & Western—champion acquisitors in the 1960s and 1970s—today are divesting scores of previously acquired businesses and operations. Today they are concentrating on what they know best and jettisoning the rest—and significantly boosting their economic performance. Big Oil, too, has struggled to divest a plethora of disastrous acquisitions.[7]

Influential business publications have repeatedly called attention to the malaise of the U.S. Bigness Complex. In recent cover stories, *Business Week* has argued that "small is beautiful";[8] in response to the question "do mergers really work?" its answer was "not very often—which raises questions about merger mania";[9] and in noting the trend toward "splitting up," it has reported that some large corporations are now "divesting assets, spinning off divisions, even liquidating themselves."[10] *Forbes* has provided case studies to document what would seem an obvious fact— that is, "soap and pastrami don't mix."[11] *The Economist* has featured articles entitled "Big Won't Work" and "Big Goes Bust."[12] As summarized by Martin S. Davis, president of Gulf & Western, "Bigness is not a sign of strength. In fact, just the opposite is true."[13] According to *Business Week*, progressive business leaders today are "turning away from bigness to find efficiency."[14]

Aside from the difficulty of merging occasionally incompatible corporate cultures, the quest for efficiency is bedeviled by the problem of bureaucracy. In a candid moment, for example, Elliott M. Estes, the past president of General Motors, confided that:

Chevrolet is such a big monster that you twist its tail and nothing happens at the other end for months and months. It is so gigantic that there isn't any way to really run it. You just sort of try to keep track of it.[15]

Similarly, H. Ross Perot told *Fortune*:

At GM, if you see a snake, the first thing you do is hire a consultant. . . . Then you get a committee. . . . The most likely course of action is—nothing. . . . We need to build an environment where the first guy who sees the snake kills it.[16]

Richard G. Darman, former Deputy Secretary of the Treasury and now director of the Office of Management and Budget, may have summed it up when he excoriated "corpocracy"—'large-scale corporate America's tendency to be like the government bureaucracy that corporate executives love to malign: bloated, risk-averse, inefficient, and unimaginative."[17]

Third, megamergers are seldom conducive to technological innovation. According to one analyst, the "vast majority of acquisitions of high-technology companies by large corporations (including acquisitions by Exxon, Burroughs, 3M, and Westinghouse) have ended in disaster."[18] An important reason, the *Wall Street Journal* reports, is that the "giants'

many layers of bureaucracy often paralyze the freewheeling entrepreneurial style typical in the high-tech world."[19] Conversely, managers of
divested operations released from control by corporate giants are "freed
from endless hours of explaining proposals to corporate headquarters
and waiting months, often years, for approvals on new projects."[20]

The atmosphere for promoting research and development (R&D) in
some large corporations was picturesquely described by one steel industry executive. Speaking of research and development facilities, he
stated:

The first time I went into one of them I thought I was entering Forest Lawn
[cemetery]. After you spend some time there, you realize you *are* in Forest Lawn.
Not because there are no good ideas there, but because the good ideas are dying
there all the time.[21]

It is not surprising that creative minds are suffocated in the bureau-
cratized R&D environment of giant corporations. For example, Sir James
Black, the 1987 Nobel laureate in physiology and medicine, renounced
the ambiance of corporate research

because he believed that big drug companies inhibit the process of discovery:
bigness breeds conservatism. . . . He is now to be found running a small team
at the Rayne Institute in London. Its aim is not to invent more drugs, but to
find out what sort of research helps others to do so.[22]

Indeed, the record is replete with established large firms that "frequently missed or overlooked important new departures or remained
unconvinced of the merits of an invention which, it might have been
thought, would have appealed strongly to them."[23] Examples include
telephone, cable, and electrical manufacturing companies that greeted
the invention of radio with indifference; aircraft engine producers who
accorded a similar reception to the jet engine; and chemical companies
that resisted penicillin even after its chemotherapeutic virtues had been
demonstrated.[24] Likewise, the nation's largest industrial concerns re-
jected xerography, while Eastman Kodak dismissed the newly invented
instant camera as a toy with no commercial appeal.[25]

Fourth, evidence regarding the futility of mergers in promoting efficiency is not confined to the United States. With respect to the United
Kingdom, for example, one authoritative study reports:

In many cases efficiency has not improved; in some cases it has declined, in
other cases it has improved but no faster than one would have expected in the
absence of merger. . . . More generally . . . merger has led to no apparent improvement in international competitiveness or export performance.[26]

Similar findings have been reported for other countries as well.[27]

It is ironic that, during the 1960s, European policymakers believed that European firms would never be able to compete with U.S. companies unless they merged together to create big, powerful concerns able to slug it out toe-to-toe with the U.S. giants. However, the results (such as British Steel and British Leyland) were disastrous—so much so that today, European governments are beginning to scrutinize the bloated, inefficient, unprogressive, and non-competitive giants they so assiduously built up over the preceding two decades. In a profound reorientation of policy, European governments now are seeking to promote small business in order to encourage entrepreneurship, dynamism, and economic growth.[28]

Fifth, if merger-induced bigness were truly conducive to world-class competitiveness, U.S. automobile and steel giants should be the efficiency and innovation marvels of the world. Clearly they are not. In automobiles, General Motors (itself the product of a number of mergers) has long stood as the world's very largest producer. Measured by dollar value, it is bigger than the two biggest Japanese auto companies (Toyota and Nissan) combined. However, bigness has been a liability, not an asset, for the firm: GM suffers the highest per-car production costs in the industry. Its high degree of vertical integration in parts and components production seriously impairs its flexibility and adaptability. Its multibillion-dollar acquisition of EDS has been a fiasco. Its acquisition of Hughes Aircraft has done nothing to protect the U.S. auto market from erosion by foreign producers. Indeed, GM has effectively abandoned the economy segment of the U.S. auto market to foreign automakers, and is now losing the medium-size and luxury segments of the market as well. Perhaps most embarrassing of all, the firm—by its own admission—has been forced to turn to "joint ventures" with smaller foreign rivals in a struggle to learn how to make cars economically.

In steel, bigness is the product of decades of combinations and consolidations, beginning at the turn of the century, and continuing—virtually uninterrupted by antitrust challenge—down to the present day. The U.S. Steel Corp. (now USX) at its inception in 1901 resulted from a massive amalgamation of nearly 180 formerly independent plants, and controlled at the outset upwards of 70 percent of the U.S. market. Bethlehem Steel was incorporated in 1904 as a combination of 10 producers; between 1914 and 1945, it acquired 33 other steel firms. Republic, Jones & Laughlin, and Armco all exhibit a similar genealogy.

Consolidation in steel has continued apace. In 1968, Wheeling Steel (then the industry's 10th largest firm) merged with Pittsburgh Steel (the industry's 16th largest firm). In 1971, National Steel (4th largest) acquired Granite City Steel (13th largest). In 1978, Jones & Laughlin (7th largest) was combined with Youngstown Sheet & Tube (8th largest), and in 1984,

Table 11.1
Corporate Expenditures on Mergers, R&D, and Net New Investment
(billions of dollars)

Year	Mergers and Acquisitions	Industry-Financed R&D	Net New Nonresidential Investment
1980	$ 33.0	$ 30.9	$ 88.9
1981	67.3	35.9	98.6
1982	60.4	40.1	65.5
1983	52.6	43.5	45.8
1984	126.0	49.1	91.1
1985	145.4	52.6	101.5
1986	204.4	55.7	81.0

Sources: "1987 Profile," *Mergers & Acquisitions*, May/June 1988; p. 45; U.S. Department of Commerce, *Statistical Abstract of the United States*, (Washington, D.C.: U.S. Government Printing Office, 1988), p. 557; *Economic Report of the President*, (Washington, D.C.: U.S. Government Printing Office, 1988), p. 266.

LTV (the owner of the combined Youngstown/Jones & Laughlin operations) acquired Republic Steel (a merger between two of the industry's five largest firms).

However, merger-induced bigness has scarcely saved Big Steel. Today it lies prostrate before the world and, even more significantly, it is an easy target not only for foreign competitors, but also for vastly smaller, non-integrated, super-efficient, hyper-advanced U.S. "minimill" producers like Worthington, Chaparral, Nucor, Raritan River, and Florida Steel. The collapse of the LTV-Republic combination into bankruptcy in 1987—only two years after its formation—underscores the point that merger-induced bigness has not promoted competitiveness in steel.[29]

Sixth, merger-mania inflicts an enormous and ultimately debilitating opportunity cost on the U.S. economy. This is because two decades of managerial energies devoted to sterile paper entrepreneurialism and the merger game are, at the same time, two decades during which management attention has been diverted from the critical task of investing in new plants, new products, and new state-of-the-art manufacturing techniques. Billions of dollars spent on shuffling ownership shares are, at the same time, billions of dollars not spent on productivity-enhancing measures for plants, equipment, and research and development. The millions of dollars absorbed in legal fees and investment banking commissions are, at the same time, millions of dollars not plowed directly into the nation's industrial base. As Table 11.1 shows, expenditures for mergers and acquisitions in recent years have far exceeded U.S. corporate spending on R&D and net new investment. These opportunity costs of merger madness are real, and they bode ill for the reindustrialization of the U.S. economy.

Seventh, autos and steel are prime examples of the opportunity cost of merger-mania in import-impacted industries, and of the devastating impact in our economy of the misdirected strategy of corporate giants. The "breathing space" afforded to the steel giants by a succession of import restraints was not used by them to revitalize domestic plants in order to stem the burgeoning tide of imports. Big Steel used the opportunity to proliferate joint ventures with foreign competitors (National/Nippon Kokan, Inland/Nippon Steel, LTV/Sumitomo, and so on) on the one hand, and to rechannel investment funds from modernization of its antiquated plants into acquisition of non-steel operations on the other. Thus U.S. Steel (now USX) spent $6.3 billion to acquire Marathon Oil and $2.9 billion to acquire Texas Gas & Oil; National bought California-based savings and loan associations; and Armco diversified into insurance—a venture that has saddled it with $500 million in losses during the 1980s.

The auto giants followed a parallel course. Instead of using the "breathing space" they enjoyed under the voluntary import quotas (in effect since 1981) to gird their loins for a battle against foreign competitors, they joined those competitors in a series of joint ventures; GM/Toyota; GM/Daewoo; GM/Isuzu; GM/Suzuki; GM/Lotus; Ford/Mazda; Ford/Mazda/Kia; Chrysler/Mitsubishi; Chrysler/Mitsubishi/Hyundai; Chrysler/Samsung; and Chrysler/Maserati. In addition, they have used the breathing space to export production and jobs to offshore installations while pursuing a strategy of progressive plant closing in the United States.

Finally, the auto giants—like their brethren in steel—embarked on a strategy of diversification that may well signal the abandonment of entire sectors of the domestic auto industry. GM's investment of $2.5 billion in Electronic Data Systems and $5 billion in Hughes Aircraft; Ford's investment of $493 million in First Nationwide Financial Corporation, the ninth largest savings and loan association in the country; and Chrysler's investment of $637 million in Gulfstream Aerospace and $125 million in the credit operations of E. F. Hutton, are dramatic cases in point.

The impact on employment has, of course, been predictable. In steel, employment has declined from 592,000 in 1950 to 572,000 in 1960, 531,000 in 1970, 399,000 in 1980, and 208,000 in 1985. In autos, the number of hourly workers employed by the Big Three has declined from a high-water mark of 755,797 in 1978 to 554,000 in 1986.

PUBLIC POLICY IMPLICATIONS

Merger-mania and corporate bigness have failed to deliver the goods. U.S. corporate giants have lost market after market to foreign producers.

They have lagged in innovation. The quality of their products has often been inferior and unreliable. They have suffered massive plant shutdowns and closings. Furthermore, taken together, the 500 largest U.S. industrial corporations have (according to one account) lost 4 to 5 million jobs over the period 1970 through 1985, while the U.S. economy as a whole has generated 29 million new jobs. This record scarcely evokes pride, nor does it inspire confidence in the bigness complex.

What, then, should be done?[30] One quick way of slowing down the pace of megamergers and acquisitions would be to pull out one linchpin of the hot corporate takeover game by controlling junk bond financing. This has been suggested by former Federal Reserve Chairman Paul A. Volcker. It would prevent corporate raiders from financing their takeovers by, in effect, using the stock of the acquired company as collateral for loans. A similar proposal would bar the financing of megamergers by bank loans or similar debt obligations.

Our own preference would be an amendment to Section 7 of the Clayton Act barring all corporate mergers involving corporations with assets of more than $1 billion, unless the acquiring corporation could affirmatively demonstrate—say, before an expert tribunal like the Federal Trade Commission—that the proposed merger would not be likely to lessen competition in any line of commerce; that it would enhance operating efficiency and contribute substantially to the firm's international competitiveness; and that it would promote technological progress in demonstrably specific ways. Such legislation would, of course, permit any firms, regardless of size, to grow by internal expansion—by building rather than buying. It would even permit growth by acquisition, but only on the basis of proven social advantage rather than on the basis of public-relations claims and media hype. Its most positive benefit would be to refocus management's attention on creative entrepreneurship and away from unproductive financial shell games.

NOTES

1. Malcolm Baldrige, "Rx for Export Woes: Antitrust Relief," *Wall Street Journal*, Oct. 15, 1985, p. 28.

2. Robert Bork, "Antitrust and the Theory of Concentrated Markets," in Eleanor M. Fox and James T. Halverson, eds., *Industrial Concentration and the Market System* (Chicago: American Bar Association, 1979), pp. 81, 86. See also Robert H. Bork, *The Antitrust Paradox* (New York: Basic Books, 1978).

3. Dennis Mueller, "The Effects of Conglomerate Mergers: A Survey of the Empirical Evidence," *Journal of Banking & Finance* Vol. 1 (1977): 315, 344.

4. See particularly David J. Ravenscraft and F. M. Scherer, *Mergers, Sell-Offs, and Economic Efficiency* (Washington, D.C.: Brookings, 1987).

5. Michael E. Porter, "From Competitive Advantage to Corporate Strategy," *Harvard Business Review* (May-June 1987), vol. 65, pp. 43–45.

6. Shaw Livermore, "The Success of Industrial Mergers," *Quarterly Journal of Economics* 50 (1935): 75–77, 87–88.

7. See the discussion of failed mergers in Chapter 3 of this volume.

8. Judith H. Dobrzynski, John P. Tarpey and Rebecca Aikman, "Small Is Beautiful," *Business Week*, May 27, 1985, p. 88.

9. Steven E. Prokesch and William J. Powell, "Do Mergers Really Work?" *Business Week*, June 3, 1985, p. 88.

10. Stewart Toy, "Splitting Up: The Other Side of Merger-Mania," *Business Week*, June 3, 1985, p. 50.

11. Phyllis Berman, "Why Pastrami and Soap Didn't Mix," *Forbes*, Dec. 2, 1985, p. 134.

12. *The Economist*, Dec. 25, 1976, pp. 60–63, and *The Economist*, Apr. 17, 1982, pp. 67–72.

13. Stewart Toy, "Splitting Up: The Other Side of Merger-Mania," *Business Week*, July 1, 1985, p. 53.

14. "Small Is Beautiful Now in Manufacturing," *Business Week*, October 22, 1984, p. 152.

15. J. Patrick Wright, *On a Clear Day You Can See General Motors* (Grosse Pointe, Mich.: Wright Enterprises, 1979), pp. 100, 114–15.

16. Ross Perot, "How I Would Turn Around GM," *Fortune*, Feb. 15, 1988, p. 48.

17. Richard G. Darman, "Looking Inward, Looking Outward: Beyond Tax Populism," remarks before the Japan Society's Conference on Tax Reform in Japan and the United States, New York City, Nov. 7, 1986 (mimeographed).

18. Laurie P. Cohen, "Raytheon Is among Companies Regretting High-Tech Mergers," *Wall Street Journal*, Sept. 10, 1984, p. 1.

19. Ibid.

20. Leslie Wayne, "Joys of Fleeing the Corporate Stable," *New York Times*, Nov. 15, 1981, Section 3, p. 1.

21. "Interview: Gordon E. Forward," *Harvard Business Review* 64 (May-June 1986), p. 99.

22. "Winning Design," *The Economist*, Oct. 22, 1988, p. 94.

23. John Jewkes, David Sawers, and Richard Stillerman, *The Sources of Invention*, 2d ed. (New York: W. W. Norton, 1969), p. 144.

24. Ibid., pp. 144–45.

25. U.S. Senate Subcommittee on Antitrust and Monopoly, *Economic Concentration Hearings*, part 3, 89th Cong., 1st sess., 1965, p. 1086; Victor McElheny, "In the Beginning was Dr. Land," *New York Times*, April 18, 1976, Section 3, p. 12.

26. K. Cowling, Paul Stoneman, John Cubbin, John Cable, Graham Hall, Simon Domberger and Patricia Dutton, et al. *Mergers and Economic Performance* (Cambridge: Cambridge University Press, 1980), pp. 370, 371.

27. See Dennis Mueller, ed., *The Determinants and Effects of Mergers: An International Comparison* (Cambridge, MA: Oeleschlager, Gunn & Hain, 1980); and Alexis Jacquemin, ed., *European Industry: Public Policy and Corporate Strategy* (Oxford: Clarendon Press, 1984), esp. pp. 168, 347, 349, and 357.

28. Walter Adams and James W. Brock, "The Bigness Mystique and the

Merger Policy Debate: An International Perspective," *Northwestern Journal of International Law and Business* vol. 9 (Spring 1988): 1–48.

29. It is highly significant that in the one instance when antitrust action blocked a major steel merger—*United States v. Bethlehem Steel*—the performance effects were singularly positive. Once the avenue of expansion via merger had been blocked, Bethlehem proceeded to do what it earlier had pleaded was impossible—it constructed a completely new, modern facility at Burns Harbor, Indiana, "the only integrated green-field blast furnace–oxygen converter rolling mill complex built during the 1960s and 1970s to provide a U.S. counterpart to the modern steel-making capacity growing by leaps and bounds abroad." F. M. Scherer, *Industrial Market Structure and Economic Performance*, 2nd ed. (Chicago: Rand McNally, 1980), p. 546. One can only wonder what the state of the steel industry might be today if the antitrust agencies had blocked the spate of mergers and acquisitions that produced Big Steel, beginning with the formation of the United States Steel Corp. in 1901.

30. See Walter Adams and James W. Brock, *The Bigness Complex* (New York: Pantheon, 1987), pp. 368–379, as well as the authors' forthcoming book on mergers, takeovers, and buyouts (Pantheon).

12

SOME FINAL POLICY REFLECTIONS

David L. McKee

It should be clear from the contributions to the current volume that the issues surrounding corporate mergers and acquisitions have become very complicated. Particularly in cases involving LBOs and hostile take-overs, the debate has not been won, meaning that there is considerable uneasiness among the ranks of both corporate and public policymakers.

At this writing (December 1988) the largest buyout in U.S. corporate history has just been consummated. Kohlberg, Kravis, Roberts & Company (KKR) was successful in its bid to acquire RJR Nabisco, the food and tobacco giant. The machinations leading up to the KKR victory were replete with many examples of what those opposed to takeovers seem to fear most—a seemingly Darwinian management group, intent on stripping the corporation with little regard for jobs and other economic niceties beyond personal gain. Fears such as those cited prompted the corporate board to accept the outside suitor, KKR, over the internal management group. In the eyes of those opposed to takeovers, the irony is no doubt complete in this case, since the white-hatted protagonist, KKR, is one of the more active players in the takeover scenario to have emerged during the 1980s.

The impact of the RJR Nabisco takeover is yet to be seen. Nonetheless it seems clear that with this latest buyout a watershed may have been reached beyond which no corporate players may be safe. *Time* magazine sums up the uneasiness generated by the case:

The sums are so vast, and so apparently out of line with any foreseeable benefits
... that they raise deep and disturbing doubts about the direction of U.S. business at a time when many firms lag badly behind in foreign competition. (Greenwald et al., 1988, p. 67)

If the above statement leaves any doubts as to *Time's* position, they are
soon dispelled: "The battle for RJR Nabisco seems to have crossed an
invisible line that separates reasonable conduct from anarchy" (Greenwald et al., 1988, p. 67).

The suspicions that the RJR Nabisco situation was unique gained further support from the fact that KKR's winning bid of $109 per share for
a total of $25.07 billion was outdistanced by the bid of the management
group that had initiated the buyout competition (Helyar and Burrough,
1988, p. 5). In accepting the KKR bid, the board was not persuaded by
the monetary factor. As reported in the *Wall Street Journal* of December
2, 1988, factors influencing the board's decision included fears concerning the management group's proposed dismemberment of the corporation, a desire to let the stockholders share as much as possible in any
profits ensuing from the buyout, concern about future debt payments,
and fears about potential job losses (Helyar and Burrough, 1988, p. 5).
If the factors cited above were what persuaded the board, it seems clear
that concerns relating to good corporate citizenship are not dead in the
face of the emergence of what may be the prototype for future giant
mergers or buyouts.

What has occurred in the RJR Nabisco case hardly places the capstone
in the case against buyouts. Nevertheless, it has focused attention on
issues that cut across corporate and public-policy concerns, in ways that
the somewhat less ambitious takeovers of the recent past have not done.
It has rightly been suggested that this particular case has raised political
concerns about "several U.S. business trends of the past decade" (Greenwald et al., 1988, p. 67). At the top of the list was "the relentless focus
on deal making rather than on long term investment" (Greenwald et
al., 1988, p. 67). Among the other considerations cited by Greenwald et
al. were the apparent disregard for company employees and the communities in which they are located. This particular group of concerns is
especially important at the state and local levels where they may encourage crisis-response legislation that may or may not be well conceived
or appropriate. Greenwald et al. also cited fears concerning debt buildup
and the cost to taxpayers.

Hopefully the present volume has brought together information and
shades of opinion that will make some contribution to the understanding
of the takeover issue as it stands. Certainly it seems clear that no quick
fix can be accomplished. Strong arguments have been presented on both
sides. The major issue at the moment may not be the overall rightness

or wrongness of takeovers as a genre. In the realm of public policy, the issue may be the prevention of negative overspills from the process where possible. Since there are both winners and losers in every takeover incident, the minimization of negatives may be more complicated than it may appear on the surface. That policy makers are aware that problems exist can be seen in the fact that "in 1985, more than fifty bills were introduced in the congress to deal with mergers and acquisitions; more than twenty hearings on the subject were held by nine different committees" (Weidenbaum, 1988, p. 151). Murray Weidenbaum went on to suggest that there was no "meeting of minds" on the issues in question.

Various levels of government have become involved with the issue of takeovers. Even the Federal Reserve Board has tried to play a role:

On December 6, 1985 . . . the Fed governors voted to propose that the use of debt in takeovers, in cases where debt was issued by shell corporations that lacked major assets of their own be limited to 50 percent of the purchase price of the target company. (Brooks, 1987, p. 274)

The intent "was to slow down to progressive leveraging of the economy" (Brooks, 1987, p. 275). Instead of accomplishing that objective, the proposal from the Fed incurred the ire of the Reagan administration: "Virtually every branch of government with even a remote interest in the matter—denounced the Fed's proposal" (Brooks, 1987, p. 276).

Weidenbaum suggests the company's own board of directors as a force more effective than government in staving off unsolicited takeovers (Weidenbaum, 1988, p. 167). "The key responsibility of board members, and one frequently unfulfilled, is to know when to say no to the management—on takeovers, investments and other strategic issues" (Weidenbaum, 1988, p. 169). Perhaps Weidenbaum's rationale differs from those of various other members of the Reagan administration. In any event, the 1980s has not been a time when any of the apparatus of the federal bureaucracy has been brought to bear on takeovers. If anything, indifference or perhaps approval by federal officialdom has encouraged takeovers, while those same officials have shown little interest in dealing with the potential for negative externalities that may accompany takeover activity.

In the rather permissive federal climate of the 1980s, it hardly seems surprising that rumblings were being heard on state and local levels as officials felt the need to respond to perceived threats to subnational economies. It is evident from the contribution of Lois Yoder to the present volume (Chapter 8) that the states are heavily involved in generating takeover legislation. It is too soon to say how interstate differences in the business climate engendered by this legislation will affect the national economy. There is little doubt that if the state laws stand they will have some impact within their jurisdictions. How such laws will affect the interstate configuration of corporate facilities remains to be seen, as does any impact that they may have on the national takeover picture.

If the impact of actual or contemplated state takeover legislation seems unpredictable, it would appear that there is even more room for uncertainty at the local level. Although takeovers generate very real concerns in urban agglomerations that house impacted corporate facilities, as of this writing it seems less than obvious that local legislation or government involvement can do much to influence the course of events. Tax concessions or other largess toward firms involved in takeovers may suffer from the same well-known problems encountered when local boosters attempt to woo potential enterprises with tax holidays and other concessions (Levy, 1981, and 1987). On the surface it would appear that public involvement, if indicated at all, may best be at the federal level. Such involvement should be designed to minimize negative overspills while at the same time not restricting legitimate acquisitive activity.

SELECTED
BIBLIOGRAPHY

Abbott, A. F., "Foreign Competition and Relevant Market Definition under the Department of Justice's Merger Guidelines," *Antitrust Bulletin*, Vol. 30, No. 2, Summer 1985, pp. 299–336.

Adams, J. W., and K. Heimforth, "The Effect of Conglomerate Mergers on Changes in Industry," *Antitrust Bulletin*, Vol. 31, No. 1, Spring 1986, pp. 133–153.

Adams, W., "Mega-Mergers Spell Danger," *Challenge*, Vol. 25, No. 1, March/April 1982, pp. 12–17.

Adams, W., and J. W. Brock, "Corporate Power and Economic Sabotage," *Journal of Economic Issues*, Vol. 20, No. 4, December 1986, pp. 919–940.

Adams, Walter, and James W. Brock, *The Bigness Complex: Industry, Labor, and Government in the American Economy*, New York: Pantheon Books, 1986.

Alexander, R. J., "Is the United States Substituting a Speculative Economy for a Productive One?" *Journal of Economic Issues*, Vol. 20, No. 2, June 1986, pp. 365–374.

Allen, B. T., "Merger Statistics and Merger Policy," *Review of Industrial Organization*, Vol. 1, No. 2, Summer 1984, pp. 78–92.

American Enterprise Institute for Public Policy Research, *Recent Proposals to Restrict Conglomerate Mergers*, Washington, D.C. and London: American Enterprise Institute for Public Policy Research, 1981.

Amihud, Y., P. Dodd, and M. Weinstein, "Conglomerate Mergers, Managerial Motives, and Stockholder Wealth," *Journal of Banking and Finance*, Vol. 10, No. 3, October 1986, pp. 401–410.

———, and B. Lev, "Risk Reduction as a Managerial Motive for Conglomerate

Mergers," *Bell Journal of Economics*, Vol. 12, No. 2, Autumn 1981, pp. 605–617.

Amoako-Adu, B., and J. Yagil, "Stock Price Behavior between the Base, Announcement, and Consummation Dates of the Merger," *Journal of Economics and Business*, Vol. 38, No. 2, May 1986, pp. 105–111.

Anders, George, "Leveraged Buy-Outs Make Some Companies Tougher Competitors," *Wall Street Journal*, September 15, 1988.

Ang, J. S., J. H. Chua, and A. M. Fateni, "An Empirical Analysis of the Use of Market Timing in Strategic Corporate Acquisition Planning," *Nebraska Journal of Economics and Business*, Vol. 21, No. 3, Summer 1982, pp. 27–33.

Ashton, D. J., and D. R. Atkins, "A Partial Theory of Takeover Bids," *Journal of Finance*, Vol. 39, No. 1, March 1984, pp. 167–183.

Asquith, K. P., and E. H. Kim, "The Impact of Merger Bids on the Participating Firms' Security Holders," *Journal of Finance*, Vol. 37, No. 5, December 1982, pp. 1209–1228.

Asquith, P., "Merger Bids, Uncertainty, and Stockholder Returns," *Journal of Financial Economics*, Vol. 11, No. 1–4, April 1983, pp. 51–83.

Asquith P., R. F. Bruner, and D. W. Mullins, Jr., "The Gains to Bidding Firms from Merger," *Journal of Financial Economics*, Vol. 11, No. 1–4, April 1983, pp. 121–139.

Atoncik, M., and P. Bennett, "Financial Consequences of Mergers," *Federal Reserve Bank of New York Quarterly Review*, Vol. 9, No. 1, Spring 1984, pp. 26–30.

Auerbach, Alan J., ed., *Corporate Takeovers: Causes and Consequences*, Chicago: University of Chicago Press, National Bureau of Economic Research Project Report, 1988a.

———, *Mergers and Acquisitions*, Chicago: University of Chicago Press, National Bureau of Economic Research Project Report, 1988b.

Bacon, Richard L., and Nicholas A. Tomasulo, "Net Operating Loss and Credit Carryovers: The Search for Corporate Identity," *Tax Notes*, Vol. 20, No. 11, September 12, 1983.

Baker, D. I., and W. Blumenthal, "Ideological Cycles and Unstable Antitrust Rules," *Antitrust Bulletin*, Vol. 31, No. 2, Summer 1986, pp. 327–339.

Ballantine, J. W., F. W. Cleveland, and C. T Koeller, "Profit Differences and Corporate Power: Some Empirical Surprises," *Journal of Economic Issues*, Vol. 19, No. 2, June 1985, pp. 355–364.

Barnes, P. A., and J. C. Dodds, "Building Society Mergers and the Size-Efficiency Relationship: A Comment," *Applied Economics*, Vol. 13, No. 4, December 1981, pp. 531–534.

Baron D. P., "Tender Offers and Management Resistance," *Journal of Finance*, Vol. 38, No. 2, May 1983, pp. 331–343.

Baur, J. F., "The Control of Mergers between Large, Financially Strong Firms in West Germany," *Zeitschrift für die gesamte Staatswissenschaft*, Vol. 136, No. 3, September 1980, pp. 444–464.

Bebchuk, L. A., "The Case for Facilitating Competing Tender Offers: A Last (?) Reply," *Journal of Law and Economics*, Vol. 2, No. 2, Fall 1986, pp. 253–271.

Benson, B. L., "Spatial Competition: Implications for Market Area Delineation in Antimerger Cases," *Antitrust Bulletin*, Vol. 25, No. 4, Winter 1980, pp. 729–749.

Bhagat, Sanjai, and James Brickley, "The Value of Minority Shareholder Voting Rights," *Journal of Law and Economics*, Vol. 27, 1984, pp. 339–365.

Bhagat, Sanjai, James Brickley, and Uri Lowenstein, "The Pricing Effects of Inter-Firm Cash Tender Offers," *Journal of Finance*, Vol. 42, 1987, pp. 965–968.

Bittker, Borris I., and James S. Eustice, *Federal Income Taxation of Corporations and Shareholders*, Chicago: Warren, Gorham, & Lamont, 1987.

Bittlingmayer, G., "Did Antitrust Policy Cause the Great Merger Wave?" *Journal of Law and Economics*, Vol. 28, No. 1, April 1985, pp. 77–118.

Black, Fischer, "Noise," *Journal of Finance*, Vol. 41, July 1986, pp. 529–543.

Boisjoly, R. J., and T. M. Corsi, "The Economic Implications of Less-Than-Truck-load Motor Carrier Mergers," *Journal of Financial Economics and Business*, Vol. 33, No. 1, Fall 1980, pp. 13–20.

————, "The Changing Nature of the Motor Carrier Acquisition Market," *Quarterly Journal of Business and Economics*, Vol. 22, No. 4, Autumn 1983, pp. 25–39.

Bradley, James W., and Donald H. Korn, *Acquisition and Corporate Development: A Contemporary Perspective for the Manager*, Lexington, Mass., and Toronto: Heath, Lexington Books, 1981.

Bradley, M., A. Desai, and E. H. Kim, "The Rationale behind Interfirm Tender Offers: Information or Synergy?" *Journal of Financial Economics*, Vol. 11, No. 1–4, April 1983, pp. 183–206.

Bradley, M., and M. Rosenzweig, "Defensive Stock Repurchases and the Appraisal Remedy," *Yale Law Journal*, Vol. 96, No. 2, December 1986, pp. 322–338.

Bradley, M., and L. M. Wakeman, "The Wealth Effects of Targeted Share Repurchases," *Journal of Financial Economics*, Vol. 11, No. 1–4, pp. 301–328.

Brennan, M. J., and E. S. Schwartz, "Regulation and Corporate Investment Policy," *Journal of Finance*, Vol. 37, No. 2, May 1982, pp. 289–300.

Brickley, J. A., S. Bhagat, and R. C. Lease, "The Impact of Long-Range Managerial Compensation Plans on Shareholder Wealth," *Journal of Accounting and Economics*, Vol. 7, April 1985, pp. 115–130.

Bronsteen, P., "A Review of the Revised Merger Guidelines," *Antitrust Bulletin*, Vol. 29, No. 4, Winter 1984, pp. 613–652.

Brooks, John, *The Takeover Game*, New York: E. P. Dutton, 1987.

Brown, Stephen J., and Jerold B. Warner, "Using Daily Stock Returns: The Case of Event Studies," *Journal of Financial Economics*, Vol. 14, 1985, pp. 3–31.

Brozen, Yale, *Concentration, Mergers, and Public Policy*, New York: Macmillan, 1982.

————, *Mergers in Perspective*, AEI Studies in Economic Policy No. 353, Washington, D.C. and London: American Enterprise Institute for Public Policy Research, 1982.

Brue, S. L., *Local Economic Impacts of Corporate Mergers: The Nebraska Experience*, Lincoln, Nebr.: University of Nebraska Studies, New Series No. 43, 1972.

————, "Local Employment and Payroll Impacts of Corporate Mergers," *Growth and Change*, Vol. 6, October 1975, pp. 8–13.

Buhner, R., "Shareholder Wealth, Synergy, and the VEBA/Gelsenberg Merger," *Zeitschrift für die gesamte Staatswissenschaft*, Vol. 140, No. 2, June 1984, pp. 259–275.

Bulmash, S., and A. Mehrez, "Mergers and Synergism—Some Chance-Constraint Perspectives," *Managerial and Decision Economics*, Vol. 7, No. 1, March 1986, pp. 57–62.

Burns, M. R., "Predatory Pricing and Acquisition Cost of Competitors," *Journal of Political Economy*, Vol. 94, No. 2, April 1986, pp. 266–296.

Carleton, W. T., D. R. Chambers, and J. Lakonishok, "An Empirical Analysis of the Role of the Medium of Exchange in Mergers," *Journal of Finance*, Vol. 38, No. 3, May 1983, pp. 813–826.

Chakrabarti, A. K., and J. Burton, "Technological Characteristics of Mergers and Acquisitions in the 1970s in Manufacturing Industries in the U.S.," *Quarterly Review of Economics and Business*, Vol. 23, No., 3, Autumn 1983, pp. 81–90.

Chappell, H. W., Jr., and D. C. Cheng, "Firms' Acquisition Decisions and Tobin's q Ratio," *Journal of Economics and Business*, Vol. 36, No. 1, February 1984, pp. 29–42.

Chappell, H. W., Jr., J. T. Pitrowski, and R. D. Wilder, "R and D, Firm Size, and Concentration: Evidence from the FTC Line of Business Survey," *Quarterly Journal of Business and Economics*, Vol. 25, No. 2, Spring 1986, pp. 32–50.

Charest, Guy, "Dividend Information, Stock Returns, and Market Efficiency—II," *Journal of Financial Economics*, Vol. 6, 1978, pp. 297–330.

Chinitz, B., "The Regional Transformation of the American Economy," *Urban Studies*, Vol. 23, No. 5, October 1986, pp. 377–385.

Choi, D., and G. C. Philippatos, "An Examination of Merger Synergism," *Journal of Financial Research*, Vol. 6, No. 3, Fall 1983, pp. 239–256.

———, "Post-Merger Performance among Homogeneous Firm Samples," *Financial Review*, Vol. 19, No. 2, May 1984, pp. 173–194.

Clark, N. E., "The Future of Antitrust Enforcement," *Antitrust Bulletin*, Vol. 31, No. 2, Summer 1986, pp. 401–408.

Conn, R. L., "Merging Pricing Policies by Owner-Controlled Versus Manager-Controlled Firms," *Journal of Industrial Economics*, Vol. 28, No. 4, June 1980, pp. 427–438.

———, "A Re-Examination of Merger Studies that Use Capital Asset Pricing Model Methodology," *Cambridge Journal of Economics*, Vol. 9, No. 1, March 1985, pp. 43–56.

Crum, M. R., and B. J. Allen, "U.S. Transportation Merger Policy: Evolution, Current Status, and Antitrust Considerations," *International Journal of Transport Economics*, Vol. 13, No. 1, February 1986, pp. 41–75.

Czamanski, D. Z., and S. Fogel, "Industrial Location and the Divorce of Management and Ownership," *Annals of Regional Science*, Vol. 19, No. 1, March 1985, pp. 77–86.

Dann, L. Y., and H. DeAngelo, "Stand-Still Agreements, Privately Negotiated Stock Repurchases, and the Market for Corporate Control," *Journal of Financial Economics*, Vol. 11, No. 1–4, April 1983, pp. 275–300.

Davidson, C., and R. Deneckere, "Horizontal Mergers and Collusive Behavior,"

International Journal of Industrial Organization, Vol. 2, No. 2, June 1984, pp. 117–132.

Davidson, Kenneth M., *Mega-Mergers: Corporate America's Billion-Dollar Takeovers*, Cambridge, Mass.: Harper and Row, Ballinger, 1985.

DeAngelo, H., and E. M. Rice, "Anti-Takeover Charter Amendments and Stockholder Wealth," *Journal of Financial Economics*, Vol. 11, No. 1–4, April 1983, pp. 329–359.

DeAngelo, Harry, and Linda DeAngelo, "Managerial Ownership of Voting Rights: Study of Public Corporations with Dual Classes of Common Stock," *Journal of Financial Economics*, Vol. 14, March 1985, pp. 33–69.

Demsetz, H., "Corporate Control, Insider Trading, and Rates of Return," *American Economic Review*, Vol. 76, No. 2, May 1986, pp. 313–316.

Demsetz, H., and K. Lehn, "The Structure of Corporate Ownership: Causes and Consequences," *Journal of Political Economy*, Vol. 93, No. 6, December 1985, pp. 1155–1177.

Dennis, D. K., and J. J. McConnell, "Corporate Mergers and Security Returns," *Journal of Financial Economics*, Vol. 16, No. 2, June 1986, pp. 143–187.

Dicken, Peter, "The Multiplant Business Enterprise and Geographical Space: Some Issues in the Study of External Control and Regional Development," *Regional Studies*, Vol. 10, 1976, pp. 401–412.

Dodd, P., "Merger Proposals, Management Discretion and Stockholder Wealth," *Journal of Financial Economics*, Vol. 8, No. 2, June 1980, pp. 105–137.

Dodd, Peter, and Richard Leftwich, "The Market for Corporate Charters: 'Unhealthy Competition' Versus Federal Regulation," *Journal of Business*, Vol. 53, 1980, pp. 259–283.

Domberger, S., S. A. Meadowcroft, and D. J. Thompson, "Competitive Tendering and Efficiency: The Case of Refuse Collection," *Fiscal Studies*, Vol. 7, No. 4, November 1986, pp. 69–87.

Donaldson, Gordon, *Managing Corporate Wealth*, New York: Praeger, 1984.

Dugger, W. M., "Power: An Institutional Framework of Analysis," *Journal of Economic Issues*, Vol. 14, No. 4, December 1980, pp. 897–907.

———, "The Shortcomings of Concentration Ratios in the Conglomerate Age: New Sources and Uses of Corporate Power," *Journal of Economic Issues*, Vol. 19, No. 2, June 1985, pp. 343–353.

———, "Centralization, Diversification, and Administrative Burden in U.S. Enterprises," *Journal of Economic Issues*, Vol. 19, No. 3, September 1985, pp. 687–701.

Dye, T. R., "Who Owns America: Strategic Ownership Positions in Industrial Corporations," *Social Science Quarterly*, Vol. 64, No. 4, December 1983, pp. 862–870.

Easterbrook, F. H., "Two Agency-Cost Explanations of Dividends," *American Economic Review*, Vol. 74, September 1984, pp. 650–659.

———, "Managers' Discretion and Investors' Welfare: Theories and Evidence," *Delaware Journal of Corporate Law*, Vol. 9, No. 3, 1984, pp. 540–571.

Easterbrook, F. H., and D. R. Fischel, "Anti-Trust Suits by Targets of Tender Offers," *Michigan Law Review*, Vol. 80, No. 6, May 1982, pp. 1155–1178.

Easterbrook, Frank H., and Gregg A. Jarrell, "Do Targets Gain From Defeating

Tender Offers?" *New York University Law Review*, Vol. 59, 1984, pp. 277–299.

Eckbo, B. E., "Mergers and the Market Concentration Doctrine: Evidence from the Capital Market," *Journal of Business*, Vol. 58, No. 3, June 1985, pp. 325–349.

———, "Mergers and the Market for Corporate Control: The Canadian Evidence," *Canadian Journal of Economics*, Vol. 19, No. 2, May 1986, pp. 236–260.

Eckbo, B E., and P. Wier, "Antimerger Policy under the Hart-Scott Rodino Act: A Reexamination of the Market Power Hypothesis," *Journal of Law and Economics*, Vol. 28, No. 1, April 1985, pp. 119–149.

Eger, C. E., "An Empirical Test of the Redistribution Effect in Pure Exchange Mergers," *Journal of Financial and Quantitative Analysis*, Vol. 18, No. 4, December 1983, pp. 547–572.

Einhorn, H. A., H. A. Rosenthal, and W. P. Smith, "Merger Litigation: Two Strategic Alternatives," *Antitrust Bulletin*, Vol. 26, No. 4, Winter 1981, pp. 669–696.

Elton, E., and M. Gruber, *Modern Portfolio Theory and Investment Analysis*, New York: Wiley, 1984.

Epstein, Edward Jay, *Who Owns the Corporation? Management vs. Shareholders*, New York: Priority Press, 1986.

Erickson, Rodney A., "Corporate Organization and Manufacturing Branch Plant Closures in Nonmetropolitan Areas," *Regional Studies*, Vol. 14, No. 4, 198, pp. 491–501.

———, "Corporations, Branch Plants and Employment Stability in Nonmetropolitan Areas," in J. Rees, G. J. G. Hewings, and H. A. Stafford, eds., *Industrial Location and Regional Systems*, London: Croom Helm, 1981, pp. 135–154.

Fairburn, J. A., "British Merger Policy," *Fiscal Studies*, Vol. 6, No. 1, February 1985, pp. 70–81.

Fare, R., "Addition and Efficiency," *Quarterly Journal of Economics*, Vol. 101, No. 4, November 1986, pp. 861–865.

Feinberg, R. M., "Conglomerate Mergers and Subsequent Industry Effects," *Review of Industrial Organization*, Vol. 1, No. 2, Summer 1984, pp. 128–137.

Ferguson, D. R., "The Monopolies and Mergers Commission and Economic Theory," *National Westminster Bank Quarterly Review*, November 1985, pp. 30–40.

Fox, E. M., "The New Merger Guidelines—A Blueprint for Microeconomic Analysis," *Antitrust Bulletin*, Vol. 27, No. 3, Fall 1982, pp. 519–591.

Fox, Eleanor M., and James T. Halverson, eds., *Antitrust Policy in Transition: The Convergence of Law and Economics*, Chicago: American Bar Association, Section of Antitrust Law, 1984.

Gagnon, J. E., "The New Merger Guidelines: Implications for New England Banking Markets," *New England Economic Review*, July/August 1982, pp. 18–26.

Geroski, P. A., "On the Relationship between Aggregate Merger Activity and the Stock Market," *European Economic Review*, Vol. 25, No. 2, July 1984, pp. 223–233.

George, K. D., "Monopoly and Merger Policy," *Fiscal Studies*, Vol. 6, No. 1, February 1985, pp. 34–48.

Giammarino, R. M., and R. L. Heinkel, "A Model of Dynamic Takeover Behavior," *Journal of Finance*, Vol. 41, No. 2, June 1986, pp. 465–480.

Gilson, Ronald J., *The Law and Finance of Corporate Acquisitions*. Mineola, N.Y.: The Foundation Press, 1986.

Gitman, Lawrence J., and John R. Forrester, Jr., "A Survey of Capital Budgeting Techniques Used by Major U.S. Firms," *Financial Management*, Vol. 6, Fall 1977, pp. 66–71.

Gitman, Lawrence J., and Vincent A. Mercurio, "Cost of Capital Techniques Used by Major U.S. Firms," *Financial Management*, Vol. 11, Winter 1982, pp. 21–29.

Giuffra, R. J., Jr., "Investment Bankers' Fairness Opinions in Corporate Control Transactions," *Yale Law Journal*, Vol. 96, No. 1, November 1986, pp. 119–141.

Gordon, J. N., and L. A. Kornhauser, "Takeover Defense Tactics: A Comment on Two Models," *Yale Law Journal*, Vol. 96, No. 2, December 1986, pp. 295–321.

Gordon, M. J., "The Postwar Growth in Monopoly Power," *Journal of Post Keynesian Economics*, Vol. 8, No. 1, Fall 1985, pp. 3–13.

Goudie, A. W., and G. Meeks, "Diversification by Merger," *Economica*, Vol. 49, No. 196, November 1982, pp. 447–459.

Gough, T. J. "Building Society Mergers and the Size-Efficiency Relationship: A Reply," *Applied Economics*, Vol. 13, No. 4, December 1981, pp. 535–538.

Grabowski, Henry, and Dennis C. Mueller, "Life-Cycle Effects on Corporate Returns on Retentions," *Review of Economics and Statistics*, Vol. 57, November 1975, pp. 400–409.

Green, Milford B., and Robert G. Cromley, "The Horizontal Merger: Its Motives and Spatial Employment Impacts," *Economic Geography*, Vol. 58, 1982, pp. 358–370.

———, "Merger and Acquisition Fields for Large United States Cities, 1955–1970," *Regional Studies*, Vol. 18, No. 4, August 1984, pp. 291–301.

Greenwald, John, with Richard Hornik, William McWhirter, and Frederick Ungeheuer, "Where's the Limit?" *Time*, Dec. 5, 1988, pp. 66–70.

Greer, D. F., "Size, Efficiency, and Fortune Magazine," *Review of Industrial Organization*, Vol. 1, No. 1, Spring 1984, pp. 53–59.

———, "Acquiring in Order to Avoid Acquisition," *Antitrust Bulletin*, Vol. 31, No. 1, Spring 1986, pp. 155–186.

Grossman, S. J., and O. D. Hart, "Takeover Bids, the Free-Rider Problem, and the Theory of the Corporation," *Bell Journal of Economics*, Vol. 11, No. 1, Spring 1980, pp. 42–64.

Gruchy, A. G., "Corporate Concentration and the Restructuring of the American Economy," *Journal of Economic Issues*, Vol. 19, No. 2, June 1985, pp. 429—439.

Hall, L., and J. Sweeney, "Profitability of Mergers in Food Manufacturing," *Applied Economics*, Vol. 18, No. 7, July 1986, pp. 709–727.

Halpern, P., "Corporate Acquisitions: A Theory of Special Case? A Review of Event Studies Applied to Acquisitions," *Journal of Finance*, Vol. 38, No. 2, May 1983, pp. 297–317.

Hamilton, J. L., and S. B. Lee, "Vertical Merger, Market Foreclosure, and Economic Welfare," *Southern Economic Journal*, Vol. 52, No. 4, April 1986, pp. 948–961.

Hannah, L., and J. A. Kay, "The Contribution of Mergers to Concentration Growth: A Reply to Professor Hart," *Journal of Industrial Economics*, Vol. 29, No. 3, March 1981, pp. 305–313.

————, "The Contribution of Mergers to Industrial Concentration: A Reply to Professor Prais," *Journal of Industrial Economics*, Vol. 29, No. 3, March 1981, pp. 331–332.

Hart, P. E., "The Effects of Mergers on Industrial Concentration," *Journal of Industrial Economics*, Vol. 29, No. 3, March 1981, pp. 315–320.

Hartz, Peter F., *Merger*, New York: Morrow, 1985.

Hasbrouck, J., "The Characteristics of Takeover Targets: q and Other Measures," *Journal of Banking and Finance*, Vol. 9, No. 3, September 1985, pp. 351–362.

Hausman, G. L., "The Merger Game Starts with Deception," *Challenge*, Vol. 29, No. 4, Sept./Oct. 1986, pp. 3–17.

Hayes, Samuel L., "Capital Commitments and the High Cost of Money," *Harvard Business Review*, Vol. 55, May–June 1977, pp. 155–161.

Helyar, John, and Bryan Burrough, "How Underdog KKR Won RJR Nabisco without Highest Bid," *Wall Street Journal*, Vol. 70, No. 35, Dec. 2, 1988, pp. 1, 5.

Herman, Edward S., *Corporate Control, Corporate Power*, Cambridge, New York and Sydney: Cambridge University Press, 1981.

Hill, C. W. L., and J. F. Pickering, "Conglomerate Mergers, Internal Organization and Competition Policy," *International Review of Law and Economics*, Vol. 6, No. 1, June 1986, pp. 59–75.

Hirschey, M., "Mergers, Buyouts, and Fakeouts," *American Economic Review*, Vol. 76, No. 2, May 1986, pp. 317–322.

Holderness, Clifford G., and Dennis P. Sheehan, "Raiders or Saviors? The Evidence of Six Controversial Investors," *Journal of Controversial Economics*, Vol. 14, December 1985, pp. 555–579.

Holl, P., "Control Type and the Market for Corporate Control: Reply," *Journal of Industrial Economics*, Vol. 28, No. 4, June 1980, pp. 443–445.

Hubbard, R. G., *Market Structure and Macroeconomic Fluctuations: Comments*, Brookings Papers on Economic Activity No. 2, 1986, pp. 328–336.

Ippolito, Richard A., *Pensions, Economics, and Public Policy*, New York: Dow-Jones-Irwin, 1985.

————, "Issues Surrounding Pension Terminations for Reversion," *The American Journal of Tax Policy*, Vol. 5, No. 1, Spring 1986, pp. 81–116.

Ireland, N. J., "A Note on Conglomerate Merger and Behavioral Response to Risk," *Journal of Industrial Economics*, Vol. 31, No. 3, March 1983, pp. 283–289.

Jahera, J. S., Jr., J. Hand, and W. P. Lloyd, "An Empirical Inquiry into the

Premiums for Controlling Interests," *Quarterly Journal of Business and Economics*, Vol. 24, No. 3, Summer 1985, pp. 67–77.

Jarrell, G. A., "The Wealth Effects of Litigation by Targets: Do Interests Diverge in a Merge?" *Journal of Law and Economics*, Vol. 28, No. 1, April 1985, pp. 151–177.

Jarrell, G. A., and M. Bradley, "The Economic Effects of Federal and State Regulations of Cash Tender Offers," *Journal of Law and Economics*, Vol. 23, No. 2, October 1980, pp. 371–407.

Jarrell, Gregg A., James A. Brickley, and Jeffrey M. Netter, "The Market for Corporate Control: The Empirical Evidence since 1980," *Journal of Economic Perspectives*, Vol. 2, No. 1, Winter 1988, pp. 40–68

Jarrell, Gregg A., and Annette B. Poulsen, "Shark Repellents and Stock Prices: The Effects of Antitakeover Amendments Since 1980," *Journal of Financial Economics*, Vol. 19, 1987, pp. 127–168.

Jensen, M. C., "Agency Costs of Free Cash Flow, Corporate Finance, and Takeovers," *American Economic Review*, Vol. 76, No. 2, May 1986, pp. 323–329.

Jensen, M. C., and R. S. Ruback, "The Market for Corporate Control: The Scientific Evidence," *Journal of Financial Economics*, Vol. 11, No. 1–4, April 1983, pp. 5–50.

Jensen, Michael C., "Takeovers: Their Causes and Consequences," *Journal of Economic Perspectives*, Vol. 2, No. 1, Winter 1988, pp. 21–48.

Jensen, Michael C., and William H. Meckling, "Theory of the Firm: Managerial Behavior, Agency Costs and Ownership Structure," *Journal of Financial Economics*, Vol. 3, 1976, pp. 305–360.

Jensen, Michael C., and Clifford Smith, Jr., "Stockholder, Manager, and Creditor Interests: Applications of Agency Theory," in Edward I. Altman, and Marti G. Subrahmanyam, eds., *Recent Advances in Corporate Finance*, Homewood, Ill.: Irwin, 1985, pp. 93–131.

John, T. A., "Mergers and Investment Incentives," *Journal of Financial and Quantitative Analysis*, Vol. 21, No. 4, December 1986, pp. 393–413.

Jorde, T. M., "Restoring Predictability to Merger Guideline Analysis," *Contemporary Policy Issues*, Vol. 4, No. 3, July 1986, pp. 1–21.

Keenan, Michael, and Lawrence J. White, eds., *Mergers and Acquisitions: Current Problems in Perspective*, Lexington, Mass. and Toronto: Heath, Lexington Books, 1982.

Kemp, K. A., "Lawyers, Politics, and Economic Regulation," *Social Science Quarterly*, Vol. 67, No. 2, June 1986, pp. 267–282.

Keyes, L. S., "The New Merger Guidelines of the Department of Justice," *Review of Industrial Organization*, Vol. 1, No. 1, Spring 1984, pp. 26–52.

Knoebar, C. R., "Golden Parachutes, Shark Repellents, and Hostile Tender Offers," *American Economic Review*, Vol. 76, No. 1, March 1986, pp. 155–167.

Koleman, Joe, "The Proxy Pressure on Pension Fund Managers," *Institutional Investor*, July 1985, pp. 145–147.

Koss, D. I., "Antitakeover Measures—Obstructions to the Market for Corporate Control?" *Contemporary Policy Issues*, Vol. 4, No. 3, July 1986, pp. 46–49.

Krattenmaker, T. G., and S. C. Salopi, "Anticompetitive Exclusion: Raising Rivals' Costs to Achieve Power over Price," *Yale Law Journal*, Vol. 96, No. 2, December 1986, pp. 209–293.

Kumar, M. S., "Do Mergers Reduce Corporate Investment? Evidence from United Kingdom Experience," *Cambridge Journal of Economics*, Vol. 5, No. 2, June 1981, pp. 107–118.

Kwoka, J. E., Jr., and F. R. Warren-Boulton, "Efficiencies, Failing Firms, and Alternatives to Merger: A Policy Synthesis," *Antitrust Bulletin*, Vol. 31, No. 2, Summer 1986, pp. 431–450.

Lam, C. H., and K. J. Boudreaux, "Conglomerate Merger, Wealth Redistribution and Debt: A Note," *Journal of Finance*, Vol. 39, No. 1, March 1984, pp. 275–281.

Lambert, R., and D. Larcker, "Golden Parachutes, Executive Decision-Making, and Shareholder Wealth," *Journal of Accounting and Economics*, Vol. 7, April 1985, pp. 179–204.

Langtieg, T. C., "An Application of a Three-Factor Performance Index to Measure Stockholder Gains from Merger," *Journal of Financial Economics*, Vol. 6, December 1978, pp. 365–384.

Langtieg, T. C., R. A. Haugen, and D. W. Wichern, "Merger and Stockholder Risk," *Journal of Financial and Quantitative Analysis*, Vol. 15, No. 3, September 1980, pp. 689–717.

Lawriwsky, M. L., "Control Type and the Market for Corporate Control: A Note," *Journal of Industrial Economics*, Vol. 28, No. 4, June 1980, pp. 439–441.

Lease, Ronald C., John J. McConnell, and Wayne H. Mikkelson, "The Market Value of Control in Publicly Traded Corporations," *Journal of Financial Economics*, Vol. 11, April 1983, pp. 439–472.

Leigh, R., and D. North, "Regional Aspects of Acquisition Activity in British Manufacturing Industry," *Regional Studies*, Vol. 12, 1978, pp. 227–246.

Leontiades, M., "Rationalizing the Unrelated Acquisition," *California Management Review*, Vol. 24, No. 3, Spring 1982, pp. 5–14.

Levin, P., and S. Aaronovitch, "The Financial Characteristics of Firms and Theories of Merger Activity," *Journal of Industrial Economics*, Vol. 30, No. 2, December 1981, pp. 149–172.

Levin, S. G., "Mergers and Corporate Control," *Rivista Internazionale di Scienze Economiche e Commercial*, Vol. 31, No. 10–11, October–November 1984, pp. 1073–1090.

Levy, D. T., "Specifying the Dynamics of Industry Concentration," *Journal of Industrial Economics*, Vol. 34, No. 1, September 1985, pp. 55–68.

Levy, John M., *Economic Development Programs for Cities, Countries and Towns*, New York: Praeger, 1981.

———, "The Limits of Local Development Programs," in David L. McKee and Richard E. Bennett, eds., *Structural Change in an Urban Industrial Region*, New York: Praeger, 1987, pp. 122–136.

Lewellen, W., C. Loderer, and A. Rosenfeld, "Merger Decisions and Executive Stock Ownership in Acquiring Firms," *Journal of Accounting and Economics*, Vol. 7, No. 1–3, April 1985, pp. 209–231.

Link, A. N., and J. Lunn, "Concentration and the Returns to R&D," *Review of Industrial Organization*, Vol. 1, No. 3, Fall 1984, pp. 232–239.

Linn, S. C., and J. J. McConnell, "An Empirical Investigation of the Impact of

'Antitakeover' Amendments on Common Stock Prices," *Journal of Financial Economics*, Vol. 11, No. 1–4, April 1983, pp. 361–399.

Little, Jane Sneddon, "The Impact of Acquisition by Foreigners on the Financial Health of U.S. Firms," Federal Reserve Bank of Boston, *New England Economic Review*, July/August 1982, pp. 40–53.

———, "Foreign Investment in the United States: A Cause for Concern?" Federal Reserve Bank of Boston, *New England Economic Review*, July/August 1988, pp. 51–58.

Lloyd, T., "The Importance of Giant Companies," *Lloyds Bank Review*, No. 160, April 1986, pp. 52–54.

Lloyd, W. P., J. S. Jahera, Jr., and S. J. Goldstein, "The Relation between Returns, Ownership Structure, and Market Value," *Journal of Financial Research*, Vol. 9, No. 2, Summer 1986, pp. 171–177.

Lofthouse, S., "Monopolies and Mergers Commission Reports: A Note," *Managerial and Decision Economics*, Vol. 4, No. 4, December 1983, pp. 221–223.

Lorch, Brian J., "Mergers and Acquisitions and the Geographic Transfer of Corporate Control: Some Evidence from Canada's Manufacturing Industry," in J. Rees, G. J. G. Hewings, and H. A. Stafford, eds., *Industrial Location and Regional Systems*, London: Croom Helm, 1981, pp. 123–134.

Lunn, J., and S. Martin, "Market Structure, Firm Structure, and Research Development," *Quarterly Review of Economics and Business*, Vol. 26, No. 1, Spring 1986, pp. 31–44.

Lye, S., and A. Silbertson, "Merger Activity and Sales of Subsidiaries between Company Groups," *Oxford Bulletin of Economics and Statistics*, Vol. 43, No. 3, August 1981, pp. 257–272.

Macey, J. R., "Takeover Defense Tactics and Legal Scholarship: Market Forces versus the Policymaker's Dilemma," *Yale Law Journal*, Vol. 96, No. 2, December 1986, pp. 342–352.

Macey, J. R., and F. S. McChesney, "A Theoretical Analysis of Corporate Greenmail," *Yale Law Review*, Vol. 95, No. 1, November 1985, pp. 13–61.

Mahajan, A., "Profitability Measures as Indicators of Post-Merger Efficiency," *Journal of Industrial Economics*, Vol. 33, No. 1, September 1984, pp. 135–138.

Malatesta, P. H., "The Wealth Effect of Merger Activity and the Objective Functions of Merging Firms," *Journal of Financial Economics*, Vol. 11, No. 1–4, April 1983, pp. 155–181.

Mandelker, Gershon, "Risk and Return: The Case of Merging Firms," *Journal of Financial Economics*, Vol. 1, December 1974, pp. 303–336.

Mann, H. M., "Discussion of 'Credible Commitments,' " *Antitrust Bulletin*, Vol. 29, No. 1, Spring 1984, pp. 85–88.

Marris, Robin, "A Model of the 'Managerial' Enterprise," *Quarterly Journal of Economics*, Vol. 77, May 1963, pp. 185–209.

Martin, S., "Testing the Interaction between Concentration and Barriers to Entry," *Review of Industrial Organization*, Vol. 1, No. 2, Summer 1984, pp. 114–126.

Marx, T. G., "Political Consequences of Conglomerate Mergers," *Antitrust Bulletin*, Vol. 27, No. 1, Spring 1982, pp. 107–133.

Means, G. C., "Corporate Power in the Marketplace," *Journal of Law and Economics*, Vol. 26, No. 2, June 1983, pp. 467–485.

Meeks, G., and J. G. Meeks, "Profitability Measures as Indicators of Post-Merger Efficiency," *Journal of Industrial Economics*, Vol. 29, No. 4, June 1981, pp. 335–344.

———, "Profitability Measures as Indicators of Post-Merger Efficiency: Reply," *Journal of Industrial Economics*, Vol. 33, No. 1, September 1984, pp. 139–142.

Melicher, R. W., J. Ledolter, and L. J. D'Antonio, "A Time Series Analysis of Aggregate Merger Activity," *Review of Economics and Statistics*, Vol. 65, No. 3, August 1983, pp. 423–430.

Mikkelson, W. H., and R. S. Ruback, "Takeovers and Managerial Compensation: A Discussion," *Journal of Accounting and Economics*. Vol. 7, No. 1–3, April 1985, pp. 233–238.

Mikkelson, Wayne H., and Richard S. Ruback, "An Empirical Analysis of the Interfirm Equity Investment Process," *Journal of Financial Economics*, Vol. 14, December 1985, pp. 523–553.

Miller, R. A., "Notes on the 1984 Merger Guidelines: Clarification of the Policy or Repeal of the Celler-Kefauver Act?" *Antitrust Bulletin*, Vol. 29, No. 4, Winter 1984, pp. 653–662.

Millner, E. L., "Concentration, Mergers and Public Policy," *Atlantic Economic Journal*, Vol. 11, No. 4, December 1983, pp. 89–90.

Modani, N. K., W. P. Lloyd, and J. H. Hand, "Behavior of Risk Proxies and Merger Activity," *Review of Business and Economic Research*, Vol. 19, No. 2, Spring 1984, pp. 81–89.

Mueller, Dennis C., "A Theory of Conglomerate Mergers," *Quarterly Journal of Economics*, Vol. 83, November 1969, pp. 643–651.

Mueller, Dennis C., ed. *The Determinants and Effects of Mergers: An International Comparison*, Cambridge, Mass.: Oelgeschlager, Gunn & Hain, 1980.

———. "Mergers and Market Share," *Review of Economics and Statistics*, Vol. 67, No. 2, May 1985, pp. 259–267.

———, *The Modern Corporation: Profits, Power, Growth and Performance*, Lincoln, Nebr: University of Nebraska Press, 1986.

Mueller, W. F., and R. T. Rogors, "Changes in Market Concentration of Manufacturing Industries 1947–1977," *Review of Industrial Organization*, Vol. 1, No. 1, Spring 1984, pp. 1–14.

Murphy, K. J., "Corporate Performance and Managerial Remuneration: An Empirical Analysis," *Journal of Accounting and Economics*, Vol. 7, April 1985, pp. 11–42.

North, D. J., "The Process of Locational Change in Different Manufacturing Organizations," in F. E. I. Hamilton ed. *Spatial Perspectives On Industrial Organization and Decision-Making*. London: John Wiley, 1981, pp. 235–254.

Ott, M., G. J. Santoni, "Mergers and Takeovers—The Value of Predators' Information," *Federal Reserve Bank of St. Louis Review*, Vol. 67, No. 10, December 1985, pp. 16–28.

Ordover, J. A., and R. D. Willig, "Antitrust for High-Technology Industries: Assessing Research Joint Ventures and Mergers," *Journal of Law and Economics*, Vol. 28, No. 2, May 1985, pp. 483–488.

Palepu, K. G., "Predicting Takeover Targets: A Methodological and Empirical Analysis," *Journal of Accounting and Economics*, Vol. 8, No. 1, March 1986, pp. 3–35.

Partch, Megan, "The Creation of a Class of Limited Voting Common Stock and Shareholders' Wealth," *Journal of Financial Economics*, Vol. 18, June 1987, pp. 313—339.

Pechman, Joseph A., *Federal Tax Policy*, 5th ed., Washington, D.C.: Brookings Institution, 1987.

Pension Benefit Guarantee Corporation, *Annual Report to the Congress, Fiscal Year 1987*, 1987.

Perryman, M/ R., "Evolutionary Aspects of Corporate Concentration and Its Implications for Economic Theory and Policy," *Journal of Economic Issues*, Vol 19, No. 2, June 1985, pp. 375–381.

Peters, Thomas J., and Robert H. Waterman, Jr., *In Search of Excellence: Lessons from America's Best-Run Companies*. New York: Warner Books, 1983.

Pickering, J. F., "The Causes and Consequences of Abandoned Mergers," *Journal of Industrial Economics*, Vol. 31, No. 3, March 1983, pp. 267–281.

Pitelis, C. N., and R. Sugden, "The Separation of Ownership and Control in the Theory of the Firm: A Reappraisal," *International Journal of Industrial Organization*, Vol. 4, No. 1, March 1986, pp. 69–86.

Pittman, R. W., "Predatory Investment: U.S. vs. IBM," *International Journal of Industrial Organization*, Vol. 2, No. 4, December 1984, pp. 341–365.

Porter, Michael E., "From Competitive Advantage to Corporate Strategy," *Harvard Business Review*, May–June 1987, pp. 43–59.

Poulsen, A. B., and G. A. Jarrell, "Motivations for Hostile Tender Offers and the Market for Political Exchange," *Contemporary Policy Issues*, Vol. 4, No. 3, July 1986, pp. 30–45.

Pratten, C., "The Importance of Giant Companies," *Lloyds Bank Review*, No. 159, January 1986, pp. 33–48.

Prais, S. J., "The Contribution of Mergers to Industrial Concentration: What Do We Know?" *Journal of Industrial Economics*, Vol. 29, No. 3, March 1981, pp. 321–329.

Pred, Allan, *Major Job Providing Organizations and Systems of Cities*, Washington, D.C.: Association of American Geographers, 1974.

Ravenscraft, David J., and F. M. Scherer, *Mergers, Sell-Outs, and Economic Efficiency*. Washington, D.C.: Brookings Institution, 1987.

Rege, U. P., "A Cross Sectional Study of Relative Take-Over Activity," *Applied Economics*, Vol. 15, No. 2, April 1983, pp. 235–242.

Rhoades, S. A., "Mergers of the 20 Largest Banks and Industrials, All Bank Mergers (1960–1983), and Some Related Issues," *Antitrust Bulletin*, Vol. 30, No. 2, Fall 1985, pp. 617–649.

Rhoades, Stephen, *Power, Empire Building and Mergers*, Lexington, Mass., and Toronto: Heath, Lexington Books, 1983.

Rohatyn, F. G., "Needed: Restraints on the Takeover Mania," *Challenge*, Vol. 29, No. 2, May/June 1986, pp. 30–34.

Roll, R., "The Hubris Hypothesis of Corporate Takeovers," *Journal of Business*, Vol. 59, No. 2, Part 1, April 1986, pp. 197–216.

Ross, David, "Learning to Dominate," *Journal of Industrial Economics*, Vol. 34, June 1986, pp. 337–353.

Rozeff, M., "Growth, Beta and Agency Costs as Determinants of Dividend Payout Ratios," *Journal of Financial Research*, Vol. 5, 1982, pp. 249–259.

Ruback, R. S. "The Conoco Takeover and Stockholder Returns," *Sloan Management Review*, Vol. 23, No. 2, Winter 1982, pp. 13–33.

———, "Assessing Competition in the Market for Corporate Acquisitions," *Journal of Financial Economics*, Vol. 11, No. 1–4, April 1983, pp. 141–153.

Salop, S. C., and J. J. Simons, "A Practical Guide to Merger Analysis," *Antitrust Bulletin*, Vol. 29, No. 4, Winter 1984, pp. 663–703.

Samuelson, W., and L. Rosenthal, "Price Movements as Indicators of Tender Offer Success," *Journal of Finance*, Vol. 41, No. 2, June 1986, pp. 481–499.

Sarig, O. H., "On Mergers, Divestments, and Options: A Note," *Journal of Financial and Quantitative Analysis*, Vol. 20, No. 3, September 1985, pp. 385–389.

Scherer, F. M., *Industrial Market Structure and Economic Performance*, Chicago: Rand McNally, 1970.

———, "Corporate Takeovers: The Efficiency Arguments," *Journal of Economic Perspectives*, Vol. 2, No. 1, 1988, pp. 69–82.

Schipper, K., and R. Thompson, "The Impact of Merger-Related Regulations on the Shareholders of Acquiring Firms," *Journal of Accounting Research*, Vol. 21, No. 1, Spring 1983, pp. 184–221.

———, "Evidence on the Capitalized Value of Merger Activity for Acquiring Firms," *Journal of Financial Economics*, Vol. 11, No. 1–4, April 1983, pp. 85–119.

Schnabel, J. A., "A Note on Takeovers and the Market Value Rule," *Atlantic Economic Journal*, Vol. 10, No. 2, July 1982, pp. 19–22.

Schwartz, S., "Factors Affecting the Probability of Being Acquired: Evidence for the United States," *Economic Journal*, Vol. 92, No. 366, June 1982, pp. 391–398.

———, "An Empirical Test of a Managerial, Life-Cycle, and Cost of Capital Model of Merger Activity," *Journal of Industrial Economics*, Vol. 32, No. 3, March 1984, pp. 265–276.

Settle, J. W., G. H. Petry, and C. C. Hsia, "Synergy, Diversification, and Incentive Effects of Corporate Merger on Bondholder Wealth: Some Evidence," *Journal of Financial Research*, Vol. 7, No. 4, Winter 1984, pp. 329–339.

Sharir, S., "A Note on the Measurement of Welfare Changes Due to a Merger," *Scottish Journal of Political Economy*, Vol. 32, No. 1, February 1985, pp. 107–110.

Shiller, Robert J., "Do Stock Prices Move Too Much to be Justified by Subsequent Changes in Dividends?" *American Economic Review*, Vol. 71, June 1981, pp. 421–436.

Shleifer, A., and R. W. Vishny, "Large Shareholders and Corporate Control," *Journal of Political Economy*, Vol. 94, No. 3, Part 1, June 1986, pp. 461–488.

Shleifer, Andrei, and Robert W. Vishny, "Value Maximization and the Acquisition Process," *Journal of Economic Perspective*, Vol. 2, No. 1, 1988, pp. 7–20.

Shughart, W. F., II, and R. D. Tollison, "The Random Character of Merger Activity," *Rand Journal of Economics*, Vol. 15, No. 4, Winter 1984, pp. 500–509.

Smiley, Robert, "The Effect of State Securities Statutes on Tender Offer Activity," *Economic Inquiry*, Vol. 19, 1981, pp. 426–435.

Smith, Clifford W., Jr., and Jerold B. Warner, "On Financial Contracting: An Analysis of Bond Covenants," *Journal of Financial Economics*, Vol. 7, 1979, pp. 117–161.

Smith, W. F., "Department of Justice Merger Guidelines (June 14, 1982)," *Antitrust Bulletin*, Vol. 27, No. 3, Fall 1982, pp. 619–620.

Spence, A. M., "The Learning Curve and Competition," *Bell Journal of Economics*, Vol. 12, Spring 1981, pp. 49–70.

Spiller, P. T., "On Vertical Mergers," *Journal of Law, Economics, and Organization*, Vol. 1, No. 2, Fall 1986, pp. 285–312.

Steinberg, Marc I., ed., *Tender Offers: Developments and Commentaries*, Westport, Conn., and London: Greenwood Press, Quorum Books, 1985.

Steindel, Charles, "Tax Reform and the Merger and Acquisition Market: The Repeal of General Utilities," *Federal Reserve Bulletin of New York*, Autumn 1986, pp. 31–35.

Stewart, J. F., R. S. Harris, and W. T. Carleton, "The Role of Market Structure in Merger Behavior," *Journal of Industrial Economics*, Vol. 32, No. 3, March 1984, pp. 293–312.

Strickland, A. D., "Conglomerate Mergers, Mutual Forbearance Behavior and Price Competition," *Managerial and Decision Economics*, Vol. 6, No. 3, September 1985, pp. 153–159.

Summers, Lawrence H., "Does the Stock Market Rationally Reflect Fundamental Values?" *Journal of Finance*, Vol. 41, July 1986, pp. 591–601.

Sutton, C. J., "Merger Cycles: An Exploratory Discussion," *British Review of Economic Issues*, Vol. 2, No. 8, Spring 1981, pp. 89–97.

Tannon, Jay M., and Cynthia L. Stewart, "Did the Indiana Decision Buoy Takeover Regulation?" *Mergers and Acquisitions*, Vol. 22, 1987, pp. 43–48.

Thompson, R. S., "Diversifying Mergers and Risk: Some Empirical Tests," *Journal of Economic Studies*, Vol. 10, No. 3, 1983, pp. 12–21.

Tollison, R. D., "Antitrust in the Reagan Administration: A Report from the Belly of the Beast," *International Journal of Industrial Organization*, Vol. 1, No. 2, June 1983, pp. 211–221.

Trebilcock, M., "Restrictive Covenants in the Sale of a Business: An Economic Perspective," *International Review of Law and Economics*, Vol. 4, No. 2, December 1984, pp. 137–161.

Tregenna-Piggott, J. V., "Acquisitions and the Public Interest," *South African Journal of Economics*, Vol. 50, No. 3, September 1982, pp. 253–262.

Udell, J. G., *Social and Economic Consequences of the Merger Movement in Wisconsin*, Wisconsin Economy Studies No. 3, University of Wisconsin, Madison, 1969.

U.S. Congress, Joint Committee on Taxation, *Federal Income Tax Aspects of Hostile Takeovers and Other Corporate Mergers and Acquisitions* (And S. 420, S. 476, and S 632), Washington, D.C.: U.S. Government Printing Office, JCS-9-85, April 19, 1985.

————, *General Explanation of the Tax Reform Act of 1986*, (H.R. 3838, 99th Congress: Public Law 99–514), Washington, D.C.: U.S. Government Printing Office, JCS–10–87, May 4, 1987.

Vancil, Richard F., *Passing the Baton*, Cambridge, Mass.: Harvard Business Press, 1987.

van den Berg, K. T., "Approval of Take-Out Mergers by Minority Shareholders: From Substantive to Procedural Fairness," *Yale Law Journal*, Vol. 93, No. 6, May 1984, pp. 1113–1126.

van der Wecle, R., "Is This Merger Right for You?" *Management Accounting*, Vol. 62, No. 9, March 1981, pp. 35–39, 47.

Wadhwani, S. B., "Inflation, Bankruptcy, Default Premia and the Stock Market," *Economic Journal*, Vol. 96, No. 381, March 1986, pp. 120–138.

Waldman, D. E., "The Impact of Conglomerate Mergers on Acquired Firms' Growth Rates," *Nebraska Journal of Economics and Business*, Vol. 22, No. 3, Summer 1983, pp. 24–43.

Wansley, J. W., and W. R. Lane, "A Financial Profile of Merged Firms," *Review of Business and Economic Research*, Vol. 19, No. 1, Fall 1983, pp. 87–98.

Wansley, J. W., R. L. Roenfeldt and P. L. Cooley, "Abnormal Returns from Merger Profiles," *Journal of Financial and Quantitative Analysis*, Vol. 18, No. 2, June 1983, pp. 149–162.

Watts, H. D., *The Large Industrial Enterprise*, London: Croom Helm, 1981.

Weidenbaum, Murray, *Rendezvous with Reality: The American Economy after Reagan*, New York: Basic Books, 1988.

Werden, G. J., "Section 7 of the Clayton Act and the Analysis of 'Semihorizontal' Mergers," *Antitrust Bulletin*, Vol. 27, No. 1, Spring 1982, pp. 135–160.

Wier, P., "The Costs of Antimerger Lawsuits: Evidence from the Stock Market," *Journal of Financial Economics*, Vol. 11, No. 1–4, April 1983, pp. 207–224.

Williamson, O. E., "Credible Commitments: Further Remarks," *American Economic Review*, Vol. 74, No. 3, June 1984, pp. 488–490.

————, "Transforming Merger Policy: The Pound of New Perspectives," *American Economic Review*, Vol. 76, No. 2, May 1986, pp. 114–119.

Windbichler, C., "Informal Practices to Avoid Merger Control Litigation in the U.S. and West Germany: A Comparison," *Antitrust Bulletin*, Vol. 25, No. 3, Fall 1980, pp. 619–662.

Wintrobe, R., and A. Breton, "Organizational Structure and Productivity," *American Economic Review*, Vol. 76, No. 3, June 1986, pp. 530–538.

Wright, M., J. Coyne, and H. Lockley, "Regional Aspects of Management Buyouts: Some Evidence," *Regional Studies*, Vol. 18, No. 5, October 1984, pp. 428–431.

Yamey, B. S., "Deconcentration as Antitrust Policy: The Rise and Fall of the Concentration Ratio," *Rivista Internaziaonale di Scienze Economiche e Commercial*, Vol. 32, No. 2, pp. 119–140.

Yarrow, G. K., "Shareholder Protection, Compulsory Acquisition and the Efficiency of the Takeover Process," *Journal of Industrial Economics*, Vol. 34, No. 1, September 1985, pp. 3–16.

INDEX

costs of, 37–38, 148–49; periods of, four, 48–52, 56–57, 118; power transferral via, 60, 68; profit decline via, 36–37, 53; public loses via, 54; regulation of, 54–56 (*see also* antitakeover legislation); shareholders lose via, 54; small investors lose via, 34; spatial dimensions and, 60–61; stock value and, 34, 54; tax laws encourage, 122–23, 127; technological innovation and, 145–46; vertical, explained, 50; volume of, 33, 48–50, 62, 103. *See also* corporate takeovers; hostile takeovers

corporate takeovers: by arbitrageurs, 80; benefits of, 3–4; capital investment and, 11; debt-financed, 71; defensive, 51; defined, 47; employment and, 10, 60, 61–62, 81; by foreigners, 77, 78; of Fortune 500 companies, 69–70; hostile (*see* hostile takeovers); illegal tactics and, 25; laws against (*see* antitakeover legislation; *specific laws*); leveraged (*see* leveraged buyouts); management inefficiency and, 33, 112; by money managers, 80–81; of Ohio-based firms, 70–71, 75–78; stock prices and, 9; tactics preventing, 5–7, 51, 67, 112; by takeover artists, 80; volume of, 16–17. *See also* corporate mergers

corporations: control of, 7–8; diversification by, 35–36, 144–45, 149; foreign investment and diversification by, 104; ideal behind, 7; merger-prone, compared with non-merger-prone, 53; stockholders' ignorance of, 8; taxes on (*see* taxes, corporate)

CTS Corporation v. Dynamics Corporation of America, 90, 94

depression, 48, 49

Economic Recovery Act, 125–26, 134
Edgar v. Mite Corporation, 86, 88, 90, 93, 94
effective influence defined, 103

employment: corporate bigness and, 150; corporate competition increases, 116; corporate diversification and, 149; corporate takeovers and, 10, 60, 61–62; ethics regarding, after merger, 81–82; foreign investment and, 111–12, 113–14; hostile takeovers and, 18, 19–20; theories about decline of, 110

Federal Trade Commission Act, 49, 56
Fleet Aerospace Corporation v. Holderman, 94
foreign direct investment: benefits of, 113; by Canada, 105, 109; costs of, 113–14; data on, 104; defined, 103; deindustrialization and, 110–12; employment and, 111–12, 113–14; by France, 105; geographic preference and, 110; increase of, 103, 104–5, 109, 118; by Japan, 105, 109; by Netherlands, 105, 109; in Ohio, 109; by Switzerland, 105, 109; types of change in, 105, 109; by United Kingdom, 105, 109; by West Germany, 105
Fortune 500 companies: mergers of, 70–71; in Ohio, 69–70, 72–75; shift of, from North, 71–72

General Utilities Doctrine, 122–23, 136
golden parachute explained, 6–7
greenmail explained, 6
Grundfest, Commissioner Joseph, 18, 19

hostile takeovers: abolition of, 27–30; communities affected by, 20; compared with friendly takeovers, 83; corporate debt via, 17–18; employment and, 18, 19–20; market crash and, 17; before mid–1970's, 51; pension surplus decrease via, 23; productivity and, 18–19; stockholder wealth increase and, 18; studies on, 19–23; volume of, 17

ABOUT THE EDITOR
AND CONTRIBUTORS

David L. McKee is Professor of Economics in the Graduate School of Management at Kent State University. He is a specialist in economic development and regional economics. His research has been widely published in professional journals in the United States and abroad, and has appeared in translation in French, Italian, and Spanish. His recent books include *Growth, Development and the Service Economy in the Third World; Canadian-American Economic Relations: Conflict and Cooperation on a Continental Scale* (edited); and *Structural Change in an Urban Industrial Region* (coedited with Richard E. Bennett).

Walter Adams is Distinguished University Professor and Professor of Economics at Michigan State University. He has also served that institution as its president. Professor Adams is a nationally known economist and a regular consultant to the federal government. He has published numerous books, the latest of which, *The Bigness Complex* (coauthored with James W. Brock) was selected by *Business Week* as one of the ten best business books of 1987. His articles have appeared in such journals as the *American Economic Review*, *Quarterly Journal of Economics*, *Yale Law Journal*, *Columbia Law Review*, and the *California Law Review*.

James W. Brock is Associate Professor of Economics at Miami University in Oxford, Ohio. His research and teaching focus on the structure and performance of U.S. industry and on public policy toward business, including antitrust, regulation, mergers and acquisitions, and import protectionism. Professor Brock has authored scholarly articles in a number of professional journals and publications. He has testified before Senate and House committees, at both the federal and state level. He is coauthor (with Walter Adams) of *The Bigness Complex* (1987). With Professor Adams, Brock is coauthor of another book on corporate mergers, takeovers, and buyouts to be published in 1989.

Edward R. Bruning is an Associate Professor in the Graduate School of Management at Kent State University where he holds a joint appointment in the Department of Economics and the Department of Marketing and Transportation. Specializing in policy analysis and transportation economics, he has published widely in the professional literature of those areas.

William D. Gunther is Professor of Economics at the University of Alabama. He has been Visiting Fulbright Professor at the University of Veracruz, Mexico, and Senior Fulbright Professor at the University of Amazonas, Brazil. His articles on regional economics have appeared in various professional journals. He is Executive Director of Omicron Delta Epsilon and has served as a consultant to various public agencies and private firms.

Gordon E. Heffern retired as Chairman of the Board of Society Corporation in 1987, a position he had held since 1983. He joined Society National Bank as President in 1974 and subsequently was elected Executive Vice President of the corporation. He was named President and Chief Operating Officer of the corporation in 1976, Chief Executive Officer of the bank in 1981, and chairman and CEO of the corporation and bank in 1983. He continues as a Director of Society Corp. and Society National Bank of Cleveland. Mr. Heffern attended Stevens Institute of Technology and was graduated from the University of Virginia. He is presently Goodyear Executive Professor in the College of Business Administration at Kent State University.

Brian P. Holly is Associate Professor of Geography at Kent State University. He has been a Visiting Research Fellow at the University of Liverpool and a Visiting Researcher at the Martin Centre for Architectural and Urban Studies at Cambridge University. He publishes regularly in professional journals in the United States and Europe.

R. D. Norton holds the Norman Sarkisian Chair in Business Economics at Bryant College. Professor Norton is a regional economist with a special interest in changes in industrial structure. He has served as a consultant to the Joint Economic Committee of Congress, the President's Commission for a National Agenda for the Eighties, and the White House Conference on Small Business. He is also the editor and originator of *The Survey of Regional Literature*.

Robert P. Strauss is Professor of Economics and Public Policy in the School of Urban and Public Affairs of Carnegie-Mellon University and Director of the Center for Public Financial Management at that institution. His research has been widely published in professional journals. He has been an active consultant to government agencies at both federal and state levels.

Leigh B. Trevor joined the law firm of Jones, Day, Reavis and Pogue in 1962, becoming a partner in 1969. His practice has been largely devoted to mergers, acquisitions, divestitures, takeovers, and related litigation. He is Vice Chairman of the Ohio State Bar Association's Corporation Law Committee, Chairman of its Cumulative Voting Subcommittee, and a member of its Tender Offer Subcommittee. He is President of Stakeholders in America (a coalition devoted to the reform of federal law relating to hostile takeovers).

Richard K. Vedder is Distinguished Professor of Economics at Ohio University. Dr. Vedder has published numerous books and more than 70 articles. An economic historian, his policy interests are evidenced by his service with the Joint Economic Committee, Congress of the United States 1981–1982, as well as by appearances before various congressional committees and federal commissions. He has also been an active consultant to the private sector and has lectured and taught at various universities throughout the United States. In 1978 he was Visiting Lecturer in Economics, MARA, Institute of Technology (Malaysia, 1978).

Lois J. Yoder is Assistant Professor of Finance in the Graduate School of Management of Kent State University. A member of the Ohio Bar, Professor Yoder was admitted to the U.S. Tax Court in 1982. She is also the holder of an Ohio Certified Public Accountant Certificate and is a member of the Ohio Society of Certified Public Accountants. Her writings on legal and financial matters appear with regularity in the professional literature.